Pedagogy in the Age of Politics

Pedagogy in the Age of Politics

Writing and Reading (in) the Academy

Edited by

Patricia A. Sullivan
University of New Hampshire

Donna J. Qualley
Western Washington University

National Council of Teachers of English
1111 W. Kenyon Road, Urbana, Illinois 61801-1096

Manuscript Editor: Lee Erwin

Production Editor: Rona S. Smith

Cover Design: Pat Mayer

Interior Book Design: Tom Kovacs

NCTE Stock Number 58900-3050

It is the policy of NCTE in its journals and other publications to provide a
forum for the open discussion of ideas concerning the content and the teaching
of English and the language arts. Publicity accorded to any particular point
of view does not imply endorsement by the Executive Committee, the Board
of Directors, or the membership at large, except in announcements of policy,
where such endorsement is clearly specified.

Library of Congress Cataloging-in-Publication Data

Pedagogy in the age of politics : writing and reading (in) the academy
/ edited by Patricia A. Sullivan, Donna J. Qualley.
p.   cm.
Includes bibliographical references and index.
ISBN 0-8141-5890-0 (paper) : $21.95
1. English language—Rhetoric—Study and teaching—Political
aspects—United States.   2. English philology—Study and teaching
(Higher)—Political aspects—United States.   3. Reader (Higher
education)—Political aspects—United States.   I. Sullivan,
Patricia A., 1956–   .   II. Qualley, Donna J.   III. National Council
of Teachers of English.
PE1405.U6P33   1994
808'.042'07—dc20   94-16004
                                                                  CIP

Contents

Introduction: Writing in the Age of Politics

Patricia A. Sullivan
University of New Hampshire

Donna J. Qualley
Western Washington University

Those teachers of writing we associate with expressivism may well be experiencing a feeling of déjà vu these days. Nearly everywhere we turn—at our conferences, in our journals, in our textbooks—we encounter calls for "empowerment," for "freedom," for "breaking silences" that echo expressivist calls for personal autonomy, self expression, and the reclaiming of voice. When Peter Elbow wrote, in his preface to *Writing without Teachers* in 1973, "Many people are now trying to become less helpless, both personally and politically; trying to claim more control over their own lives" (vii), he was responding to the social upheavals of the 1960s and early 1970s (the Vietnam War, the Civil Rights movement, the beginnings of Watergate) that rendered some of our most powerful institutions suspect and left many people feeling powerless in an increasingly impersonal and dehumanized society. As a college writing teacher, Elbow was also responding to the debilitating effects of a language curriculum that made students fully responsible for, but granted them no authority over, their own literacy. "One of the ways people most lack control over their own lives," he continues, "is through lacking control over words. Especially written words" (vii).

The "establishment" against which the counterculture of the 1960s rebelled included not only the government, the corporate world, and the military but also our nation's schools, with their demands for conformity to modes of learning and a prescriptive set of truths that were thought to suppress individual creativity and deflect the individual's search for personal meaning and understanding. Elbow observed the ways that his students' adherence to the formal rules and conventions of standard English threatened their very desire to generate words. Therefore, like other expressivists, he imagined a pedagogy that would help students recover and assert their own voices, to write "with power," to become the authors of their own literacy. Ken Macrorie similarly exhorted student writers not to imitate the "dull and lifeless" prose of the schools, but to recover and value "the language within." And Donald Murray prodded writing teachers in 1969 to be "revolutionary," to "welcome an age of dissent," to "glory in [their students'] diversity," but above all to encourage their students to be "individuals." For such teachers, the discovery of one's "own" voice was necessary if one was to gain control over the written word. And controlling the written word was a necessary condition of freedom, the ability to exercise choice in a democratic society, or what Murray called a "responsible Babel" (140).

"The events of the sixties," Richard Ohmann writes, "were hard on complacency; they provoked self scrutiny, and an effort to connect the large with the small, the abstract with the concrete" (4–5). Looking back, we can see that the politically charged atmosphere of the 1960s generated a composition pedagogy that responded in kind, a pedagogy that implicitly pitted the individual against society's institutions and centers of authority. Today, as we move into the 1990s, we find ourselves again in an age of politics, but a politics of a different sort. Today, when we talk of empowerment, of freedom, of resistance, we are not talking about the individual's struggle to discover his authentic voice or her own personal truths against the impersonal and dehumanizing discourses of academe, but about the social forces, inscribed in relations of power, by which selves, and texts, are constituted. Our discussions today are more apt to be centered on issues of multiculturalism, ethnic diversity, gender, feminism, the canon, freedom of expression, cultural literacy. Indeed, the liberated, autonomous self that stood as one of the goals of writing instruction when expressivists introduced personal writing and freewriting into college curricula has itself come into question as composition has moved from studies of the inner life of the writer to studies of the social contexts of writing. The texts a student composes are now widely perceived as a function of the writer's cultural identity and experience, including his or her social location in matrices of race, class, and gender, as well as the institutional contexts in which he or she reads and writes. Our focus, in other words, has shifted from the self that writes to the sources of that self—the social, cultural, and historical conditions by which selves, or "subjects," are formed, and which make particular acts of writing possible.

With this shift in focus from the private to the social has come a shift in the purpose of writing instruction: teachers who once invited students to master or to transcend the strictures of written discourse now call upon students to participate critically in the discourses that shape their lives. Pedagogies that once aimed at self-actualization now aim at social transformation. Here lies the key source of contention in the composition community, the issue upon which all our polemics turn. For while we might agree in principle about the socially ameliorating potential of a curriculum that empowers student writers across the cultural spectrum, we are by no means in agreement about what teaching practices might best be put to this end, or indeed, whether a composition course should be used to this end at all.

Recent events at the University of Texas at Austin provide a lens through which to view the specific nature of these disagreements. The director of composition at Texas, working in concert with other instructors and teaching assistants, devised a curriculum around a set of texts—essays and court cases based on charges of discrimination— that were intended as case studies for the students' own reading and writing. One of the explicit goals of the course was to foster students' critical consciousness, to encourage students to view rhetoric as consequential in a participatory democracy. The proposed curriculum quickly met with resistance from other writing faculty, from university administrators, and eventually from self-elected representatives of the public, who perceived a political agenda, and specifically a liberal politics, operating at the curriculum's core. In his syndicated column, for example, George Will decried the Texas model and similar curricula at other state universities for indoctrinating students in politics at the expense of the literacy skills that constituted the "true" purpose and objective of first-year composition. The Texas curriculum, in the end, advanced no further than the proposal stage, but the circumstances of its making and unmaking (or its "unmasking," as some would have it) provided the catalyst for ongoing debates within the composition community about what we teach—or ought to teach—in courses devoted to writing.

While few of us were surprised that an outsider and conservative like George Will would sound the liberal scare against academe and advocate a back-to-basics approach to a course he himself had never taught, many compositionists were taken off guard when their colleague, Maxine Hairston, an insider notably to the left of Will, sounded themes similar to his in a recent article in *College Composition and Communication*. Hairston's essay, "Diversity, Ideology, and Teaching Writing," "provoked more Counterstatement submissions," according to editor Richard Gebhardt, "than any *CCC* article since the start of 1987" (295). In this essay, Hairston takes to task those of her colleagues who are using the composition course as a platform from which to espouse ideology rather than to teach the writing process. Echoing the criticisms of Will, Hairston denounces the "new model emerging for freshman writing programs, . . . a model that puts dogma before diversity, politics before craft, ideology before critical thinking, and the social goals of the teacher before the educational needs of the student" (180).

What is important to notice in Hairston's formulation of the problem currently dividing teachers of writing is how each term of the "new" model for freshman English—"dogma," "politics," "ideology," and "the social goals of the teacher"—is paired with a term that we are meant to read as ideologically pure, devoid of the political commitments of anyone in particular. "Diversity," "craft," "critical thinking," and "the educational needs of the student" are cast into a politically neutral space, or more accurately, into a prepoliticized time in composition's history when it was possible for us to teach writing untainted by the social values and institutional conditions in which our practices and theories were forged. In his chapter, "When Is Something 'Political'?" in *Beyond the Culture Wars*, Gerald Graff detects "a double standard" at work in arguments like Hairston's:

> Change is political, but keeping things as they are is not. A status quo that we are used to and comfortable with is not seen as political; one who says, "Western culture has made the world we know and therefore should be preeminent in the curriculum," is seen simply as stating a fact, not endorsing an agenda. Like the oxygen that we notice only when it is taken away, the orthodox or established side does not stand out from its background and seems therefore not to be a "side" at all but just the way things are. (164)

Whether or not we see a double standard operating in Hairston's argument, what we can see in her essay is the expressed desire for a utopian past, a longing for those days when writing teachers could teach the writing process and craft to diverse students with the same detachment and disinterest with which the New Critic approached a text. In expressing this desire, Hairston herself is endorsing an agenda; she is taking a stand against any curricular change that would insert the local and particular interests of culturally situated subjects— students and teachers—in the place she, and others, wish to reserve for a universalized and decontextualized notion of literacy. The main problem with Hairston's argument, however, is not its refusal to see itself as a "side," as a stance with its own political investments, but that this stance is premised on an elisive reading of composition's history. In her attempt to depoliticize the teaching of writing, Hairston imagines for composition studies an apolitical past that even those of us sympathetic to her cause would be hard-pressed to recall.

The course we now identify as Freshman Composition was, as we know, instituted in the nineteenth century to prepare students for the "real" subjects that formed higher education. Students' ability to master standard English and to imitate models of effective prose became the key measure of their academic potential, their intellectual and moral worthiness to participate in the discourses of higher learning. Composition's perceived nature as a service industry, in turn, helped to cement the marginalized status of its teachers—an increasingly female labor force that was thought to need no specialized training or higher degree to practice its trade, nor adequate compensation for its efforts. Even the process movement of the 1960s and 1970s, with its plural but persistent calls to teach writing as a process, not a product, may be read as a reclaiming of power on the part of writing teachers—the power to name and define what writing is, what writers do—on behalf of students. And if we look only to our most recent past, to the 1980s, we will recall the sheer quantity of publications (including Hairston's "Breaking Our Bonds") that criticized the perceived hegemony of literary studies and appealed either for reconciliation of composition and literary studies or for composition's secession from English departments.

What the various texts of composition's history teach us is that change is inevitable, and that the changes that matter most will be forged out of struggle—of competing viewpoints, of opposing sides. Those teachers who, yesterday, were the most self-consciously political, the most active in questioning and criticizing the status quo, are often, now, the same people who are most intent on defending the perspectives they worked so hard to achieve. What has changed, then, is not composition's nature as a site of struggle, nor is it the "politicization" of the work we now do. The teaching of writing has always been steeped in politics—in the configurations of power that invest certain groups with the privilege to determine the meanings and value we accord to literacy and pedagogy. What is different today are the specific terms of the struggle and the positions or "sides" of some of the key authors of (and in) composition's still-unfolding story. Composition is no longer absorbed in the identity politics, the "us" versus "them" polemics, that marked our coming of age; we have for the most part won the struggle to name ourselves, wresting from others the power to define the nature of our work. Now we have turned our critical gaze within, and what we see are deep divisions, conflicts that threaten our sense of a shared identity, the "community" that has allowed us to present a unified front to the world outside our disciplinary borders.

But as Maxine Greene writes in the opening essay of this volume, the "dialectic struggle" that defines the teaching of reading and writing is "never quite resolved. We would not need to be wide-awake to ourselves and our lives . . . if we could exist somehow without contraries or contradictions, ascending with nothing in our way." As we debate the nature and purposes of writing among ourselves, we need to attend carefully to the sounds of our own dissonance, for they are pointing us to the work we have still to do. We are engaging an increasing plurality of literacies in our classrooms—multiple ways of learning, knowing, and expression. As we struggle to define the educational needs of this new generation of students, we must resist the lures of nostalgia and complacency and confront the politics of our practice—the ideological tensions that now stand in our way. For if our work is indeed consequential (the one point, perhaps, about which we all agree), then we have a decisive role to play in both the academy's and society's transformation as sites of cultural power.

The purpose of this volume is to further discussion of issues that social theories of writing have opened to question—to examine critically our own and our students' assumptions and practices as makers of meaning situated within sociopolitical contexts of composing. The title of our book is meant to signal its central theme: that acts of writing and reading *in* the academy reflect and produce a writing *of* the academy. The discourses through which knowledge is made and shared (whether the personal truths of lived experience or the social constructions of collective inquiry) comprise at once the subjects we teach and the means by which the academy does its intellectual work. Inasmuch as this work is always inscribed in, and reinscribing, relations of power, it is important that we continually visit and revisit such questions as what we teach and why, where and how we position ourselves as we teach, and what conditions constrain and enable our students' acts of making meaning.

A number of recent publications take the politics of writing instruction as their central concern (see, for example, Miller; Harkin and Schilb; Bullock and Trimbur). What distinguishes this volume from others is largely a matter of the perspective, or positioning, from which its authors write. Here, authors locate their inquiry in their own practices as teachers, scholars, and theorists, writing from their own narratives and not merely from (or about) the master narratives currently circulating in academe. They situate their analyses in the classrooms, institutions, and regions in which they work and live, in the personal and academic literacies of their students, in the textual transactions and human interactions that form their own readings and writings of the academy. This collection does not aim to achieve ideological consensus, nor does it privilege a single political viewpoint. Rather, it plays host to a series of essays that revolve around a common theme: what it means to study and teach writing and reading in "the age of politics," a time of intense institutional examination and social critique.

This book comprises sixteen essays arranged into three interrelated sections, each dealing with a subset of issues related to the larger theme. Essays in the first section acknowledge the centrality of pedagogy to composition studies and make the implicit argument that it is in classroom practices that our politics become most visible. In this section, contributors explore the specific ways that students and teachers resist, acknowledge, mediate, or embrace the dialectical tensions that emerge through encounters with "others"—other ideas, people, texts, and technologies.

Maxine Greene's essay, "Teaching for Openings: Pedagogy as Dialectic," sounds a keynote for the essays that follow by exploring what it means to "break from immersion" and view "the universal" as a set of "points of view," both textual and cultural. Arguing that literacy "is and must be a social undertaking to be sought in pluralist classrooms," Greene conceives pedagogy as a fluid and dynamic dialectic, as an always-vigilant praxis in which students and teachers "work together to unconceal what is hidden, to contextualize what happens to us. . . ." While acknowledging that she is still drawn to the idea of "a view from nowhere," to "the blinding light of disembodied reason," she affirms the importance of reading and rewriting texts against the background of lived experience: "We are going to be increasingly a community of newcomers in the years ahead . . . some stunned by lives in refugee camps, some unabashedly in search of economic success." We have to keep texts open to "endless, restless interrogation," to the "play of differences . . . through which meanings can emerge," if we are "to provoke the young to be free."

In "Advocacy and Resistance in the Writing Class," Karen Fitts and Alan France argue for a critical pedagogy of writing on the grounds that teaching writing as a "politically neutral process" in effect reproduces institutionalized inequities of race, class, and gender. Analyzing the rhetorical strategies that students invent to resist political engagement, Fitts and France describe how their pedagogy, "conceived of as oppositional," actually results in "a dialectical process" that "precludes the one-sided imposition of 'truth' or 'political correctness.' " In counterpoint to Hairston, the authors suggest that writing teachers who acknowledge their own political investments are in a better position to "cultivate an open and honest dialogue about public events" and help students take personal responsibility for their own literacy and advocacy in the public forum.

Like Fitts and France, Donna Qualley is interested in the ways writing instructors can help students develop more complex perspectives. She cautions, however, that students cannot be expected to adopt multiple perspectives at once. In "Being Two Places at Once: Feminism and the Development of 'Both/And' Perspectives," Qualley suggests that "the road to 'both/and' often runs through many intellectual, emotional, and political 'either/ors.' " She argues that essentialist thinking can be an important step in the development of feminist consciousness and group solidarity, while a premature focus on difference may simply contribute to radical individualism—something that is already endemic in many of today's young women. Nonetheless, Qualley takes up Greene's admonition that teachers continually strive to provide occasions for students to "break loose from anchorage," especially those students comfortably and uncritically situated in the social and cultural mainstream. Toward this end, she describes a collaborative inquiry project that offers students the chance to experience, and not merely encounter, the perspectives of others.

In "Naming Harlem: Teaching the Dynamics of Diversity," Daniel Reagan approaches the concept of the "double perspective" from another angle. Citing the controversy that arose when white writer Carl Van Vechten attempted to use "a black . . . psychological perspective" to write his 1926 novel, *Nigger Heaven*, Reagan suggests that white teachers of African American texts today face a similar problem: What grants such teachers the authority to speak about the other's texts and traditions? Reagan contends that white teachers must find ways to "engage black literature while accepting the position of outsider." He describes three strategies he uses to help students "explore the doubleness that lies at the heart of many African American texts" so they can become "aware of the process of naming they undertake" when reading and writing about "other" cultures, traditions, and texts.

Michael J. Kiskis is interested in the ways adult students complicate our theories of teaching and learning. In "Adult Learners, Autobiography, and Educational Planning: Reflections on Pedagogy, Andragogy, and Power," he explores the conflicts that adult students negotiate as they undertake degree programs in an institution that was originally structured to serve younger students and, historically, to prepare males to assume professional roles in the workplace. Kiskis describes, as an administrator and teacher, a program in which students work collaboratively with faculty and compose ongoing autobiographical essays that show how the practice of reflective writing gives nontraditional students power over their educational choices. But he also cautions us to pay attention to the differences among adult students, especially to gender differences, lest we repeat some of the universalizing tendencies of early composition scholarship and the developmental models on which such research relied.

In the last essay in this section, we learn that the "other" may take the form of a new technology. In "Whose Machines Are These?" Elizabeth Klem and Charles Moran examine how the introduction of computers affects the politics of ownership in writing centers and classrooms. Just as the students in Fitts and France's class invented strategies to resist political engagement, many of the writing instructors in Klem and Moran's study displayed a resistance to the reallocation of power and authority that resulted from teaching "online." Klem and Moran contend that computerized classrooms alter the nature of student-teacher relationships as well as the kind of "work" that gets done. Teachers need to acknowledge these changes in the learning environment and "reflect on their own pedagogical assumptions" to "work with and around points of dissonance."

Contributors in the second section reflect on the evolution of particular practices and genres of writing in the academy, and offer revisionary readings of the events, theories, and concepts that have shaped and still inform some of our assumptions about pedagogy and literacy. These essays focus on reading and rereading as political acts, underscoring the importance of critique and self-reflection as we locate and reposition ourselves in the various (historical) "texts" that frame present experience.

Mariolina Salvatori's essay, "Pedagogy and the Academy: 'The Divine Skill of the Born Teacher's Instincts,'" illuminates a particular and still-dominant conception of pedagogy that was constructed and inscribed in the academy at the end of the nineteenth century. She contends that this construction, which led to the bifurcation of theory and practice as well as of art and science, was "a determining factor for certain seizures of power within universities that served *then* and . . . serve *now* as a pretext to relegate pedagogy to an ancillary position." Salvatori's essay, part of a larger study aimed at recuperating the history of American pedagogy from "singular and collective acts of forgetfulness," invites readers to think about whose interests are being served when pedagogy is either trivialized—reduced to a set of techniques anyone can master—or mystified, construed as the inborn skill of a privileged few.

Like Salvatori, Peter Mortensen asks us to reconsider where the narratives that inform our perceptions originate. In "Representations of Literacy and Region: Narrating 'Another America,'" Mortensen presents findings from a yearlong study that show how devaluing the traditions and patterns of a local culture—the Appalachian region of eastern Kentucky—has not only contributed to the "creation and perpetuation" of the myth of an "Appalachian otherness" but has also authorized certain notions of literacy that conflict with the ways inhabitants of the region themselves choose to represent the literacy events that inform their lives. He argues that we can "challenge restrictive definitions of literacy," such as those that "equate a narrow range of literacies with intelligence, even humanity," by working to "unveil" the double-sided history of literacy, a history that reveals that literacy "can subjugate as well as liberate."

In "The Essay Dies in the Academy, circa 1900," Jean Donovan Sanborn traces the development of the "thesis-driven," "hierarchical" essay to the late nineteenth century and shows how its form and pedagogy served an authoritarian model of education that still lingers today. Sanborn suggests that in adopting this linear model of the essay we may be "perpetuating a model of learning we no longer espouse" and a "political unity" that turns out to be fiction, given the diversity of students most teachers encounter in their classrooms. She argues that the "conversational essay" as envisaged by Montaigne may be a more accessible and appropriate form for our students, may be "closer to the ways we now talk about learning and thinking," and may more fruitfully extend our notions of "academic discourse."

In the next essay, Sharyn Lowenstein, Elizabeth Chiseri-Strater, and Cinthia Gannett examine the historical, pedagogical, and political contexts of the journal as a complex social construction rather than a simple book of the self. In "Re-envisioning the Journal: Writing the Self into Community," the authors unravel the criticisms that have led to the marginalization of this (feminized) genre in the academy and recover a history that shows how the journal has been and can be a source of individual and collective empowerment. Maintaining that the journal acts as a mediator among selves and between self and community, they suggest that teachers can more fully exploit its multiple possibilities for the classroom if they regard the journal not only as a place for the "construction and transformation of the self . . . but also as a means to define, maintain, and transform one's connection" to a community of others.

Linda M. LaDuc explores the "thorny nexus of feminism, pedagogy, and power" in her essay, "Feminism and Power: The Pedagogical Implications of (Acknowledging) Plural Feminist Perspectives." LaDuc contends that feminist teachers can avoid the "abhorrent uses/abuses of our professorial power" that occur through univocalized teaching by developing an understanding of multiple feminist perspectives, practicing methodological flexibility, and engaging in self-critique. LaDuc describes the reflexive process she used to read and clarify her own positions on a number of critical issues, including the relationship between feminism and authority. Such a process, LaDuc suggests, not only serves to expose the contradictions in one's own perspective, it also provides a way for feminism and pedagogy to "go hand in hand."

In the last essay of this section, "Rereading the Discourses of Gender in Composition: A Cautionary Tale," Susan Wall reexamines the assumptions that guided a case study she completed ten years ago of a young woman's struggle with language and self in a first-year composition course. Her case study was conducted at a time when composition studies both "lacked any feminist theory of composing" and confined our attention to the individual writer. Thus, while she saw the student's struggles as gendered, she also saw gender "in terms of a largely stereotyped, ready-made discourse for defining the self that a writer had to resist in order to 'grow'." Wall rereads her case study through critical readings of Carol Gilligan and of Mary Belenky and her colleagues, and shows how her earlier attempts to make unified and conclusive sense of her student's writing, despite its conflicting moves of self-assertion and self-censorship, were shaped by her own situated desire to bring her narrative to a unified and hopeful closure.

The essays in the third section focus on issues of content in composition courses and across a range of textual, curricular, and cultural settings. Each explores the ways that particular assignments and kinds of writing draw from, inform, and affect other discourses and situations within the academy and in the larger culture.

In "The Myth of Transcendence and the Problem of the 'Ethics' Essay in College Writing Instruction," David Jolliffe draws from classical rhetoric to consider the efficacy and place of the "ethics" essay in composition courses—the traditional assignment that asks students to take a stand on a moral or ethical question that may have little or no immediate bearing on their daily lives. He questions whether students can transcend their material culture by criticizing it and envisioning "moral" solutions in their writing. Our expectation that the kind of critical thinking and writing we ask students to do in composition classes will automatically be transferred to other classes and real world situations runs counter, he argues, to the ways students actually incorporate coursework into their lives. What *can* be transferred from composition courses to other fields and domains, he says, is an understanding of the specific dynamic that exists in all fields "between the way an intellectual community constructs knowledge in writing and the genres it uses to configure that knowledge." For this reason, Jolliffe maintains that composition courses must have a specific content so that students can "participate in an inquiring community" and "learn about writing by investigating this subject matter."

In "The 'Kinds of Language' Curriculum," David Bleich suggests that the classroom become a place for the "interrogation" and "collective critique" of the kinds of language students use inside and outside of school. Citing instances of student writing from a course he taught, a course in which students from diverse backgrounds studied the language they used in both academic and informal settings, Bleich argues for a curriculum that would accept "the widest variety of existing 'kinds' [of language] . . . proper and improper, culturally masculine or feminine, private and public, scientific and humanistic." Such a curriculum would be derived from both the existing knowledge and the interpersonal and societal relations of its constituents. As these relations are always in flux, the uses of language that would form the content of a writing course would contribute to "changing the social relations of the classroom" as well as to integrating "the memberships of different academic interests and classrooms more fully."

Rhonda C. Grego proposes another way for integrating knowledge and lived experience in the academy. In "Writing Academic Autobiographies: Finding a Common Language across the Curriculum," Grego observes that writing-across-the-curriculum workshops typically focus on discipline-specific modes of discourse or on vocabularies derived from rhetorical theory rather than on the "interpersonal, peopled contexts of our individual academic experiences." Maintaining that "the only shared languages available to us are the languages of primary subjective experience," she advocates an approach to WAC workshops that enlists the personal stories and writing histories of the faculty participants. Inviting participants to explore and compare "academic autobiographies," she says, would foster "a much-needed exchange of ideas and information about disciplines."

Concluding this volume is an essay on intertextuality that is itself an example of how texts are made out of other texts. In "So Happy a Skill," Robert Scholes claims (and illustrates) that all writing is "directed toward the boundaries of our knowledge" and that writing always involves the reworking of old ideas in new contexts. En route to his conclusion that "we must find topics for our writing courses that enable students to focus on their culture at the points where it most clearly impinges upon them," he advocates both creative "stealing" and the disfiguring of texts we regard as examples of good writing. Subversive exercises such as these, he suggests, remind us that "the topic of any course exists as the object of a discourse, a body of texts connected by a certain way of naming its objects that is ultimately metaphorical." Since "culture," for Scholes, is always textual, bound by the discourses that produce and reproduce it, acts of writing that interrogate or disrupt are metaphorical, involving a "skill" that he terms a "happy one" because it is "based on play."

This volume is meant to be both provocative and instructive, to stimulate thinking and debate among educators across a broad political spectrum and to provide strategies for those teachers asking practical questions similar to those of our contributors. As we've put this volume together, however—as we've selected essays, organized them into their present sequence, summarized them, written this introduction—we have been made all the more aware that reading and writing are, indeed, political acts. While no ideas can be said to escape ideology, few ideas are inherently political, their politics self-evident at the point of utterance. Rather it is our particular acts of reading and writing, against the background of our own situated frames of reference, that make them so. Thus, as we've compiled and edited this text, we have been drawn inescapably into the book's own vortex, aware at each step that ours is a point of view, a way of reading and rendering that privileges our own agendas and at times conceals those agendas—even from us. In light of these necessary omissions and commissions both flagrant and otherwise, and in the dialectical spirit that pervades this book, we invite readers to construct their own itineraries for reading this volume rather than feel compelled to follow the course suggested by the present organization. We encourage readers to consider the different ways individual essays complement or complicate the others (such as Mortensen's and Reagan's; Qualley's and LaDuc's); to notice how different issues emerge when an essay in one section is paired with an essay in another (for example, the chapters by Sanborn and Jolliffe); and to explore the intertextual tensions that result when discrete essays are juxtaposed. We note with special interest in this last regard that the essays framing this volume, those of Greene and Scholes, enact a philosophical tension emblematic of the present field of composition. As Scholes stages the type of textual performance he advocates for writing courses, he seems to occupy the "view from nowhere" that Greene implores writing teachers to resist. Scholes engages in a textual practice, a play of differences, which he construes as metaphorical rather than political; thus, even as it foregrounds the materiality of language, Scholes's essay transcends any stance in particular, a perspective Greene feels we can ill afford when the material circumstances of our students' lives—the social conditions which foster their literacies—are at stake.

Although we have placed Scholes's essay last in this volume, we would preempt a linear reading of this collection that would grant him the last word, so to speak, by pointing out that his essay, in effect, returns us to Hairston. In the composition pedagogy Scholes imagines, we find echoes of Hairston's assertion that we can and should leave dogma, politics, and ideology at the door of our classrooms and attend to the work that unites us: teaching writing as process and craft. In confronting Hairston once again, we also confront the central question this book poses: whether politics belong in the composition course and, if so, what teaching practices might best be put to this end. We believe this collection provides answers to both questions, answers that are well-considered and informed, but answers that are, finally, "sides" in a larger debate, points of departure in an ongoing dialectic. We invite our readers to join with the authors here and enter this dialectic, to examine the processes and genres they teach, and, with an eye directed toward composition's still unwritten chapters, confront what it means to teach writing and reading in this most interesting of times.

Works Cited

Bullock, Richard, and John Trimbur, eds. *The Politics of Writing Instruction: Postsecondary*. Portsmouth, NH: Boynton/Cook, 1991.

Elbow, Peter. *Writing without Teachers*. New York: Oxford UP, 1973.

Gebhardt, Richard. "Theme Issue Feedback and Fallout." *College Composition and Communication* 43 (Oct. 1992): 295–96.

Graff, Gerald. *Beyond the Culture Wars: How Teaching the Conflicts Can Revitalize American Education*. New York: Norton, 1992.

Hairston, Maxine. "Breaking Our Bonds and Reaffirming Our Connections." *College Composition and Communication* 36 (Oct. 1985): 272–82.

———. "Diversity, Ideology, and Teaching Writing." *College Composition and Communication* 43 (May 1992): 179–93.

Harkin, Patricia, and John Schilb, eds. *Contending with Words: Composition and Rhetoric in a Postmodern Age.* New York: MLA, 1991.

Macrorie, Ken. *Telling Writing.* 4th ed. Portsmouth, NH: Boynton/Cook, 1985.

Miller, Susan. *Textual Carnivals: The Politics of Composition.* Carbondale, IL: Southern Illinois UP, 1991.

Murray, Donald. "Finding Your Own Voice: Teaching Composition in an Age of Dissent." In *Learning by Teaching: Selected Articles on Writing and Teaching.* Portsmouth, NH: Boynton/Cook, 1982. 139–45.

Ohmann, Richard. *Politics of Letters.* Middletown, CN: Wesleyan UP, 1987.

1 Teaching for Openings: Pedagogy as Dialectic

Maxine Greene
Teachers College, Columbia University

Risking a charge of hubris, I choose to start with a quotation from Michel Foucault's *Discourse on Language*:

> I would really like to have slipped imperceptibly into this lecture. . . . I would have preferred to be enveloped in words, borne way beyond all possible beginnings. At the moment of speaking, I would like to have perceived a nameless voice, long preceding me, leading me merely to enmesh myself in it, taking up its cadence, and to lodge myself, when no one else was looking, in its interstices as if it had paused an instant, in suspense, to beckon to me. There would have been no beginnings; instead, speech would proceed from me. (215)

I am tempted, you see, to remain within what Foucault called "the established order of things"—pedagogical things, liberal educational things. I am drawn to affirm the timelessness of what I have come to love over the years, of what I choose to think of as the very sources of my self. Allowing myself to be carried along by the great conversation initiated by others (and, indeed, maintained by others), I do not have to disrupt it. I do not have to begin anything; I need only be swept along by what the great ones have said and remain partly submerged.

But then I think of how much beginnings have to do with freedom, how much disruption has to do with consciousness and the awareness of possibility. And I think that if I truly want to provoke others to break through the limits of the conventional and the taken-for-granted, I myself have to experience breaks with what has been established in my own life; I have to keep arousing myself to begin again. I recall the philosopher Maurice Merleau-Ponty writing that "choice and action alone cut us loose from anchorage" (*Phenomenology* 456), and Virginia Woolf writing about the "shock-receiving capacity" that probably made her a writer (72). Both of them move me to reach into my own story, into the ambivalence of my own choosing and the desire to stir others—along with me—to act in such a way that we do break loose

1

from anchorage, that we become different, that we reach beyond where we are.

I must recognize, however, how hard it has been to confront the controls, the principle of exclusion and denial that have allowed me a certain range of utterances and prevented others. I have not easily come to terms with the ways in which what education permits and forbids in different people's experiences too often follows the lines of class, gender, and race. (I think at once of the performance artist Karen Finley talking about the fear of naming and what doesn't get talked about, and of the children Michelle Fine discovered who expressed a "terror of words" [159], and of what Mina Shaughnessy called the "trap" set by academic writing for entering students at the City University in New York [71].) I say the words but evade the implications of what most of us acknowledge by now: that "every educational system is a political means of maintaining or of modifying the appropriation of discourse, with the knowledge and powers it carries with it" (Foucault 227). I have wanted to believe that education has been a means of giving every living person access to any sort of discourse that person might prefer. I have believed that literacy is a personal achievement, a door to personal meaning. It has taken an effort (and still takes an effort) to realize how much literacy is involved in relations of power, how it must be understood in context and in relation to a social world.

I have to keep choosing myself and my project in connection with what I keep trying to learn in these domains. If my teaching is indeed to lead to openings in experience, I must continually discover and rediscover (as a practitioner among other practitioners) what it signifies to encounter openings myself. I have to be willing to "surmount the boundaries in which all customary views are confined, and to reach a more open territory" (Heidegger 13). Yes, it is a matter of transcending the given, of entering a field of possibles. We are only likely to do that, however, when we become aware of something lacking in the world around as seen from our situated vantage points. We have to exert ourselves to *name* what we see around us (the hungers, the passivity, the homelessness, the inarticulateness) and reach out somehow, not only to envisage and imagine, but to repair. (Saying that, I cannot but recall Dr. Rieux's voice at the end of Camus's *The Plague*, speaking of those "unable to be saints but refusing to bow down to pestilences" who "strive their utmost to be healers" [278]. To do that, I have always thought, requires the ability to see clearly through our own eyes, to speak clearly—as Dr. Rieux does—in our own voices.)

In my own case, immersed as I was for so long and immersed as I wanted to be, it took years before I realized that the tradition I had entered required that I look through the eyes of the Other, that I master a way of speaking that was not my natural way of articulating the world. It came as a painful shock to realize that what I had believed was universal, transcending gender and class and race, was a set of points of view. I had considered it a kind of beneficence for someone like me to be initiated into this dimension of the culture's conversation, even if it were only a stream or a rivulet of "nameless voices" made faintly available to those who did not quite belong. Now, in the very midst of remembered delights and still-beckoning desires, I found myself challenged (*directly* challenged) to think about my own thinking and, at once, about that in which I was submerged. And that meant singling out the determinants in my life, the seductions as well as the controls; and it meant fending them off, if I could, resisting them, widening the spaces in which I could choose for myself.

That is what I mean by the dialectic: the recognition of the determinants and of the inevitable tension between the desire to *be* and the forces that condition from within and without. Not to identify those forces is, very often, to acquiesce in oppression. It may be to live what Milan Kundera describes as the "unbearable lightness of being" among chance happenings and fortuitous encounters, without possibility. The alternative to such "lightness" does not have to be a submission to determinism, or to what Kundera calls *es muss sein*. It can be a life lived in tension and a kind of ardor, with the dialectical struggle never quite resolved. We would not need to be wide-awake to ourselves and our lives if it could be resolved—if we could exist somehow without contraries or contradictions, ascending with nothing in our way.

When I ponder my own history, I realize that I can never quite overcome the unease caused by the tension between my unalloyed love for, say, the works of Flaubert, Baudelaire, Melville, Cézanne, Debussy, and Stevens, and my recognition that theirs are male speakings and imaginings and soundings which demand a diversity of decodings and interpretings, not reverential uncoverings of what is objectively illuminating, objectively *there*. It was the presumed capacity, the learned capacity, to uncover in that fashion that gave me the feeling of being one with those artists. Following the rules, I thought, I could make their visions mine. Today there is unease because the very metaphor of uncovering no longer serves, nor does the idea of a preexistent vision. *I* am obligated to achieve those works as meaningful by paying heed to them through a range of shifting perspectives, including those created by my own embodied consciousness. How do I break through the circles I am likely to create? What do I do about what Gadamer calls my "prejudgments" (9)? It is with that sort of unease and in the midst of interrogation that I find my freedom, it seems to me, because the initiatives I find myself required to take open spaces in which I must make choices and act upon the choices I make. I recall Martin Buber speaking about teaching and about the importance of "keeping the pain awake" (116); and, for me, the pain he had in mind must be lived through by teacher as well as student, even as the life stories of both must be kept alive.

It is important for me, for example, to summon up the ways in which I was demeaned in my early days of college teaching by being told I was too "literary" to do philosophy. That meant I was ill-equipped to do the sort of detached and rigorous analysis of language games and arguments that for a long time dominated the academic world. I could not objectify, nor separate my subjectivity from, what I was perceiving. I could not separate my feeling, imagining, wondering consciousness from the cognitive work assigned for me to do. Nor could I bracket out my biography and my experiences of embeddedness in an untidy, intersubjective world. Only now, trying to understand the contexts of the dominant intellectual preoccupations and their connection with gender issues and sexuality, trying to name the relationship between academic norms and the demands of an advanced technological society, trying to grasp the real meaning of instrumental rationality in a universe of suffering children and desperate mothers and thousands of struggling poor, can I begin to identify what stopped me and stood in my way. Gaining perspective on it now, pondering a better state of things, I can try to achieve my freedom in an expanded sphere. I hope it is one in which I can act—as teacher, as practitioner—somehow to transform what is inhuman, what alienates people from themselves.

Still caught in turmoils of interrogation, in what Buber called the pain, I am likely to feel the pull of my old search for certainty. I find myself now and then yearning after the laws and norms and formulations, even though I know how many of them were constructed in the interests of those in power. The appeal of those norms to me was not only due to the ways in which they provided barriers against relativism. It was also due in a strange way to my marginality: I wanted so much to be accepted in the great world of wood-panelled libraries, authoritative intellectuals, sophisticated urban cafés. My response to the criticisms I received early on was to turn away from the local and particular in my life, to strive for an incarnation of values that promised to transcend gender and class and race. And, indeed, we are frequently exhorted today that self-interest and provincialism can best be overcome through mastery of a monological "cultural literacy" justified by an almost transcendent notion of "national community" (Hirsch 137). Rejecting that for a range of reasons, I can still feel drawn to the idea of what Hilary Putnam calls a "view from nowhere" (27). I always liked feeling like one of Plato's prisoners released from the cave and standing in the blinding light of disembodied reason. Knowing better, I even liked the idea of the objectively universalizable, the overwhelmingly True.

It took time for me to realize that the Great White Father, along with the eternal verities, was as much a construct as the indifferent God paring his nails in Joyce's *Portrait of the Artist as a Young Man*. But that did not leave me quiescent in the face of loss. I think of the "forlornness" about which Jean-Paul Sartre used to write, about what it signifies to be alone with no excuses (*Existentialism*). A kind of homesickness accompanies such a response, even when the individual realizes that he or she is not literally alone but caught up in intersubjectivity. That is why so many people still turn eagerly toward the stable, the monolithic, the monological. We want a foothold in an era of collapsing hierarchies, when the world is increasingly viewed as "continuously changing, irreducibly various, and multiply configurable" (Smith 183). The debate over the National Endowment for the Arts is evidence of this, as is the defensiveness displayed by some with respect to the canon in the humanities, or the resistance to curricula "of difference," wherever they appear.

It has taken many shocks of awareness to make me realize how I existed within the tradition (or the "conversation") as within a container. Merleau-Ponty, warning against this, reminds us of the importance of keeping our ideas open to the field of nature and culture which they must express. "The idea of going straight to the essence of things is an inconsistent idea if one thinks about it. What is given is a route, an experience which gradually clarifies itself, which gradually rectifies itself and proceeds by dialogue with itself and with others. . . . What saves us is the possibility of a new development" (*Primacy* 21). The dialogue can be generated and enriched by the writing some of us try to do, the journals we keep along with others. Even now it helps me to be in search of words, to break with immersion by seeing and saying. Yes, working in a dialogical relation with students, I want to communicate what this can mean; but, at the same time, I want them to make their perspectives available so that we can all see from many vantage points, make sense from different sides. I want us to work together to unconceal what is hidden, to contextualize what happens to us, to mediate the dialectic that keeps us on edge, that may be keeping us alive.

I have to keep summoning up the experiences that gave me what Woolf calls "moments of being" and the ones that buried me in cotton wool, in the hope that that will arouse others to couch some of their stories in similar ways. I have to communicate what it signifies to treat the texts we read together as "open" in Umberto Eco's sense. The reader in the presence of an open work, writes Eco, supplies her or his own existential credentials, a sense of conditioning particularly her or his own, a defined culture, a "set of tastes, personal inclinations, and prejudices" (49). The reader's own perspective, in other words, affects and modifies comprehension of the work. Then Eco goes on to say that "the form of the work of art gains its aesthetic validity precisely in proportion to the number of different perspectives from which it can be viewed and understood." There are important connections between this and Robert Scholes's treatment of interpretation in his *Protocols of Reading*, of the importance of protocols, and of the idea (taken from Barthes and similar to Freire's) of "rewriting the texts that we read in the texts of our lives . . . and rewriting our lives in the light of those texts" (155).

I am moved to offer examples, surely not unique, of how a tapping of perspectives while reading enabled me and still enables me to read my world differently. To articulate what can be discovered and to make it part of the dialogue in a classroom may in time move those of us who are teachers to wonder about going beyond reading the world to, as Freire says, "transforming it by means of conscious, practical work" (35). There are ways of being dialogical in relation to the texts we read together; and it can become crucial to reflect—opening to one another—upon the texts of our lives.

My first examples are taken from the poetry of Elizabeth Bishop. In "At the Fishhouses," she writes about a childhood experience with an old man repairing nets at a fishhouse, with seals now and then appearing in the cold dark water, and the fir trees behind. She speaks of how the water swings indifferently and icily above the stones, and how your hand would burn if you were to dip it in the water. And then:

> If you tasted it, it would first taste bitter,
> then briny, then surely burn your tongue.
> It is like what we imagine knowledge to be:
> dark, salt, clear, moving, utterly free,
> drawn from the cold hard mouth

of the world, derived from the rocky breasts
forever, flowing and drawn, and since
our knowledge is historical, flowing, and flown.
(65-66)

The very idea of flow, of change, of history is to me a challenge and
a critique, whatever Elizabeth Bishop intended. Not only systems but
discrete and formalized particles of knowledge are put into question
here, as is ungrounded knowledge that is its own excuse for being.
All this constituted a shock for me on first and second reading, a
rupture of some of the containers in which I had lived and thought I
wanted to live. And when students began pouring in their own
inclinations and prejudices and memories (especially in response to
the bitter taste, and the salty clarity, and the startling flow as from a
stone fountain) I found something like a common text emerging among
us, one that—in our diversity—we began to read and reread, and
even began to rewrite.

Something similar happened when I read Bishop's poem called "In
the Waiting Room," recounting a seven-year-old child's wait while her
aunt is in the dentist's office, one winter during the First World War.
The child (the Elizabeth child, presented in the first person) is looking
at a *National Geographic* magazine and then at the grown-up people
sitting around the room.

I said to myself: three days
and you'll be seven years old.
I was saying it to stop
the sensation of falling off
the round, turning world
into cold, blue-black space.
But I felt: you are an *I*,
you are an *Elizabeth*,
you are one of *them*.
Why should you be one, too?
I scarcely dared to look
to see what it was I was. (160)

The interrogative mode; the painful particularity; the sensation of
falling into space; all these introduce a vantage point that subverts
the systematic, the complete. At once, at least for me and some of
those with whom I learn, it enhances the tension, the consciousness
of dialectic. Feeling ourselves on a kind of verge, we all try to carve
a space in which we can break the peculiar silences and choose.

Christa Wolf, in her novel *Cassandra*, creates a narrator who tells
us that the excluded always recognize and understand each other. This
makes me ponder the ways in which my own acquaintance with

silence and the uncertainty involved in seeking my own voice might help me begin to understand how it is with people of color—African American men and women, Hispanics newly arrived or long resident. Ralph Ellison's narrator, at the start of *Invisible Man*, makes very clear that his "invisibility" (perhaps the invisibility of any minority) "occurs because of a peculiar disposition of the eyes of those with whom I come in contact. A matter of the construction of their inner eyes, those eyes with which they look through their physical eyes upon reality" (1). How am I to look? How am I to hear? Ellison's narrator speaks of the importance of recognition; and I understand that I can only recognize a person like him (like the others whom I meet) against my own lived situation, my own life history. I need to try to see, whenever possible, through their eyes as well as my own, if they are willing to engage in dialogue, if they are willing to offer clues. I think, for example, of the clue that appears in *Invisible Man*, where the narrator begins and ends his story "underground," treating (it might be) *Notes from Underground* as open text. When I reach the concluding pages, I read:

> In going underground, I whipped it all except the mind, the *mind*. And the mind that has conceived a plan of living must never lose sight of the chaos against which that pattern was conceived. That goes for societies as well as individuals. Thus, having tried to give pattern to the chaos which lives within the pattern of your certainties, I must come out, I must emerge. (502)

Not only does reading Ellison's text raise questions that might affect my own "inner eyes." He allows us to discover (perhaps uncomfortably) a new intertextuality, enabling us in some way to rewrite *Notes from Underground*—as well as Emerson's "The American Scholar" and Mark Twain's *Adventures of Huckleberry Finn*—within the texts of our lives.

There are, too, the amazing shocks stimulated by Toni Morrison's works, opening yet other modes of recognition, against the background of our own lives. In *The Bluest Eye*, for example, we engage with the story of Pecola Breedlove and the ways in which she was destroyed by two of the culture's master narratives: the "Dick and Jane" basal readers, and the myth of Shirley Temple with her blue eyes. For Pecola, the standard of human reality is set by those blue eyes; and, whether or not her situation matches ours in its particulars, it may still move us to rewrite those parts of the texts of our world that have similarly constrained us. The text's vantage point on the unloved Pecola is that of two other children, loved ones, who defend themselves by considering "all speech a code to be broken by us, and all gestures subject to careful analysis" (149). They are proud and arrogant because they have to be; unlike Pecola, they survive. "We tried to see her without looking at her, and never, never went near. Not because she was absurd or repulsive, or because we were frightened, but because we had failed her. Our flowers never grew." The years go on; Pecola picks and plucks her way between the tire rims and milkweed, "among all the waste and beauty of the world, which she herself was." Then the narrators talk of feeling wholesome after cleaning themselves on Pecola: "Her simplicity decorated us, her guilt sanctified us, her pain made us glow with health, her awkwardness made us think we had a sense of humor. Even her waking dreams we used to silence our own nightmares" (159). There are descriptions like these in Morrison's *Sula* as well. Sula's friend Nel thinks that Sula's return home is like getting an eye back. "Talking to Sula had always been a conversation with herself. . . . Sula never competed; she simply helped others define themselves" (82).

Can it be that, in the struggle to define ourselves, strangers like Sula do indeed enter the dialectic when it comes to choosing who we are? Again, I am drawn to wonder about how we can all discover together against the diversity of our backgrounds, write together, draw upon each others' existential realities to create what Hannah Arendt has called an "in-between" (182). "Everyone's liberation must be self-won," writes Catherine Stimpson (35); I know this, but I want to go further with her and with those around me to open terrains, to communities where our engagements can be wide and deep at once. I am driven to wonder about looking through the perspectives of more and more persons at the history we have made, at a society that may or may not survive. And then I remind myself again that there is no objective reality, not even with regard to someone else's life. Receptive, wondering as we try to be, we can only understand through the play of our own assumptions, our own prejudgments, our own memories and, perhaps, what Toni Morrison's Sethe in *Beloved* calls our "re-memory" (191). There is no information or knowledge anywhere that can be taken in or absorbed by empty consciousnesses. We can only attend from our own interpretive communities, if we can learn to name the appropriate strategies and make them understandable to those we are trying to engage with and somehow understand. And, at the same time, we need to continue enlarging those communities until (using Edward Said's words) we create a secular realm with "a more open sense of community as something to be won and of audiences as human beings to be addressed" (152).

That must mean a transformation of what Elizabeth Fox-Genovese has called the elite culture white male scholars tend to create, one that has "functioned in relation to women, the lower classes, and some white races analogously to the way in which imperialism functioned for colonized people. At worst, it denied the values of all others and imposed itself as an absolute standard" (140-41). She also points out that the canon, "or the power to speak for the collectivity, results from social and gender relations and struggles, not from nature. Those who fashioned our collective elite tradition were the victors of history." I am thrust back again into the contradictions of my life when I read that; and again I am reminded of the differential meanings of literacy. As a set of techniques, it has often silenced persons and disempowered them. Our obligation today is to find ways of enabling the young to find their voices, to open their spaces, to reclaim their histories in all their variety and discontinuity. Attention has to be paid to those on the borders, on the margins, the too frequently smothered voices from Latin America, Africa, the Middle East, Southeast Asia. Writers like Freire today and Du Bois in time past ask, as increasing numbers are beginning to do, that we pay special heed to the defeated, the submerged, the oppressed. Again, it is a matter of releasing them, if we can, to make their claims, to break with their silences, to thematize and articulate their worlds. And we can only do this against our own lived stories, from the situations in which we are living our lives.

This is not romantic or simply a matter of goodwill. We are going to be increasingly a community of newcomers in the years ahead: some of us from the danger of the neglected ghettos, some exhausted from their suffering under dictators, some stunned by lives in refugee camps, some unabashedly in search of economic success. The texts are and will be all around us. We have to make them accessible, offer the protocols, keep them open. We have to insist on opportunities for persons to structure their experiences by means of those texts, by means of books men and women have made. Sartre speaks of such works as gifts and says:

> And if I am given this world with its injustices, it is not so I might contemplate them coldly, but that I might animate them with my indignation, that I might disclose them and create them with their nature as injustices, that is, as abuses to be suppressed. Thus, the writer's universe will only reveal itself in all its depth to the examination, the admiration, and the indignation of the reader; and the generous love is a promise to maintain, and the generous indignation is a promise to change, and the admiration is a promise to imitate; although literature is one thing and morality a quite different one, at the heart of the aesthetic imperative we discern the moral imperative. For, since the one who writes recognizes, through the very fact that he takes the

> trouble to write, the freedom of his readers, and since the one
> who reads, by the mere fact of his opening the book, recognizes
> the freedom of the writer, the work of art, from whichever side
> you approach it, is an act of confidence in the freedom of men.
> (*Literature* 62–63)

Wishing he had said "human beings" rather than "men," I still find it deeply important that Sartre saw literature as an imaginary presentation of the world "insofar as it demands human freedom." I even find in that passage a source of paradigms for teaching, if teaching is indeed for openings, if we are concerned that choices be made. Not having time to explore the ways there are of involving people with the necessary protocols (something Sartre took as seriously as Scholes), I want to keep emphasizing the dialectical character of the reading experience as I do the dialectical character of the teaching act.

And, finally, I want to suggest once more the sense in which literacy is and must be a social undertaking, to be sought in pluralist classrooms where persons come together "in speech and action" to create something in common among themselves (Arendt 19). There will be a play of differences, inevitably, through which meanings can emerge. There will be, there ought to be, moments of recognition, moments of doubt. But there will be endless, restless interrogation as diverse persons strive to create themselves in their freedom. I think of *The Plague* again and Tarrou saying that "all our troubles spring from our failure to use plain, clean language. So I resolved always to speak—and to act— quite clearly.... That's why I decided to take the victims' side, so as to reduce the damage done" (230). And, of course, that is the point of the novel: in times of pestilence to take the victims' side. These may be times of pestilence for us. That is why, like Camus's Tarrou, we need to be attentive, to be vigilant, if we are to open texts and spaces, if we are to provoke the young to be free.

Works Cited

Arendt, Hannah. *The Human Condition*. Chicago: U of Chicago P, 1958.

Bishop, Elizabeth. *The Complete Poems, 1927–1979*. New York: Farrar, Straus and Giroux, 1983.

Buber, Martin. *Between Man and Man*. Boston: Beacon, 1957.

Camus, Albert. *The Plague*. New York: Knopf, 1948.

Eco, Umberto. *The Open Work*. Cambridge, MA: Harvard UP, 1984.

Ellison, Ralph. *Invisible Man*. New York: Signet, 1952.

Fine, Michelle. "Silencing in Public Schools." *Language Arts* 64.2 (Feb. 1987): 157–74.

Foucault, Michel. *The Archaeology of Knowledge* and *The Discourse on Language*. New York: Pantheon, 1972.

Fox-Genovese, Elizabeth. "The Claims of a Common Culture: Gender, Race, Class, and the Canon." *Salmagundi* 72 (Fall 1986): 101–63.

Freire, Paulo. "The Importance of the Act of Reading." In *Literacy: Reading the Word and the World*. Ed. Paulo Freire and Don Macedo. South Hadley, MA: Bergin and Garvey, 1987.

Gadamer, Hans-Georg. *Philosophical Hermeneutics*. Berkeley and Los Angeles: U of California P, 1976.

Heidegger, Martin. *What Is Called Thinking?* New York: Harper and Row, 1968.

Hirsch, E. D. *Cultural Literacy: What Every American Needs to Know*. Boston: Houghton Mifflin, 1987.

Kundera, Milan. *The Unbearable Lightness of Being*. New York: Harper and Row, 1984.

Merleau-Ponty, Maurice. *Phenomenology of Perception*. New York: Harcourt, Brace and World, 1967.

———. *The Primacy of Perception*. Evanston, IL: Northwestern UP, 1964.

Morrison, Toni. *The Bluest Eye*. New York: Bantam, 1970.

———. *Sula*. New York: Bantam, 1975.

———. *Beloved*. New York: Random House, 1987.

Putnam, Hilary. "After Empiricism." In *Post-Analytic Philosophy*. Ed. John Rajchman and Cornel West. New York: Columbia UP, 1975.

Said, Edward W. "Opponents, Audiences, Constituencies and Community." In *The Anti-Aesthetic*. Ed. Hal Foster. Port Townsend, WA: Bay Press, 1983.

Sartre, Jean-Paul. *Existentialism*. New York: Philosophical Library, 1947.

———. *Literature and Existentialism*. New York: Citadel, 1954.

Scholes, Robert. *Protocols of Reading*. New Haven, CT: Yale UP, 1989.

Shaughnessy, Mina. *Errors and Expectations*. New York: Oxford UP, 1977.

Smith, Barbara Herrnstein. *Contingencies of Value*. Cambridge: Harvard UP, 1988.

Stimpson, Catherine R. *Where the Meanings Are: Feminism and Cultural Spaces*. New York: Routledge, 1989.

Wolf, Christa. *Cassandra: A Novel and Four Essays*. Trans. Jan Van Heurck. New York: Farrar, Straus and Giroux, 1984.

Woolf, Virginia. *Moments of Being*. New York: Harcourt Brace Jovanovich, 1976.

2 Advocacy and Resistance in the Writing Class: Working toward Stasis

Karen Fitts
Loyola College in Maryland

Alan W. France
West Chester University

These are trying times for those attempting to teach writing as a critical, rhetorically sophisticated engagement with questions of language and power. In the first place, many in the academy continue to believe, honestly or strategically, that teaching writing can and ought to be a politically neutral process. Then, recently, conflicts over the pathology and prognosis of institutionalized social inequities (particularly those of race and gender) have been portrayed by conservatives—and those in the press who understand that anti-intellectualism is good copy in America—as evidence of a radical academic fifth column. This new Red Scare of "political correctness" has frightened even that stalwart of rhetoric and composition studies, Maxine Hairston, who has recently condemned "turning . . . [the] composition course into a forum for debate on social issues" (1). Teachers of rhetoric and writing should avoid political controversies, Hairston argues, because students are not interested in them and instructors lack "expertise" in "complex psychological and social problems" like racism and sexism. She believes that grade-conscious students will simply "parrot" their instructors' opinions on controversial issues (1).

To be clear from the outset, we write in this essay from a "politically correct" standpoint in the sense that that term is understood on the right and in the popular press. Our politics are materialist-feminist, and they are central to our pedagogical and professional ethos. It is important to us, for example, that our teaching practices actively challenge the white, middle-class consensus that Americans can afford to ignore the poverty strangling inner-city life, the general erosion of

13

women's reproductive rights, and the growing ecological threat of Western technologies. We share with other "politically correct" academics the concern that the democratic and liberatory ideal of a university education is increasingly being reduced to "disciplines" that will make Americans more productive in the workplace.

At the same time, as professors of rhetoric, we are also committed to open democratic forums, free expression of conflicting arguments, and an empathetic classroom environment for our students' apprenticeship in the public discourse of self-governance. We are, in short, as opposed to the institution of "thought police" as any conservative critic of "political correctness." But unlike those on the right, we do not believe that writing can be separated from politics, that there are ideologically neutral topics that students can write about. Hairston's insistence that students write about "their own ideas" merely confirms the ideology of privatization which shepherds students away from questions of social equity unpalatable to beneficiaries of the status quo.

The issue, simply put, is this: can the writing instructor, inevitably committed to some ideological position or another, cultivate an open and honest dialogue about public events? Or, in other words, does fairness require limiting the topoi of composition classes to the supposedly personal or objective so that students are not forced to bend the knee to their teachers' political agendas?

We argue that in order to be ethical, instructors should articulate their political commitments; furthermore, that when governed by sound pedagogical practice, this approach is a great advantage to students of rhetoric and writing. In the first place, teaching rhetoric requires "modeling" political advocacy. And advocacy itself is necessary to any dialogue—to any authentic, therefore rhetorical, exchange. In fact, we will argue that the dialectical exchange anticipated by a "forensic" (Sloane) or "sophistic" (Jarratt) pedagogy actually precludes the one-sided imposition of "truth" or "political correctness" that critics on the right fear.

There are two basic reasons that political advocacy should be considered an appropriate rhetorical stance for teaching rhetoric in introductory writing courses. The first has to do with the rhetorical nature of truth-claims. As Thomas Sloane maintains, all discourse is one or another kind of argument, and the forensic approach to establishing truth is "paradigmatic of rhetorical thinking itself" (468). It aims at discovering *stasis*: the point at issue, "the precise point on which the dispute seems to turn" (466). The discovery of stasis, as Richard Fulkerson suggests, proceeds by interrogating a claim as if it were a prima facie case presented at law: "the case (extended argument) made for a claim is structurally and substantively complete so that if no counter-case were presented then the claim would stand" (448).

Approaching an argument's point of stasis means exhausting, as nearly as possible, all the perspectives—not just binary, pro-and-con "sides"—into which arguments have been conventionally sedimented. In this sense, stasis is a critical method appropriate to rhetorical invention and analysis in much the same way poststructural literary theory is suited to "discovering" or inventing critical readings of literary texts. It isolates or "freezes" the topos, allowing the writer to observe minutely the social, cultural, and psychological implications of its claim to veracity. This technique encourages students to step back and walk around a proposition, examining its construction and looking, in particular, for the gaps and fissures, the telltale signs of covert interests, dogmas, and desires. The instructor's job is to keep the complex process bubbling, and for this reason political advocacy is a valuable catalyst. Avoiding political issues as Hairston counsels, even if possible, would fail to engage students in those very rhetorical practices that articulate and validate knowledge.

The second reason that "political correctness" in the writing classroom poses no threat to academic freedom is the inexorable and protean operation of culture that we refer to loosely as ideology. Our own experience indicates that Hairston's fears—that students will merely learn to "parrot" the political rectitude of their writing teachers—are largely without basis, if for no other reason than that students find ways (invent rhetorical strategies) to subvert or resist oppositional pedagogies. We would first like to explore the operation of ideological resistance in our own writing classes, returning at the end of this paper to a brief discussion of stasis-seeking pedagogy at work as classroom praxis.

Over the last several semesters, we have attempted to make our classrooms the scene for confronting cultural practices that replicate social inequities. Our objective, therefore, has been to awaken students to the role of culture in giving meaning to—or overlaying with significance—female or male physiology, to use a prominent example. In short, we consider our role to be that of *teaching resistance* to cultural definitions of biological sex by provoking dissonance between egalitarian expectations, on the one hand, and social and cultural asymmetries of power and perceived worth, on the other. We have developed a number of assignments to accomplish this project.

In one assignment we have used, small groups of students research gender in non-Western societies, reporting to the class on the cultural differences they detect. The aim here is to denaturalize and relativize students' own understanding of sexual difference. A second assignment asks students to investigate the ways in which gender restricts or expands people's lives. Our hope is that as they inquire into "real world" social practices—athletics, police work, the arts, domestic arrangements, domestic violence—they will discover that inequities exist and that they may well be rooted in gender.

Another assignment that we have found most provocative of the "critical tension" Dale Bauer recommends to feminist teachers (391) asks students to examine the *visual* representation of gender in a specific cultural text of their own selection—films, print advertising, record album art, and the like. In class, we practice the use of "thick description" and script narratives of textual diegesis. Student research often draws on the growing body of work in film criticism and the rhetoric of advertising, which are most often informed by feminist theory. Inquiry like this, we have come to believe, problematizes these visual representations, helping students to distinguish nature (sex) from culture (gender). The object of their research and criticism is for the students to answer this question: "Anatomy aside, how are men and women different in the world constructed—or imaged—by your text?"

The purpose of these pedagogical practices is to give students the critical ability to recognize and to resist the flood of visual media in which we are all immersed and which to a significant degree determines our identities. Electronic media place an entire ideological apparatus, including the control of visual representations of gender, in the hands of the entertainment and advertising industries. Under this regime, to quote Annette Kuhn, "subjectivity is always gendered and every human being is, and remains, either male or female. . . . Moreover, in ideology gender identity is not merely absolute; it also lies at the very heart of human subjectivity" (52). This is an enormous institutional power over our students, and because it is used to reproduce sexual inequality and stereotypes, we believe that literacy must include a critical awareness of how subjects become engendered in an age of electronic images.

As we began to analyze student responses to our assignments, we noticed that they often invented ways (some rather subtle) to resist the conclusions of their own inquiries. That is to say, they invented rhetorical strategies to reconcile their findings to the ideology of sexual difference that the assignments were calculated to problematize. An awareness of these strategies, or of the directions students' contentions were liable to take, assisted our goal of calling up an alternative world view. In any case, however, it became increasingly clear that our pedagogy—conceived of as oppositional—had indeed become a dialectical process. We had set out to teach students a construction of reality that *we* find just and compelling; but the students, for the most part, clung to the essentialist realities authorized by the dominant culture.

Before we explore the basis of this *aporia*, a statement of pedagogical credo seems in order. We believe that our students, like most Americans who have not developed for themselves any theory of subject-formation, cannot adequately account for the influence of culture on the individual. And to paper over this theoretical absence they must posit the existence of an autonomous self. Since we will be criticizing this vitalist rhetoric with citations from student texts, we risk presenting ourselves as privileged subjects, somehow standing outside culture. How did our understanding of sexual difference seemingly escape the dominant culture that we oppose? The short answer is—we suppose—that our own subjectivity results from the accidental confluence of social forces on our lives, which subverted to some degree the dominant gender patterns and demanded more egalitarian ones. Thus, the internal contradictions of our personal histories have situated us at the critical margin. And it is from this critical margin that we engage our students.

As suggested above, we have discovered that students deploy a number of recurring and interrelated rhetorical strategies to avoid confronting the subjectivity of gender, as opposed to the objective nature of biological sex. We will list these strategies briefly and then illustrate them with specific applications in student texts.

1. Objectification: there exist in nature various objective categories like separate spheres (the public realm for men, the private realm for women).

2. Social meliorism: in the past things were bad, but they are getting better.

3. Pragmatism: solving specific problems—like ending discrimination in the workplace—will lead to sexual equality.

4. Demonology: oppression and exploitation of women are the result of a few bad people or institutions that can be distinguished from "society."

5. Individual autonomy ("freedom of choice"): we can "just say no" to stereotypes and inequities.

It should be pointed out that the student papers we will be quoting from are not the failures, the inferior work of poorer students that is easy to cite invidiously, but the efforts of strong writers who understand what is at stake and who are insisting on their own construction of the world—the dominant one that we are opposing.

We will begin with objectification. Our students still inhabit a world of Cartesian dualism. The result is that they have a hard time distinguishing between *sex*, patently an objective characteristic existing in the "real world," and *gender*, a cultural formation that ascribes meaning to biological identity but is a quality of subjective experience. Without a clear concept of cultural subjectivity, our students often rendered sex and gender as distinct but complementary qualities, the former ascribed by birth, the latter "learned," most often by observation and mimesis, from "society." The continual blurring of biology and culture reduces gender to a set of objective characteristics that the subject must consciously learn to match with her or his physiology. Gender itself thus becomes an objective category. And this, as we hope to show, opens up the space for the privileged subject of experience— the self.

This "naturalization" of gender caused one student, in an essay examining homophobia, to speculate in these words:

> Some individuals are born with a gender problem. They are brought up . . . in a way that goes against proper gender traits, *sexually* a male or female but gender-wise the opposite. Our society still believes that a man should be a man and a woman should be a woman. If the sex of a person conflicts with the gender of that person, operations can be done to alter the problem.

In this case, clarification of the blurred categories seems to require surgery. More commonly, it entails the recognition of separate, and unequal, spheres for men and women. The underlying conviction repeatedly surfaced that men's physical strength determined their dominance in public life and as providers while women's "weakness" and their physiological role in procreation determined their subordination to the domestic sphere. In a paper on gender roles in a native Alaskan society, for example, a student writes that "the men work" (they go on hunting expeditions lasting up to six months) while "the women stay at home with the children." Staying at home turns out to include all kinds of work essential to the group's survival: fishing, making and repairing tools, and trapping and butchering seals. However, the student imposes her own culturally determined understanding of the natural order—including the denigration of women's work— on the cultural arrangements she was investigating, *even though*, by the student's own evidence, that work was highly valued by the group under consideration.

In terms of students' interpretive strategies, the objectification of cultural productions makes for a more or less simplistic realism. Because objects exist "out there" in nature, students have difficulty distinguishing between "representation" (which is constructed) and "reflection" (which implies a direct access to nature). They often use the words interchangeably. In a study of how representation of women on television programs "reinforce[s] our definition of gender," a student concludes:

> Because television needs to be realistic, sometimes it goes too far and isn't representative of our society. On TV, women that have important executive jobs can stay late at work and don't worry about a family when, realistically, most women do have to come home to a family.

Here, even though the student announces the influence of the media in "reinforcing gender," as she puts it, she still holds on to a naive realism according to which TV must reflect or "keep up" with objective social changes (from *The Donna Reed Show* to *Growing Pains*) but not get too far ahead and thereby "misrepresent" the reality of women's changing roles.

This text provides a bridge to the second rhetorical strategy our students use to bring their knowledge into line with their ideology: social meliorism. No matter how bad the world revealed to them by research, students are ready to find that it is getting better. The idea of progress is a venerable and distinctly American response to social problems, and we find that students use it consistently. Most papers, no matter how critical of the status quo, conclude on an upbeat note. A young woman writing on what she calls "the good old boys' club" of TV newscasting concludes with these words:

> If the television news industry starts now, perhaps it can catch up with all the other professions and realize that women can be just as serious, capable, and intelligent as men. Maybe even more so.

Another student, examining the coverage of the 1988 Calgary Winter Olympics, found, in her words, "plenty of babble on women's appearance, their unhappy personal lives, their vulnerabilities and jealousies." Nevertheless, she concludes that "attitudes towards women's involvement in sports are becoming more positive, [and] the perception of women athletes is also improving." When students take such a stance, their commitment to social activism or to the individual's responsibility for political action is significantly eroded because they feel that time itself will somehow improve conditions.

The discovery of progress in the flow of events is closely related to a third technique students use to harmonize the dissonance between what they find and what they believe: pragmatism. The most deeply embedded cultural inequities are cast as "problems" to be solved. This technique appears most commonly in student investigations of the "second-shift" conflicts faced by working women. One student sees the solution as teaching "husbands to get involved with the kids and housework," which can be done by "encouraging the children of the present time that they can play with anything they want to, such as dolls or pretend kitchens." Although this strategy is certainly laudable, we would argue that what children want to play with is determined by complex social forces unresponsive to pragmatic intervention. A male child, for instance, experiencing the profound force the media can bring to bear, is not likely to abandon "male" identity (packaged in the form of G.I. Joe, etc.) at the urging of his mother, a devalued agent in contemporary culture.

Students often contend that inequities, discrimination, and harassment in the workplace can be overcome by winning the respect of colleagues or demonstrating competence to the public. After noting the set arrangement and gestures that subordinate *The Today Show*'s Deborah Norville to her male colleagues, and her assignment to "softer" stories like premature babies and National Secretaries' Day, a student concludes:

> Due to our culture, women are perceived as being weaker and more emotional than men. . . . Until [they] are able to convince the public that they are capable of reporting "hard" news stories, they will be limited in their advancement to the top positions on the television news.

Once the problem of public perception is solved, the student implies, women will be treated equitably. This is probably true, of course, but it fails to consider the monumental cultural transformation involved in changing public perception.

If things are getting better, either because of a natural law of progress or the solution of specific problems, students must still account for much that is wrong in the present. The most common rhetorical strategy for this ideological theodicy is demonology. This move is most often associated with student analyses of advertising or the rock music industry. In a study of jean advertisements, for example, a student finds that the exploitation of women in Calvin Klein, Jordache, and Guess ads has "a negative influence on our culture." Advertisers' exploitation of women in these ads as "seductresses and sexual playthings . . . make[s] women appear cheap and easy, [and] humiliates them in society." The student conceives of the ads as moral corrosives attacking—"fraudulently," as the student puts it—the society to which they pander. The notion that society itself produces as well as consumes the ads is missing entirely from the otherwise incisive analysis. The student conjures up a vision of middle America as basically pristine; in other words, Mom and Dad and the folks back on Poplar Street are not implicated. Sexism can be safely ignored as the product of a few reprehensible sociopaths.

Another student follows the same logic in her genuinely disturbing inquiry into violence and sadism in rock lyrics like those of 2 Live Crew. The author laments the passing of clean-cut "teenie bopper groups" and the rise of music "that contains very corrupting messages. Satanism, sex, rape, drug and alcohol abuse, and suicide [she writes] are just a few of the [messages] that are being sent to innocent and impressionable kids by heavy metal and other groups." Again, the larger social context which governs the production as well as the reception of these messages is not considered.

Finally, we want to consider the most ubiquitous—and the most obvious—rhetorical strategy that students use to contain the political implications of their findings: the positing of an autonomous self capable of being insulated from the corruptions of social life. The ideology of individualism, like the subject-object split which is its philosophical basis, is of course implicit in our categories of social meliorism, pragmatism, and demonology. We will conclude, therefore, with a few examples of the form it has taken in our students' work.

Cultural formation—especially gender—is commonly represented in student discourse not as a set of axes intersecting at the point of the individual subject, but as "learned gender roles." This formulation is common in the sources our students use in their papers, and it is not surprising, therefore, that they frequently separate the "actor" from the "role" he or she learns. As a result, student texts reconstruct for themselves an inner and autonomous self as the player who can choose whether or not to play assigned cultural roles. Thus, a student writes: "Gender refers to the psychological, social, and cultural components of a person's upbringing *and* how that person identifies himself [sic] as a male or female."

Another student writes that "a child is taught to think, feel, and act in ways considered natural, morally appropriate, and desirable for a person of that sex. [With these] lessons we learn to achieve a given gender." Notice that the movement from the cultural subject ("a child") to the self within is marked by the movement from third to first person ("we"). For the student, the shift in person might well represent the desired distancing of the self—the defense of his autonomy—from the necessity of cultural subjectivity.

In terms of the politics of gender, the pervasiveness of individualism is decidedly conservative because it obviates the need for social change. As one student put it with uncharacteristic bluntness: "We all agree change is necessary, but . . . we can begin to change society's attitudes only by changing our own personal attitudes [first]." Another writes somewhat despairingly, in concluding an inquiry into the social significance of blondness, "Women have always been objects or showpieces simply to be looked at. We cannot deny the fact that we have no one to blame for these stereotypes except for ourselves. We created them, and now we will have to destroy them."

From our politically interested perspective, therefore, the efforts to get students thinking in terms of cultural subjectivity instead of individual autonomy were apparently in vain. The "critical tension"—the oppressive identity that Jennifer, the student quoted immediately above, blames on herself—has been relieved or recuperated by the culturally predominant rhetoric of individualism. But from Jennifer's perspective the assignment is a success. In the course of constructing her argument (of achieving stasis), she had been compelled repeatedly to reconfigure her experience in terms of opposing (i.e., feminist) interlocutors, her instructor and several classmates. She finally came to rest at a point, a "structurally and substantively complete" claim, which represents her own prima facie case for individual autonomy. Jennifer has, to warp the legal metaphor, returned the ball to our court. To continue the dialogue, her instructor would have to make a case against the individual's ability to "destroy" stereotypes.

In our classes, we strive to create environments in which the negotiation of truth-claims provides a continual source of critical tension. Our pedagogy is inquiry-driven; we avoid providing the authority for arguments. The instructor's role is stubbornly sophistic; we remain sideline coaches, joining in only to stir up contention when students begin to fall over themselves agreeing with each other. Students, individually and in research groups of three or four, present their claims with supporting evidence to the class. Participation in this public forum often works changes in both speakers and audience. The speakers begin to anticipate their classmates' counterarguments and to recognize them as significant to their purpose. The audience gains an understanding of its role in pressing "experts," or knowledgeable authorities, for the evidence on which their claims rest. As a result, the major research projects, in final form, generally reflect more careful analysis and authorial responsibility than might otherwise have been the case.

Typical of this process was one student's investigation of "welfare abuse." In her first presentation to the class, the student argued that public-assistance programs often support people who are too lazy to work and who want a cushy lifestyle. Some of her classmates, who had first- or secondhand knowledge of cash assistance, medical assistance, food stamps, or job training, countered her claim that "anyone can get a job who is willing to work" and challenged her to examine the standard of living made possible by welfare. As a result of this response to her first presentation, she visited the public-assistance offices in downtown Philadelphia, acquired pamphlets on types of aid available, and interviewed staff workers. She constructed a budget for a family consisting of an unmarried woman with two school-age children and attempted to make the assistance meet the family's most basic needs. By semester's end, she wrote the following:

> A stereotypical folklore story often cites the example of the welfare mother driving up to the district office in her Mercedes-Benz to pick up welfare checks. This has caused the general public to condemn people on welfare as lazy, unmotivated, and system cheaters. The truth is, though, that public assistance programs provide only the minimum survival level for individuals in need.

Student-led argument necessitated by forensic pedagogy impelled this student to modify her claims significantly. Her project clarified for her, as well as for the students who contested her claims, not only the issue of "welfare abuse" but also the larger interactive, or dialogic, process of asserting claims to knowledge.

Lest it appear that we see students change each time in the direction of "political correctness," we should mention the student who determined, following his semester-long research, that a "man's movement" is needed. We are comfortable with the fact that, in spite of the instructor's opposing arguments, the student was able to build a consensus among his classmates for his prima facie case.

Far from stifling the free exchange of ideas, therefore, political advocacy—in the context of a forensic or stasis-seeking pedagogy— facilitates and enriches the dialogue of writing classes. We would agree with Thomas Sloane that advocacy and resistance are the very nature of rhetorical practice. In the struggle to advance our own political agenda against our students' resistance, we have found a way to create a space, an occasion, and a method for cultivating public discourse.

Works Cited

Bauer, Dale M. "The Other 'F' Word: The Feminist in the Classroom." *College English* 52.4 (Apr. 1990): 385–96.

Fulkerson, Richard. "Technical Logic, Comp-Logic, and the Teaching of Writing." *College Composition and Communication* 39.4 (Dec. 1988): 436–52.

Hairston, Maxine. "Required Writing Courses Should Not Focus on Politically Charged Social Issues." *Chronicle of Higher Education* 23 Jan. 1991, sec. 2:1+.

Jarratt, Susan C. "Feminism and Composition: The Case for Conflict." In *Contending with Words: Composition and Rhetoric in a Postmodern Age.* Ed. Patricia Harkin and John Schilb. New York: MLA, 1991. 105–23.

Kuhn, Annette. *The Power of the Image: Essays on Representation and Sexuality.* London: Routledge and Kegan Paul, 1985.

Sloane, Thomas O. "Reinventing *Inventio.*" *College English* 51.5 (Sept. 1989): 461–73.

3 Being Two Places at Once: Feminism and the Development of "Both/And" Perspectives

Donna J. Qualley
Western Washington University

> We live in both/and worlds full of paradox and uncertainty where close inspection turns unities into multiplicities, clarities into ambiguities, univocal simplicities into polyvocal complexities.
>
> —Patricia Lather, *Getting Smart*

Early this semester, Janice, a student in my first-year composition course, stopped by my office and asked if I knew any good books or articles on feminism that she could read. Like many young women today, she had always associated feminism with gruff, strident, male-bashing behavior; however, she had recently seen a play in which the feminists were the "good guys." She found herself sympathizing, even agreeing, with the feminist position depicted. She had begun to wonder if she might be a feminist after all.

To help Janice, a fairly traditional middle-class student, construct an understanding of feminism, I want to suggest texts that will allow her to examine her own experience in light of other people's knowledge and experience. I want to provide her with the means to articulate a perspective, and then find ways to help her to complicate and challenge that perspective. As I think of the titles of feminist tracts that currently absorb me and deepen my own thinking about feminism, however, I need to remember that these texts are not necessarily the best texts for Janice to begin with in her exploration of feminism. I cannot expect Janice to learn to negotiate the thickets of "multiplicity," "ambiguity" and "complexity" immediately. That would be like asking her to arrive without having traveled. After all, I don't want her simply to replace one uncritical or absolute conception of reality with another. Nonetheless, as I listen to discussions in feminist theory concerning essen-

tialism and difference, similarity and diversity, it seems to me that
when we begin to translate our current ideas into classroom practice,
many of us forget how we came to occupy these theoretical positions
ourselves.

At a panel on feminist pedagogy at the 1992 NCTE Convention in
Louisville, a young woman in the audience innocently asked one of
the presenters, Alice Pitt, if she had heard of Carol Gilligan. The
woman spoke passionately about how reading Gilligan's work had
transformed her way of thinking about students. At the mention of
Carol Gilligan, a few of the more "seasoned" feminists in the audience
(myself included, I'm sorry to say) smiled and raised their eyebrows
at the young woman's seeming naiveté. Pitt responded carefully,
however, saying that although when she first read Gilligan's work she
had experienced a wonderful "a-ha!" feeling, now she would read it
much more critically. As teachers, I think, we need to show the same
care that Alice Pitt did for that young woman's sense of discovery;
we cannot afford to forget those "a-ha!" moments in our own histories.
If we are to help our students construct richer, more complex ways of
thinking, we would do well to remember our own developmental
journeys.

While some of us may live in "both/and worlds" filled with
"multiplicities," "ambiguities," and "complexities" now, the problem
is, we didn't always. As Janet Emig recently observed, we weren't
born into our present, sophisticated theoretical positions; we struggled,
we climbed, we evolved. The road to "both/and" often runs through
many intellectual, emotional, and political "either/ors." The inspiration
for the title of my essay comes from the name of a 1970s album by
the Firesign Theater, "How Can You Be Two Places at Once When
You're Not Anywhere at All?" It is meant to suggest how difficult it
can be to negotiate "multiple, fragmented or contradictory" positions
(Lather). My intention in this chapter is not to describe what books I
suggested Janice read, but rather to talk about how Janice's question,
as well as the kind of student Janice herself represents[1], complicated
my own thinking about feminism, learning, and development. As
teachers of reading and writing, I believe, we can help our students
learn to see their ideas and experiences in new ways, but new ways
of seeing take time to evolve.

We need only think about the history of feminism over the last
twenty-odd years to realize that as our thinking develops, so does our
critique of (and in some cases intolerance for) the very ideas that have
enabled us to reach our present understandings. This tendency has

been especially apparent in recent discussions of what constitutes (or if anything does constitute) female experience.

Over fifteen years ago in her famous essay, "Taking Women Students Seriously," Adrienne Rich argued that it was women's ignorance of their own history and situations as women that was the "key" to their "powerlessness." She suggested that women students could begin to take themselves seriously by "believing in the value and significance of women's experience, traditions, perceptions" (240). And indeed, the identification and validation of "women's experience, traditions, perceptions" has made up a significant portion of the feminist agenda. By calling attention to the value of those activities relegated to the "reproductive" realms of society, the place most women occupied (by force or by choice), women could begin to author the meanings of their own life stories. However, we are discovering that the push to distinguish and value women's experience is giving rise to what Ann Berthoff has called "killer dichotomies" and what Diane Brunner refers to as "oppressive binarisms"—for example, the notion that women are connected knowers and men are separate knowers—that many feminists are now rejecting.

Although it has become increasingly clear that there is no single, unified, undifferentiated category called female experience, nonetheless I want to argue that we had to assume there was to begin with. Before we could begin to distinguish differences across categories and within categories, we needed to first formulate a sense of the category itself. What recent charges about the dangers and limitations of universal assumptions and essentialist thinking about women fail to understand is that, before we could identify and grasp the significance of gender as a social and political construct, we had first to assume that women's perceptions of themselves and their worlds differed from how men perceived themselves and their worlds. Without a general concept of "woman," as Kathleen Jones has observed, a concept like "exploitation of women" no longer makes sense. When the category "woman" is pluralized (as some poststructuralists suggest) into the heterogeneous "women," the concept "exploitation of women" is diminished to " 'exploitation of persons who happen to be women' [and] the category itself is emptied of its contents; it becomes a disposable, ultimately dispensable label" (121). In other words, women's experience is once again "disappeared."

Diana Fuss has argued that essentialism serves an important function in the development of group identity: "The adherence to essentialism is a measure of the degree to which a particular political group has been culturally oppressed" (98). Slogans like "I Am Woman," "Black

Is Beautiful," and "Gay Pride" all suggest the birth of new, unified, political group consciousness. Thus, "in the hands of the dispossessed themselves, essentialism can be a powerful strategic weapon" (Fuss 40). Conceived in this way, universalism and essentialism may be both useful and necessary positions that individuals and groups pass through in their construction of (gender) identity and philosophy. For my student, Janice, to see herself as a "feminist," she may first need to see her experience as "female" in essentialist or exclusive kinds of ways. At the same time she may also identify her experience as "Other," as "not-male." In other words, she may need to temporarily engage in binary thinking.

But as Fuss reminds us, " 'female experience' is never as unified, as knowable, as universal and as stable as we presume it to be" (114). Janice must eventually learn, as Joan Scott suggests, to refuse "the *fixed and permanent* quality of the binary opposition" (1065, my emphasis). She must discover ways to "treat the opposition between male and female as problematic, rather than known, as something contextually defined, repeatedly constructed . . ." (1074). The way we make binary oppositions less oppressive, then, is not by pretending they don't exist, or by getting rid of them, but rather by keeping them fluid and open to redefinition.

In the next part of the essay I discuss Julie Nelson's model for complicating gender oppositions and then use it to suggest the role that universal and essentialist thinking might play in the development of a feminist perspective. Although I focus on feminism and gender oppositions here, what I talk about can be applied to the development of any complex perspective. Then, using the consciousness-raising groups of the 1960s and 1970s as an example, I show how political action was tied to the assumption of a shared commonality among women. Going back to Nelson's model, I discuss how a premature focus on difference might induce radical individualism, or the mutant brand of feminism, we see many of our women students embracing today. In the last parts of the essay I suggest that consciousness raising, the experiencing of alternative perspectives through what Maria Lugones calls " 'world'-travelling," is important for all students, but especially for students like Janice who are comfortably and uncritically situated in the mainstream of society. As composition teachers, of course, we are in an excellent position to help students keep their thinking fluid and open to redefinition by emphasizing the concept of revision—by which I mean the re-envisioning of ideas rather than the surface editing of text. To that end I close the essay by describing a collaborative project that can create occasions for students to rethink and reflect by inviting them to experience, at least temporarily, what it is like to be two places at once.

A Model for Complicating Gender Binarisms

Julie Nelson has recently proposed a way that we might complicate our conception of gender as a hierarchical, binary opposition. Nelson suggests that by using a "more complex metaphor" we can identify and differentiate the value labels that get attached to gender categories. Instead of representing gender as a "uni-dimensional" line or continuum with masculine at one end and feminine at the other, Nelson proposes a model that depicts opposition in terms of a three-dimensional relationship (fig. 1). The model depicts relationships of complementarity (horizontal dimension), perversion (vertical dimension), and lack (diagonal dimension).

Nelson uses the example of the hard-soft opposition to illustrate the ways gender and value have been culturally construed. Hardness in terms of strength and softness in terms of flexibility are both positive complements representing "durability." Hardness in terms of rigidity and softness in terms of weakness are negative complements. They depict "brittleness." The lack or absence of the masculine (+) quality, hard-strong, is the feminine (-) quality, soft-weak. The lack or absence of the feminine (+) quality, soft-flexible, is the masculine (-) quality, hard-rigid. Rigid is a negative perversion of strong, and weak is a negative perversion of flexible. Thus, Nelson's diagram is capable of depicting three different theoretical relationships rather than a single binary opposition.

In a sexist society, only one kind of relationship is perceived. The feminine-positive is perverted into feminine-negative and then contrasted or opposed with the masculine-positive. For instance, instead of seeing the emotional (feminine-positive) as the complement of the

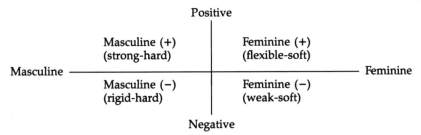

Figure 1. A Three-Dimensional Model of the "Hard-Soft" Opposition.

rational (masculine-positive), the emotional is given a negative value; it is perverted to mean "emotionalism" and depicted as the opposite of rational (Nelson 140–41). As Nelson points out, a central part of the feminist agenda, then, has consisted of inverting the terms of this relationship by highlighting the feminine-positive and exposing the male-negative. Adrienne Rich's call for women to begin to identify and believe in "the value and significance of women's experience" was really an invitation to explore and reclaim the value of the feminine-positive. Carol Gilligan's concept of the "different voice," Mary Field Belenky and her colleagues' "connected knowing," Sara Ruddick's "maternal thinking," Carolyn Heilbrun's work on women's writing, and Patricia Spacks's exploration of gossip as feminine discourse can all be seen as efforts to recover female experience and correct an imbalance in the dimension of complementarity. Recuperating the value of the feminine-positive doesn't get rid of the opposition, but it does "un-fix" it. In a similar sense, the practice of women's "consciousness raising" in the 1960s and early 1970s can be seen as an attempt to replace the "false consciousness" of the masculine-positive/feminine-negative opposition with the "raised consciousness" of the feminine-positive/masculine-negative opposition.

Consciousness Raising: Revaluing the Feminine Positive

Writing about the evolution of feminist consciousness in 1975, Sandra Lee Bartky noted that "to become a feminist is to develop a radically altered consciousness of oneself, of others and of . . . 'social reality' " (426). However, this change is not a straightforward or linear process of simply revaluing the feminine-positive. A feminist consciousness begins to emerge when it perceives what Marxists refer to as "contradictions" in society. The developing feminist consciousness is first a divided consciousness, "the consciousness of being radically alienated from her world and often divided against herself" (Bartky 437). For women, a divided consciousness can mean being in two places at once—the place the culture has put them and in the new place they now wish to put themselves—without any way to resolve the tension. And as Bartky suggests, merely apprehending a situation as contradictory or even "intolerable" is not enough to transform it.

A "raised" consciousness comes about when a woman is able to perceive alternative explanations and new possibilities for what she had previously taken for granted or seen as natural and inevitable. A raised consciousness is no longer divided against itself. Instead of being caught between "either/or," a woman begins to experience the possibility of "both/and." What is needed for this transformation, this raised consciousness, of course, is power. And for many women in the 1960s and early 1970s, this power came from their "growing sense of solidarity with other feminists" (Bartky 438), their coming together with other women in consciousness-raising groups.

The consciousness-raising movement is often remembered today (along with EST and group therapy) as simply an individual or psychological vehicle for *personal* growth and *self*-assertion; however, according to Kathleen Weiler, the first women's consciousness-raising groups were committed to the political and social transformation of society based on a "common sharing of experience in a collective, leaderless group" (457). These early groups were based on the assumption that most women were alike; they shared common experiences and perceived their worlds in similar ways. Consciousness raising occurred through the collective exploration and self-critique of these common feelings and experiences manifested in the group. Thus, it was women's recognition of their similarity as women (or as Paulo Freire might say, the discovery of their common oppression) that was the starting point for their feminist transformation and political action. Personal agendas were intimately connected with the political ideals of the group. The "personal was political" precisely because the personal was considered to be the common denominator for all women.

Interestingly, as the women's movement gradually broadened to encompass more and different kinds of women, "consciousness raising tended to lose its commitment to revolutionary change" (Weiler 458). In these heterogeneous settings, the sharing of experiences led "not to a common knowledge and solidarity based on sameness, but to the tensions of an articulation of difference" (Weiler 469). In her study of women's consciousness-raising groups in the 1960s and 1970s, Naomi Rosenthal notes that by the mid-1970s, consciousness-raising groups had drifted away from their political roots and evolved into discussion centers "for women moving out of the orbit of traditional family life" to talk about the ways in which individual women had been "socialized." This agenda led to an "increasing emphasis on *personal* analysis for *personal* life adjustments" (323, my emphasis). The loss of a shared or common vision among women contributed to the depoliticizing of consciousness raising. It's not surprising, then, that consciousness-raising groups eventually came to be exclusively associated with the self-actualization of the individual. Its ideological roots dispersed, consciousness raising became simply a "feel-good" vehicle for individual affirmation. As Rosenthal notes, while women in these latter groups admitted to experiencing an increased sense of "self-esteem, autonomy and assertiveness," as isolated individuals they lacked the power to make lasting or significant changes in their own lives or the lives of other women (324). Rosenthal concludes that if consciousness raising is only concerned with the personal, focusing exclusively on matters of

> self esteem, assertiveness and 'personal liberation,' then two conditions follow: (1) that personal circumstances and relations are independent of the social environment and can be altered if the individual is strong enough to do so, and (2) [that] failure to alter personal circumstances and relations is a personal failure or a result of the socialization process. In either case, the message is that women must change and that political action is either unnecessary or futile. (324)[2]

Mediating Similarity and Difference

Today, feminists find themselves at a similar impasse. While on the one hand, we want to avoid essentialist and universalist representations of women's experiences in an effort to respect the uniqueness and diversity of women, on the other hand, as Rosenthal, Nelson, and other feminists have cautioned, "the emphasis on difference may degenerate into a thoroughgoing individualism and political conservatism" (Nelson 150). Maybe it already has. For many of my women students feminism is not a political, social, or humanistic morality or way of life. To students like Janice, feminism simply means that an *individual* woman can do whatever she wants to do. Feminism has given them permission to repackage the "American Dream" for themselves.[3] And my more "radical" women students merely subscribe to a more radical brand of individualistic feminism, as exemplified by such pop culture icons as Madonna:

> I may be dressing like a traditional bimbo, whatever, but I'm in charge. . . . And isn't that what feminism is all about, you know, equality for men and women? And aren't I in charge of my life, doing the things I want to do? (Graeber 11)

If women have no basis for establishing any kind of similarity among themselves, not only do they lack political clout, but the assumptions that form the basis of much feminist pedagogy (e.g., the connected classroom) are also called into question. Focusing exclusively (and prematurely) on uniqueness and difference among women before any common ground has been established will probably not help my student, Janice, decide if she is a feminist. We must be careful that this present emphasis on difference doesn't lead us once again to "pervert" our oppositions by privileging diversity to the exclusion of commonality. Another of Julie Nelson's models can help to complicate and clarify the dualisms of difference and similarity, individualism and community, universalism and relativism (fig. 2). Each quadrant in Nelson's model suggests one way we might compare ourselves to another. We can see ourselves as the same, as similar, as distinct, or as radically different, disjunctive. (Interestingly, the postmodern emphasis on difference—including both the positive [distinct] and negative [disjunctive] versions—is located entirely on the masculine half of the model. We might wonder if the "feminine" is once again being "erased," and if so, why. Does it represent a temporary developmental overswing or does it suggest another example of backlash?)

Nelson suggests that our goal should be to stress the masculine-feminine relationship depicted by the positive complement: "Can we see others as similar? This is a basis for solidarity. And can we see others as distinct? This is a basis for respecting differences" (150). However, it is important to note that the positive masculine-feminine complement embodies a "both/and" perspective. While I believe that we must always strive for a "both/and" conception of gender and gender-linked traits, I don't think our students can easily embrace such a perspective if they have only experienced one side of the either/or binary. I am also suggesting that it may be more valuable for students like Janice, who are already drenched in the ethic of individualism, to seek out what is common in their own and other feminists' beliefs before they examine what is different. As Janice explained when she came to my office, she had always seen herself as different from—not like—feminists. Feminists were the "Other." What she needs is an opportunity to explore commonalities—then move to a double perspective.

However, while identification and connection might be an important first step in the creation of feminist or any kind of group solidarity, it shouldn't be the last step. The connected classroom with its emphasis

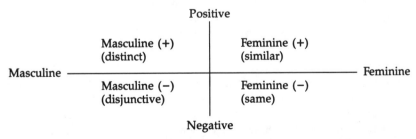

Figure 2. A Three-Dimensional Model of the "Different-Same" Opposition.

on commonality and community can just as easily oppress as it can empower women. Susan Jarratt sees a tendency in both feminist and composition pedagogy to avoid conflict, an avoidance that can make it more difficult to apprehend "contradictions" and can therefore diminish the possibility of "consciousness raising." The overemphasis on connection and community can also leave students unprepared "to negotiate the oppressive discourses of racism, sexism and classism" that can arise in the classroom (Jarratt 106) and in the larger community. As Frances Maher reminds us, it is difficult (and can be dangerous) to use "a 'power with' model in a 'power over' society" (98).

It's one thing for women to share their personal experiences and feelings in a group of like-minded, sympathetic individuals in a supportive consciousness-raising group; it's quite another for women to share their stories in a setting marked by indifference and/or hostility. During a recent performance of a play put on by the Sexual Harassment and Rape Prevention Program at the University of New Hampshire and designed to reveal the violent nature of rape, a number of male athletes in the audience disrupted both the performance and the question-and-answer portion of the program by whistling, jeering, and making sexually explicit comments. What was intended as a move to "raise consciousness" and build understanding between males and females was eclipsed by the actions of the male audience and only served to prevent any real dialogue from getting started.

Jarratt warns that teachers attempting to validate student experience "can't neutralize by fiat" the differences that already exist in the classroom. Certain kinds of pedagogical practices when used uncritically can put women (as well as students from underrepresented races, classes, sexual orientations) at a disadvantage. For example, Nel Noddings's emphasis on caring for others or Peter Elbow's "believing game" can be problematic when used by "oppressed" people as a means of entering into or accepting the positions of their oppressors (the very conditions that have led to their oppression).[4]

Perhaps what is needed, then, is not simply a pedagogy based on connection and like-mindedness, but a better way to initiate and sustain dialogue among groups as well as within groups. We need a dialogue that seeks to build connection and solidarity while at the same time respecting differences. Raising the consciousness of women or other marginal persons, however, is not enough. Both feminist and critical pedagogies (most notably Paulo Freire's process of conscienti-zation) suggest that the self-reflexive recognition of one's oppression can lead to empowerment, but recognition does not always spark collective change. The heightened awareness that individuals obtain from such practices can generate confidence and feelings of worth, but if transformation occurs, it may only be actualized on an individual basis. What Victor Villanueva says about the lure and appeal that individual success holds for African American high school students applies to many others who reside on the boundaries but desire access to the center. These students realize that

> individuals have gone further than the race. All castelike minorities have their successful individuals—big stars, successful business-men, prominent politicians. The impetus for a radical collective is not readily apparent. . . . One successful figure . . . is not likely to persuade these students that a revolutionary consciousness is a better definition of success than the possibility for individual fame or fortune. (257)

This belief in individual power and achievement can also serve to keep students who are already in the center firmly and uncritically entrenched where they are. If change is to occur, consciousness raising of the outsider or "Other" needs to be accompanied by efforts to develop the consciousness of those currently in positions of power or privilege. As educator Lisa Delpit contends, "Those with the most power, those in the majority . . . must take the greater responsibility for initiating" the dialogue (297).

"World"-Travelling

Genuine dialogue can be difficult to foster and harder to sustain in the heterogeneous classroom. It is not enough to ensure that women— that all students—have equal access to the floor and that they are free to speak in their own voices without interruption. As the incident at the University of New Hampshire suggests, simply encouraging women to speak does not guarantee dialogue and can reproduce the very feeling of powerlessness we are trying to overcome. We must also seek ways for those persons already located in positions of privilege to develop the habit of self-reflexiveness and the capacity for being in two places at once.

Magda Lewis tells the story of a male student, who, after hearing a woman classmate's presentation on violence against women, asks "why we had to talk about women and men all the time and why the presenter did not offer 'the other side of the story' " (177). Lewis realizes that encouraging this man's classmate "to 'speak up' and intervene on [her] own behalf would [reproduce] exactly the margin-alization that the young man's demand was intended to create" (179).

Instead, she throws the ball back in the young man's court. First she
praises him for remembering the importance of including all voices in
discussions. Next she asks him if he would (or could) tell the class
about " 'the other side' of violence against women" (179). What is the
other side of the story of violence against women? In the silence that
ensues, Lewis has succeeded in opening a space for self-reflexivity, a
space for the development of a different way of seeing. But seeing
different things is not easy, as Lisa Delpit reminds us:

> We do not really see through our eyes or hear through our ears,
> but through our beliefs. To put our beliefs on hold is to cease to
> exist as ourselves for a moment—and that is not easy. It is painful
> as well, because it means turning yourself inside out, giving up
> your own sense of who you are, and being willing to see yourself
> in the unflattering light of another's angry gaze. It is not easy,
> but it is the only way to learn what it might feel like to be
> someone else and *the only way to start the dialogue*. (297, my
> emphasis)

Whether this young man will or can "put his own beliefs on hold,"
so as to better understand his female classmate's experience, remains
to be seen. The point is, an opportunity has been created for him to
do so. Lewis has "opened a space" (as Maxine Greene's suggests in
this volume) for the young man to see himself in "the unflattering
light of another's angry gaze." Self-reflexivity seems crucial for the
development of both the divided and double perspectives.

For some of our students, a divided perspective already exists. Maria
Lugones points out that the immigrant or outsider has learned to adopt
this double position out of necessity, as a matter of survival: "The
outsider has necessarily acquired flexibility in shifting from mainstream
constructions of life where she is constructed as an outsider to other
constructions of life where she is more or less 'at home' " (3). Lugones
calls the ability to shift from one position to another " 'world'-
travelling." While "world"-travelling may be a matter of survival for
those persons who occupy the "borderlands" (as Gloria Anzaldua puts
it) of mainstream culture, it can be valuable and enlightening—indeed,
I would argue essential—for all students to become "world"-travellers.
However, for students like Janice, students who are only beginning to
experience the faintest inkling of "contradiction," a divided or split
consciousness does not already exist; it must be "constructed."

Collaboration as "World"-Travelling

One way I have discovered that encourages "world"-travelling and
sets up the conditions for the development of a divided perspective is

to have groups of two or three students immerse themselves for four and a half weeks in collaborative and self-reflexive research and writing projects. These projects are collaborative because students write a single paper together. As a group, they select a topic based on their common interests, conduct research, interview authorities, develop a point (or points) of view, choose (or invent) a genre and decide on a method of composing that will allow each member to contribute to the writing of the paper. The projects are self-reflexive because students keep individual journals in which they record and think about their information and their own and one another's developing perspectives toward it. Students also use their journals to document their reactions, insights, and feelings about the processes of learning and writing with others. Conversations with the group and with themselves help them to discover, articulate, and criticize their own positions and preferences as thinkers and writers. These projects are not designed to produce consensus (although they can), but rather to uncover both similarities and differences in thinking and writing. By working closely with others for an extended period of time, students can examine how ideas develop and change. In the following journal entry, Carrie not only notices the different perspectives that emerge in her group, but more important she begins to understand and value these differences.

> We all had our own ideas and conceptions coming into our talk, yet as we talked, they seemed to bend, stretch, and grow under the weight of the other's words [as well as] our thoughts about these words. At first I noticed this in listening to Liz and in truth was annoyed. I thought, "How can she change her mind like that? Didn't she just say . . . " That's where I stopped. I realized that it was not a fault as I had wanted to believe, but that it was someone trying to amalgamate all of her present thoughts and that she was merely trying to articulate them . . . I think through having to learn to communicate our ideas and feelings you can't help but come to appreciate the person more. . . . Unless there is some great gulf (so great that people cannot, or shall I say will not, consider the thoughts of others), you can't help but come to . . . respect a person for the fact she stands for something and is basically a thinking person with ideas and feelings.

For Carlos, the process of collaboration allows him the opportunity to travel to his partner's world (where he risks "going native") and then to examine his own world from her position. Near the end of their self-styled project on how men and women choose mates, he offers these reflections in his journal:

> I can't get [my partner] to agree to what I think and believe; but I can get her to appreciate it. She's helped me to [also] be this

way just by working with her. . . . Oh Christ! I'm turning into a
woman! It's a conspiracy! . . . [But] that's what collaboration means:
accepting and appreciating another writer/person for what they
are and what they value. . . . I'm learning that my value to other
people intellectually is not to put them in a position to defend
themselves. I'm listening to others. I'm thinking about how my
thoughts are interpreted by them.

However, "world"-travelling can also be threatening to persons
uncritically or comfortably situated in their present positions. For
example, a woman who wants to travel within the world of the
academy may be compelled to learn "a discourse not intended for
her" (Lewis and Simon). She may find entering a new world difficult
or uncomfortable, but she knows she must do it (as she has always
done it) if she wants to enter and become a part of the academic
mainstream. However, of what benefit is it for the young man in
Lewis's class to leave his relatively safe and privileged position to
enter the world of victims of violence? Why would he choose to leave
a world where he is in control and enter a world where he experiences
himself as victim? Why would Janice (who has admitted to seeing
most people's problems as simply stemming from "a lack of confidence") choose to see herself or other women as oppressed? Until
these students have an opportunity to experience the contradictory
feelings of "false consciousness," as does Carlos, they may not find
"world"-travelling so empowering.

Jamie, another student, questions whether he *should* "put his beliefs
on hold" and enter into another perspective. He asks if entering into
the Other's perspective might be a violation of individual space, but
he never actually questions his own position.

> The most difficult moments occurred when their thoughts seemed
> stupid, irrelevant, or useless to me. What should I do? Reject the
> thoughts? Work with what I perceived to be inferior [ideas]? . . . If
> I see them as wrong, I have to say so, no matter who it
> hurts. . . . But . . . when a group member "took" my thought and
> changed it beyond recognition, I felt used, abused and lost. . . . A
> thought is your property. I didn't like having [them] take it over,
> change it, and spurt it back to me. The biggest *weakness* is that
> collaboration requires effort, self-sacrifice and trust. . . . Do you
> realize what I've done? I've gone into the very minds of Phil and
> Chas to hear what they think. They trusted me with themselves.
> I don't ever want to go through this again. (Emphasis added)

Jamie finds his first venture at collaborating—"world"-travelling—
disturbing, unsettling. It is important to remember that I have not
asked Jamie to travel to worlds vastly different from his own. He is

in a self-selected group with two other males writing about a topic (the university's general education requirement) that he and his group have chosen themselves. Jamie is unable to adopt the "both/and" position needed to make his collaborative experience illuminating. Because he sees his partner's thoughts as "different" (and, in this case, inferior), he adopts an "either/or," an agonistic "them/us," stance, and as Lugones points out, "the agonistic attitude [is] inimical to travelling across 'worlds'" (15). And yet, I think, as teachers, we have an obligation to continue to provide occasions for students to engage in "world"-travelling encounters because "travelling to someone's 'world' is a way of identifying with them . . . we can understand *what it is to be them and what it is to be ourselves in their eyes*" (Lugones 17, emphasis in original). While I want all my students to experience "world"-travelling, I want especially to give students who might not otherwise find a sufficient reason to "expand their horizons" the chance to become "un-fixed." I hope that as Janice reexamines what it means to be a feminist, she will discover—even at the risk of becoming an essentialist for a while—how she is connected in basic ways to all women, to all people.

It strikes me as interesting that when students remake themselves by "world"-travelling from the periphery to the center ("Any poor 'boy' can be President"), the culture says that education (the great "equalizer") has done its job, has been successful. And yet when we ask students to reflect on this remaking, to examine what is lost and what is gained, education is seen as being too "political," just as it is when we encourage students to "world"-travel, to go exploring, in the *opposite* direction—from the mainstream to the back streets. I now realize, however, that living in a "both/and" world is always a political, and not easily accomplished, act in an "either/or" society.

Notes

1. In this essay I will sometimes refer to Janice as female, whereas female means "not-male," and "not-male" is construed as "Other"; but I will also talk about Janice as being a member of the privileged majority who occupy the mainstream in society. Janice reminds us that the positions we occupy are always shifting and relative. As Kathleen Jones points out, we can avoid the essentialist/absolutist/universalist trap without losing the conceptual power of our categories if we keep in mind "the existential difference . . . between the *analytic utility* of a concept and the *material reality* which it seeks to express" (123, emphasis in original). Thus, the "material reality" that Janice signifies is never just one thing.

2. What Rosenthal has to say about women's consciousness-raising groups sounds remarkably like James Berlin's concerns about expressivist rhetoric in composition theory. In "Rhetoric and Ideology in the Writing Class," Berlin argues that expressivist rhetoric, with its focus on the individual writer, cannot mount an effective critique against the academy. Berlin notes that "gestures genuinely threatening to the establishment are difficult to accomplish" when mounted by individuals acting in isolation (487).

3. Sociologist Ruth Sidel's book *On Her Own: Growing Up in the Shadow of the American Dream* (1991) provides an interesting discussion of the way many young women in their teens and early twenties have bought into the belief that individual effort, independence, and hard work will get them a piece of the American pie. She wonders if women have been "hoodwinked" into believing that they can " 'can have it all, do it all, be it all' while society itself changes minimally" (224).

4. In "Prolegomena to Future Caring," a paper discussing the implications of Nel Noddings's morality of care, Barbara Houston notes that given women's history of oppression, we might assume "that women are a damaged people and susceptible to a use of the ethics of care which will entrench their subordination, or at least not challenge it" (21). Susan Jarratt notes that Peter Elbow's "believing game" can pose similar problems for women.

Works Cited

Anzaldua, Gloria. *Borderlands–La Frontera: The New Mestiza*. San Francisco: Aunt Lute, 1987.

Bartky, Sandra Lee. "Toward a Phenomenology of Feminist Consciousness." *Social Theory and Practice* 3.4 (1975): 425–40.

Belenky, Mary Field, Blythe McVicker Clinchy, Nancy Rule Goldberger, and Jill Mattuck Tarule. *Women's Ways of Knowing: The Development of Self, Voice, and Mind*. New York: Basic Books, 1986.

Berlin, James. "Rhetoric and Ideology in the Writing Class." *College English* 50.5 (Sept. 1988): 477–94.

Berthoff, Ann. "Killer Dichotomies: Reading In, Reading Out." *Farther Along: Transforming Dichotomies in Rhetoric and Composition*. Ed. Kate Ronald and Hephzibah Roskelly. Portsmouth, NH: Boynton/Cook, 1991.

Brunner, Diane D. "Dislocating Boundaries in Our Classrooms." *Feminist Teacher* 6.3 (1992): 18–24.

Chiseri-Strater, Elizabeth. *Academic Literacies: The Public and Private Discourse of University Students*. Portsmouth, NH: Boynton/Cook, 1991.

Delpit, Lisa. "The Silenced Dialogue: Power and Pedagogy in Educating Other People's Children." *Harvard Educational Review* 58.3 (1988): 280–98.

Elbow, Peter. *Writing without Teachers*. New York: Oxford UP, 1973.

Emig, Janet. "Our Missing Theory." *Conversations: Contemporary Critical Theory and the Teaching of Literature*. Ed. Charles Moran and Elizabeth Penfield. Urbana, IL: NCTE, 1990. 87–96.

Freire, Paulo. *Pedagogy of the Oppressed.* Trans. Myra B. Ramos. New York: Continuum, 1970.

Fuss, Diana. *Essentially Speaking: Feminism, Nature and Difference.* New York: Routledge, 1989.

Gilligan, Carol. *In a Different Voice: Psychological Theory and Women's Development.* Cambridge, MA: Harvard UP, 1982.

Graeber, Laurel. "Sound Bites of Our Times: A Quiz." Rev. of *The New York Public Library Book of Twentieth-Century American Quotations,* ed. by Stephen Donadio, Joan Smith, Susan Mesner, and Rebecca Davison. *New York Times Book Review* 6 Dec. 1992: 11.

Heilbrun, Carolyn G. *Writing a Woman's Life.* New York: Norton, 1988.

Houston, Barbara. "Prolegomena to Future Caring." Paper delivered to the Association for Moral Education, Toronto, November 1985.

Jarratt, Susan C. "Feminism and Composition: The Case for Conflict." In *Contending With Words: Composition and Rhetoric in a Postmodern Age.* Ed. Patricia Harkin and John Schilb. New York: MLA, 1991. 105–23.

Jones, Kathleen B. "The Trouble with Authority." *differences: A Journal of Cultural Studies* 5.1 (1991): 104–27.

Lather, Patricia. *Getting Smart: Feminist Research and Pedagogy with/in the Postmodern.* New York: Routledge, 1991.

Lewis, Magda. "Interrupting Patriarchy: Politics, Resistance, and Transformation in the Feminist Classroom." In *Feminisms and Critical Pedagogy.* Ed. Carmen Luke and Jennifer Gore. New York: Routledge, 1992. 167–91.

Lewis, Magda, and Roger I. Simon. "A Discourse Not Intended for Her: Learning and Teaching within Patriarchy." *Harvard Educational Review* 56.4 (1986): 457–73.

Lugones, Maria. "Playfulness, 'World'-Travelling, and Loving Perception." *Hypatia* 2.2 (1987): 3–19.

Maher, Frances A. "Toward a Richer Theory of Feminist Pedagogy: A Comparison of 'Liberation' and 'Gender' Models For Teaching and Learning." *Journal of Education* 169.3 (1987): 91–100.

Nelson, Julie. "Thinking About Gender." *Hypatia* 7.3 (1992): 138–54.

Noddings, Nel. *Caring: A Feminine Approach to Ethics and Moral Education.* Berkeley and Los Angeles: U of California P, 1984.

Rich, Adrienne. "Taking Women Students Seriously." *On Lies, Secrets, and Silence: Selected Prose 1966–1978.* New York: Norton, 1979. 237–46.

Rosenthal, Naomi Braun. "Consciousness Raising: From Revolution to Re-Evaluation." *Psychology of Women Quarterly* 8.4 (1984): 309–26.

Ruddick, Sara. *Maternal Thinking: Toward a Politics of Peace.* Boston: Beacon, 1989.

Scott, Joan W. "Gender: A Useful Category of Historical Analysis." *American Historical Review* 91.5 (1986): 1053–75.

Sidel, Ruth. *On Her Own: Growing Up In the Shadow of the American Dream.* New York: Viking, 1991.

Spacks, Patricia Meyer. "In Praise of Gossip." *The Hudson Review* 35.1 (1982): 19–38.

Villanueva, Victor, Jr. "Considerations of American Freireistas." In *The Politics of Writing Instruction: Postsecondary*. Ed. Richard Bullock and John Trimbur. Portsmouth, NH: Boynton/Cook, 1991. 246–62.

Weiler, Kathleen. "Freire and a Feminist Pedagogy of Difference." *Harvard Educational Review* 61.4 (1991): 449–74.

4 Naming Harlem: Teaching the Dynamics of Diversity

Daniel Reagan
Saint Anselm College

> This perpetual dealing with people very different from myself caused a shattering in me of preconceptions I scarcely knew I held. . . . They may love or hate or admire or fear or envy this country—they see it, in any case, from another point of view, and this forces the writer to reconsider many things he had always taken for granted. This reassessment, which can be very painful, is also very valuable.
>
> —James Baldwin, "The Discovery of What It Means to Be an American"

Recently, I was giving a public lecture on Zora Neale Hurston's *Moses, Man of the Mountain,* when I found myself in a dilemma. It began when a white woman in the audience questioned my role as teacher. "What gives you, a white male, the authority to talk about this book?" she asked. Her question prompted me to return to a disturbing passage from Hurston's collection of folklore, *Mules and Men,* that I had quoted in the lecture. Hurston explains the black storyteller's strategy for dealing with white audiences as follows: "The white man is always trying to know into somebody else's business. All right, I'll set something outside the door of my mind for him to play with and handle. He can read my writing but he sho' can't read my mind. I'll put this play toy in his hand, and he will seize it and go away. Then I'll say my say and sing my song" (4–5). If taken seriously, Hurston's remark and the woman's question effectively preempt any public statement I might make about African American literature. The question posits that one's race and gender, rather than one's professional expertise, grant the authority to speak about particular texts and traditions, and Hurston further complicates the problem by suggesting that only those who share the black storyteller's world will understand her song. These statements make white readers exiles from the discourse of African American literature, and as outsiders we have no authority to speak about it.

This rhetorical position would be less troubling were I not a teacher of American literature. My profession, however, forces me to confront it. Over the past twenty years, in our anthologies and syllabi, we have abandoned the melting pot as the predominant metaphor of the American experience. Rather than searching for a single voice of consensus, we now interpret our national identity as a fabric of interwoven voices and traditions. Before we can weave a fabric out of these various voices, however, we must understand the color and texture of each. We must discover, as Henry Louis Gates urges, "whatever is black about black American literature" (*Signifying Monkey* xxiv). My dilemma, then, is this: even though I am committed to teaching courses in African American literature and including that material in my American literature courses, I find myself in a rhetorical position that proscribes discovering and discussing the distinctive features of that tradition.

Three solutions, it seems, are open to me. First, I could simply ignore the compelling imperative to teach traditions which have not directly shaped my personal history. This position, however, would force me to marginalize again much American literature and thus ignore the past twenty years of scholarship in my field. Further, establishing a relation between traditions and personal history is a slippery business. Has the New England tradition shaped the experience of midwesterners? Does Sherwood Anderson speak more forcefully than Willa Cather to a white male midwesterner? What impact do past traditions have on present histories? In one important sense, at least, all past American traditions bear upon my personal history. We all are implicated in the consequences of our nation's history; we all have historical identities. Therefore, I would erase both professional and historical aspects of myself by ignoring African American and other cultural traditions.

A second very tempting option is to refuse the position of outsider. Teachers who treat literary texts as sociological or historical treatises and emphasize the social content of the work effectively ignore the formal and rhetorical strategies that position them as outsiders. Certainly, though, there are better ways to teach the history of slavery than by having students read slave narratives or novels about slavery, and we misrepresent these texts if we teach them only as social documents, however much they may appear to be conveyors of information about realms of human existence we cannot directly experience. By refusing the position of outsider, I would, in fact, deny the text the position it claims in relation to white cultural traditions and therefore misrepresent a distinctive feature of the African American literary heritage.

Embedded in my reasons for rejecting the first and second options, however, is a third, more viable option: White teachers must engage black literature while accepting the position of outsider. We need to develop strategies for teaching that do not preempt, but rather actively engage, the formal imperatives and rhetorical strategies within such texts. Before describing three such strategies, however, I should explain the position of outsider I am advocating.

The stance of outsider can best be explored, perhaps, by examining a moment in history when a white writer violated that stance. Such a moment occurred in 1926 with the publication of white novelist Carl Van Vechten's controversial *Nigger Heaven*. Langston Hughes observed in his memoir, *The Big Sea*, that Van Vechten's use of the word "nigger" in the novel's title was "like a red rag to a bull" (268), and the contemporary reviews of the book in African American magazines, journals, and newspapers support Hughes's judgment. The story of the controversy surrounding this text presents a compelling cautionary tale for teachers of diverse traditions.

If any white writer could claim authority over Harlem as a subject during the 1920s, Van Vechten could. He was a popularizer of Harlem Renaissance art and literature. He helped persuade his publisher, Alfred A. Knopf, to publish books by James Weldon Johnson, Rudolph Fisher, Nella Larsen, Chester Himes, and Langston Hughes. He threw frequent and famous integrated parties that, according to Langston Hughes, "were so Negro that they were reported as a matter of course in the coloured society columns, just as though they occurred in Harlem" (251). He was also the foremost tour guide of downtown black nightlife for uptown white patrons. Indeed, James Weldon Johnson claimed: "In the early days of the Negro literary and artistic movement, no one in the country did more to found it" than Van Vechten in his "frequent magazine articles and by his many personal efforts in behalf of individual Negro writers and artists" (*Along This Way* 382).

The movement to which Johnson refers was a self-conscious effort among many Harlemites to forge a cultural and communal identity through art. Various artists turned to black vernacular traditions for inspiration and experimented with new forms of music, poetry, narrative, painting, and sculpture in an attempt to give expression to the black experience in America. In the short-lived Harlem literary magazine, *Stylus*, Montgomery Gregory summed up the aim of the Harlem

Renaissance when he argued that "any individual or people must depend upon the universal appeal of art, literature, painting, and music—to secure the real respect and recognition of mankind" (Johnson and Johnson 366). The belief that artistic expression could not only define and communicate a black cultural identity, but could also create racial harmony, was central to the Harlem Renaissance program, and Van Vechten earned the respect of many Harlemites because he was a forceful advocate of that faith.

Indeed, he conceived of *Nigger Heaven* as a contribution to the effort of securing white respect and recognition for blacks. A letter to Knopf written several months before the book's publication indicates that Van Vechten considered his primary audience to be white Americans who lived outside New York City. That audience, he wrote, needed advance warning about the book so that it would "not come as an actual shock" (Kellner 86). Van Vechten himself had been preparing this audience during 1925, writing "countless articles on Negro subjects" (Kellner 87) for various national publications and leading tours of Harlem for "outoftowners . . . so that they would carry some news of . . . [the life of Harlem] back to where they came from" (Kellner 87). The belief that knowledge of a people would breed respect and ultimately help forge racial harmony inspired all these efforts.

The process by which art forges social attitudes, however, is not as simple as Van Vechten and the Harlem writers conceived it to be. As Henry Louis Gates argues in "Canon-Formation, Literary History, and the Afro-American Tradition," it is not enough for black artists and critics to enter "culture" through a door opened by white society. The power of the "master's tongue" (20) to define the conditions by which the "real respect and recognition of mankind" could be earned led Phillis Wheatley to write poetry as a refutation of "racialists such as Hume and Kant" (17) who insisted that poetic expression was a mark of humanity, and led Alexander Crummell to learn Greek syntax as a refutation of John C. Calhoun's insistence that blacks were not fully human because none knew Greek. Simply "learning the master's tongue," (20), rather than creating a synthesis of that tongue with the black vernacular, leads to erasure of African American cultural traditions. Langston Hughes acknowledged the limits of the Harlem Renaissance program when he recalled, somewhat cynically: "some Harlemites thought . . . the race problem had at last been solved through Art. They were sure the New Negro would lead a new life from then on in green pastures of tolerance created by Countee Cullen, Ethel Waters, Claude McKay, Duke Ellington, Bojangles, and Alain Locke" (228). Our current attitude toward integrating diverse traditions into the curriculum suggests that we have not wholly abandoned the idea today, even if we no longer impose certain forms of artistic and intellectual accomplishments as tests of human status. By presenting the art of various traditions to our students in an effort to secure a larger "respect . . . and recognition" for those voices, we assume a role as advocates of those traditions which differs little from Van Vechten's self-proclaimed role as white patron of the Harlem Renaissance.

As long as Van Vechten functioned as a knowledgeable outsider bringing news of Harlem to the world, at any rate, his efforts were universally applauded by Harlem artists and intellectuals. In the opinion of some Harlem Renaissance writers, however, Van Vechten crossed the delicate line between advocacy and appropriation when he wrote *Nigger Heaven*. Indeed, while writing the book, Van Vechten claimed identity as a Harlem insider, a member of the black community. During 1924, he explored the people and the sites of Harlem that would become the characters and settings of his novel, and he became so immersed in Harlem life that he wrote to a friend in August of 1925, "if I were a chameleon my colour would now be at least seal-brown" (Kellner 80). But during this intense period of research, he attempted to adopt more than the physical world of Harlem, for he also tried to absorb what he considered to be the psychological makeup of blacks. He wrote to H.L. Mencken, for example: "Ain't it hell to be a Nordic when you're struggling with Ethiopian psychology?" (Kellner 84).

Van Vechten, then, claimed to have written *Nigger Heaven* from a black rather than a white psychological perspective. However, Hurston's caution that black storytellers "set something outside the door" of their minds for the white man "to play with and handle" suggests that Van Vechten could not know if he had successfully adopted an "Ethiopian psychology." If he saw and heard only the protective masks of Harlem, his novel would present not black psychology, but rather the reflection of his own attitudes and prejudices mirrored from those masks. Langston Hughes suggested that Hurston's observation also described Harlem when he wrote:

> Ordinary Negroes [did not] like the growing influx of whites toward Harlem after sundown, flooding the little cabarets and bars where formerly only colored people laughed and sang, and where now the strangers were given the best ringside tables to sit and stare at the Negro customers—like amusing animals in a zoo.
>
> The Negroes said: "We can't go downtown and sit and stare at you in your clubs. You won't even let us in your clubs." But they didn't say it out loud—for Negroes are practically never rude to white people. (225)

Van Vechten, as I have noted, was in the vanguard of that influx, and most of the action in *Nigger Heaven* occurs in the cabarets and other nightspots he visited. Even though he asked Knopf to market the book as a black novel by advertising it in his lists of titles by black writers, Hurston's and Hughes's observations about the rhetorical reticence of blacks before a white audience in the 1920s calls into question the "blackness" of Van Vechten's representation of Harlem.

Van Vechten's appropriation of Harlem as a subject for fiction and his claim to be a spokesperson for black life elicited harsh criticism from many black reviewers. W.E.B. Du Bois, for example, wrote that "Carl Van Vechten's 'Nigger Heaven' is a blow in the face. It is an affront to the hospitality of black folk and the intelligence of white" ("Books" 81). J. A. Rogers, writing in *The Messenger*, echoed Du Bois's sentiments: "Negroes all over the country are wrathful at Van Vechten's 'Nigger Heaven'—a book which may be characterized as smut with a sympathetic setting" (Dec. 1926, 365). Although reviewers objected to Van Vechten's portrait of the seamy side of Harlem life, their primary concern was, as Hughes noted, the novel's title.

Van Vechten considered this objection to be trivial and insulting. In a letter to James Weldon Johnson, one of the few positive black reviewers of *Nigger Heaven*, Van Vechten wrote, "Langston [Hughes] suggested to a few of the ... [book's critics] that they might read the book before expressing their opinion, but this advice seems to be regarded as supererogatory" (Kellner 89–90). Van Vechten's irritation was provoked by a comment in the New York *News*, a black daily. Their reviewer wrote "that any one who would call a book Nigger Heaven would call a Negro Nigger" (Kellner 89). Van Vechten was surprised that reviewers would not look past the title before branding him a racist, but even his father warned him before the book's publication, "If you are trying to help the race, as I am assured you are, I think every word you write should be a respectful one towards the black" (Ikonne 31). It is a mark of his naiveté about audience that Van Vechten did not anticipate the anger the title would provoke.

Nonetheless, acute sensitivity to the power of naming lies at the heart of the debate over the appropriateness of "Nigger Heaven" as a title for Harlem. In response to the title, critics raised questions not only about Van Vechten's racial attitudes, but also about the significance of Harlem as a race capital, and ultimately about Van Vechten's right to name Harlem and describe black life.

In Van Vechten's defense, he meant the term "Nigger Heaven" in its ironic sense as a common expression for the balcony of racially segregated theaters. In the novel, the struggling writer and protagonist,

Byron Kasson, moans, "Nigger Heaven! That's what Harlem is. We sit in our places in the gallery of this New York theater and watch the white world sitting down in the good seats in the orchestra" (149). Van Vechten considered Harlem the "Mecca of the New Negro" (*Nigger Heaven* 45), but deplored the fact that New York City was segregated. Indeed, as James Weldon Johnson sympathetically observed, Van Vechten frankly discussed "every phase of the race question, from Jim Crow discriminations to miscegenation" in the novel ("Romance" 330). Interwoven with the discussion of race questions, however, is a portrait of blacks as primitive exotics who have either sold or claimed their birthrights. In his description of Mary Love, Byron Kasson's girl, Van Vechten defines the exotic as the "love of drums, of exciting rhythms, this naive delight in glowing colour—the colour that exists only in cloudless, tropical climes—this warm sexual emotion" (89–90). Reviewers who focused on Van Vechten's discussion of race issues liked the novel; those who noted his stereotyping wrote about the book's controversial title. Most objected to the material that Du Bois disliked: "one damned orgy after another, with hate, hurt, gin, and sadism" ("Books" 82). Because Van Vechten's primary goal was to present blacks to whites, he did not sufficiently consider the range of his audience. And because he did not anticipate the reaction of black readers to his novel, he did not mediate between his ideological motives in writing it and the actual representation of Harlem he presented. His stereotyping and his title presented and named a Harlem that potentially confirmed white prejudices.

Therefore, most of those who did not reject the novel out of hand still debated the appropriateness of "Nigger Heaven" as a name for Harlem. Though the term is meant ironically in the novel, the irony itself becomes problematic when discussed by the Harlem Reviewers. If Du Bois, who missed Van Vechten's irony, considered the term "as applied to Harlem . . . [to be] a misnomer" ("Books" 81), James Weldon Johnson considered the term to be appropriate because of its ironic implications. J. A. Rogers indicated that he understood the full irony of Van Vechten's title, perhaps better than Van Vechten himself, when he argued that Harlem deserved the title "Nigger Heaven," not because it was a race capital, but because it existed for the entertainment of those who lived uptown. He argued that Van Vechten's very act of naming accurately identified Harlem as a place and a concept. Harlem, he said, was "a place where the chief excuse for one's existence is to furnish a living for exploiters, white and colored" (Feb. 1927). He felt that Harlem was owned by those, like Van Vechten, who could use it to their advantage. Its residents, as victims of the exploiters, truly lived

in a Nigger Heaven. They had no control over their fate and they had
no power to choose the name and image the world knew them by.

Indeed, Van Vechten recognized the inevitability of his role as
exploiter. In an article written for W.E.B. Du Bois's *Crisis* just five
months before the publication of *Nigger Heaven*, he wondered, "Are
Negro writers going to write about this exotic material while it is fresh
or will they continue to make a free gift of it to white authors who
will exploit it until not a drop of vitality remains?" Van Vechten's
choice of the adjective "exotic" is key. The word suggests that he
viewed Harlem as a foreign place, as something unfamiliar. Certainly
if the defining quality of the place is strangeness, to familiarize it
through writing must inevitably drain the material of its vitality. Further,
no Harlem Renaissance writer could write about Harlem as an exotic
place, because to do so would literally be an act of alienation. Simply
by considering Harlem to be exotic literary material, then, Van Vechten
claims it as a white rather than a black literary province.

Ultimately, therefore, Van Vechten's act of naming Harlem was an
act of appropriation. J. A. Rogers argued, "When Van Vechten says
'Nigger Heaven' what he really means is 'Van Vechten Heaven' since
Harlem furnishes a release of soul for white people" (Feb. 1927).
African American folklore and slave narratives emphasize repeatedly
the relation of naming to owning. The act of self-naming is a claim
to power in such contemporary works as Alice Walker's *The Color
Purple* and Toni Morrison's *Song of Solomon*. Losing the power to name
oneself and one's place forfeits identity. In the most complex and
ambivalent review of *Nigger Heaven* I have found, Wallace Thurman
suggests with a hint of sarcasm that Van Vechten so successfully
appropriated Harlem as a place and a concept that "a latter day
abolitionist statue to Carl Van Vechten" should be erected "on the
corner of 135th Street and Seventh Avenue" (279). The question is,
what did Van Vechten abolish? Thurman suggests that the idea of
Harlem as the center of African American culture was erased. A
number of critics echoed James Weldon Johnson's wistful observation
that "a Negro reviewer might pardonably express the wish that a
colored novelist had been the first to take this material and write a
book of equal significance and power" ("Romance" 316). The fear of
many was that the material, and thus the place, once appropriated
and labeled "exotic" by white writers, could not be reclaimed.

One lesson this story teaches is that if our role as teachers of
minority voices is similar to Van Vechten's role as patron of the Harlem
Renaissance, we must not write our own version of African American
literature with the same naiveté that Van Vechten displayed in writing

Nigger Heaven. Certainly we act as patrons of diverse literatures when we encourage our students to view texts by minority writers as central rather than marginal contributions to American literature. However, when we create our syllabi, construct our lectures, and help students read texts, we must constantly avoid the acts of naming and appropriating that Van Vechten fell prey to. We must resist not for fear of censure; many students may not understand the power that naming wields as well as the Harlem Reviewers did, and thus they are not likely to challenge our right to name. Students, in fact, expect us to provide a context and justification for the material we ask them to read. We face not only the temptation, but also the responsibility, of providing a (perhaps fictional) continuity and coherence in our courses. Because I teach at a small, predominantly white New England college, moreover, my students are as much outsiders to the discourse community of African American literature as I am. I do not teach many students who would position themselves as insiders when reading African American literature, and I am reluctant to thrust the role of spokesperson on those who do. We deny black students their personal identities if we force them to represent the black experience in racially mixed classrooms and thereby define their relationship with the texts. It is precisely because my students would not challenge or even detect my act of renaming and thus appropriating the landscape of African American literature that my insistence on remaining outside the tradition is essential. I must allow the texts I teach to name, and thus empower, themselves.

But how? Making this demand is simple; implementing it is not. Whenever I choose texts for a course, and thus exclude others, I immediately draft a version of African American literary history. When I construct a reading schedule, I outline a logic for understanding and naming the tradition. And every word I and my students say during the class adds to the history we are writing. We cannot, it seems, avoid naming the texts and traditions of African American literature. The temptation, of course, is to adopt Van Vechten's method of casting the material as an exotic landscape that mirrors our own and our students' preconceptions. Van Vechten represented Harlem as exotic in many ways, but none is more revealing than the glossary he provides for "the reader . . . of the unusual Negro words and phrases employed in this novel" (*Nigger Heaven* 3). This glossary casts the vernacular as exotic and claims for Van Vechten the role of cultural translator—a role teachers of diverse traditions must resist. Instead, we must derive our names from the tradition itself and make students more aware of the process of naming they undertake.

I have developed three strategies that allow my students to watch themselves in relation to the texts they read. I encourage students to identify the rhetorical situation different texts establish; I present the vernacular traditions—folklore, slave narratives, blues and jazz—out of which the form and substance of much African American literature arise; and I teach texts by white writers alongside texts by black writers to raise the issue of appropriation explicitly. I will close by briefly describing examples of each strategy.

The double audience inherent in many African American texts is conveniently introduced by Hurston's account of the storyteller with which I began this essay, and we find an even more dynamic use of this rhetorical doubleness in Harriet Jacobs's *Incidents in the Life of a Slave Girl*. As a narrator, Jacobs frequently envisions and addresses a Northern, Victorian, white, Christian reader, whose heart may be in the right place, but whose life has been so limited that she may consider Jacobs's story unbelievable. Obviously, I and my students are no more members of this audience than we are participants in Jacobs's experience; however, we are positioned in the role of the white Northerner by Jacobs's frequent exhortations. She asks, for example, "In view of these things, why are ye silent, ye free men and women of the north? Why do your tongues falter in maintenance of the right?" (29–30). As no black reader would be, we are aligned with those confronted by their own silence. Our tongues falter in the face of Jacobs's privations. We are repeatedly reminded that we cannot fully imagine Jacobs's experiences, that her pen cannot fully reveal her heart and mind. As a result we become sympathetic outsiders to her experience, called upon to listen as she names it. This dialogic act of positioning white and black readers differently is an important strategy in much African American literature, and I encourage my students to accept and read from the rhetorical position the text establishes. Often that position will lead to shocks. More than one of my white students has confessed to throwing *Native Son* against the wall in anger, not at Bigger's plight, but at the representation of many white characters as racists. Interestingly, Van Vechten failed to account for his double audience partly because he was so concerned to alleviate the "actual shock" he feared the novel would provoke in white readers. Only by confronting the shock, however, can we, to echo James Baldwin's words, shatter the preconceptions we scarcely know we hold.

Next, I encourage students to explore the intertextual relationship between the vernacular and formal literary traditions that Henry Louis Gates, Houston Baker, and others identify. To do this, I create a sequence of readings that yoke the two. For example, I have taught

Frederick Douglass's and Harriet Jacobs's slave narratives next to Arna Bontemps's *Black Thunder* (a historical novel about Gabriel's slave revolt), Ernest Gaines's *The Autobiography of Miss Jane Pittman*, and Alice Walker's *The Color Purple*. I have taught African and African American folktales next to Charles Chesnutt's *The Conjure Woman* and Toni Morrison's *Song of Solomon* and *Tar Baby*. Students can observe firsthand the interplay between vernacular expression and literary shaping by comparing these works. As they see the texts referring to each other, in a sense talking to each other, students will learn that African American literature is not simply informed by a tradition of protest and opposition to dominant culture, but that it arises out of a rich cultural tradition of its own.

Finally I pair texts such as Joel Chandler Harris's *Uncle Remus* and Zora Neale Hurston's *Mules and Men*, Harriet Beecher Stowe's *Uncle Tom's Cabin* and Harriet Jacobs's *Life*, Carl Van Vechten's *Nigger Heaven* and Nella Larsen's *Quicksand*, to explore explicitly the issues I have raised in this essay. For example, I compare Van Vechten's representation of the exotic "naive delight in glowing colour—the colour that exists only in cloudless, tropical climes" (*Nigger Heaven* 89) with this passage from *Quicksand*:

> Helga Crane . . . [had] some unanalyzed driving spirit of loyalty to the inherent racial need for gorgeousness [which] told her that bright colours *were* fitting and dark-complexioned people *should* wear yellow, green, and red. Black, brown, and gray were ruinous to them, actually destroying the luminous tones lurking in their dusky skins. One of the loveliest sights Helga had ever seen had been a sooty black girl decked out in a flaming orange dress, which a horrified matron had next day consigned to the dyer. (18)

Larsen represents the love of color as a mark of beauty. This passage reads as a defense, on the one hand, against Van Vechten's representation of color as a sign of the primitive exotic and, on the other, against the matrons of Naxos (the white-funded "school for Negroes" where Helga works) who insist that blacks should wear dull clothes *because* a love of color is primitive. Helga finds herself squeezed by both attitudes, but wears colorful clothes as an assertion of independence from white acts of naming. Where Van Vechten presents a simple stereotype, Larsen revises the stereotype into a version of the double bind. By comparing black and white representations of similar material, then, students can begin to identify "whatever is black about black American literature," and explore the doubleness that lies at the heart of many African American texts. This doubleness grows out of the constant awareness of two audiences, one black, the other white, that many black writers feel compelled to address.

In *The Souls of Black Folk*, W. E. B. Du Bois says that the psychological state of black Americans is defined by a double consciousness. "It is a peculiar sensation," he writes,

> this sense of always looking at one's self through the eyes of others, of measuring one's soul by the tape of a world that looks on in amused contempt and pity. One ever feels his twoness— an American, a Negro; two souls, two thoughts, two unreconciled strivings; two warrings in one dark body, whose dogged strength alone keeps it from being torn asunder. (45)

This doubleness is reflected in the term "Afro-American" itself, and even that term is now being transformed into "African American" by those sensitive to the problems both of naming and doubleness that I have been discussing. We have become increasingly sensitive to the use of names—Negro, black, others more disparaging—which have been imposed upon African Americans by whites, or have been rejected and replaced. I am uncomfortable each time I type or read the title of Van Vechten's book. But this discomfort, as my prefatory quotation from James Baldwin notes, is extremely valuable, because it allows us to look back at ourselves. My reading strategies attempt to make white students adopt doubleness for a while. I want them to see themselves as the text presents them, to measure themselves against an image mirrored from a world apart. Doubleness, Du Bois argues, is the defining characteristic of black art and experience. By confronting it, however temporarily, my students may respect and recognize more fully a tradition which informs their own historical identities.

Works Cited

Baker, Houston A., Jr. *Blues, Ideology, and Afro-American Literature: A Vernacular Theory*. Chicago: U of Chicago P, 1987.

Du Bois, W. E. B. *The Souls of Black Folk*. 1903. New York: New American Library, 1969.

———. "Books." Rev. of *Nigger Heaven*, by Carl Van Vechten. *The Crisis* Dec. 1926: 81–82.

Gates, Henry Louis, Jr. *The Signifying Monkey: A Theory of Afro-American Literary Criticism*. New York: Oxford UP, 1988.

———. "Canon-Formation, Literary History, and the Afro-American Tradition: From the Seen to the Told." *Afro-American Literary Study in the 1990s*. Ed. Houston Baker and Patricia Redmond. Chicago: U of Chicago P, 1989.

Hughes, Langston. *The Big Sea*. New York: Viking, 1933.

Hurston, Zora Neale. *Mules and Men*. 1935. Bloomington: Indiana UP, 1978.

———. *Moses, Man of the Mountain: A Novel*. 1939. New York: HarperCollins, 1991.

Ikonne, Chidi. *From Du Bois to Van Vechten: The Early New Negro Literature: 1903–1926*. Contributions in Afro-American and African Studies 60. Westport, CT: Greenwood, 1981.

Jacobs, Harriet A. *Incidents in the Life of a Slave Girl: Written by Herself*. Ed. Jean Fagan Yellin. Cambridge: Harvard UP, 1987.

Johnson, A. A. A., and R. M. Johnson. "Forgotten Pages: Black Literary Magazines of the 1920s." *Journal of American Studies* 8 (1974): 363–82.

Johnson, James Weldon. *Along This Way*. New York: Viking, 1933.

———. "Romance and Tragedy in Harlem—A Review." Rev. of *Nigger Heaven* by Carl Van Vechten. *Opportunity: A Journal of Negro Life* Oct. 1926: 316–17, 330.

Kellner, Bruce, ed. *Letters of Carl Van Vechten*. New Haven: Yale UP, 1987.

Larsen, Nella. *Quicksand* and *Passing*. Ed. Deborah E. McDowell. New Brunswick, NJ: Rutgers UP, 1986.

Rogers, J.A. "The Critic." *The Messenger: World's Greatest Negro Monthly* Dec. 1926: 365.

———. "The Critic." *The Messenger: World's Greatest Negro Monthly* Feb. 1927: 47.

Thurman, Wallace. "A Stranger at the Gates." Rev. of *Nigger Heaven* by Carl Van Vechten. *The Messenger: World's Greatest Negro Monthly* Sept. 1926: 279.

Van Vechten, Carl. *Nigger Heaven*. 1926. New York: Harper and Row, 1971.

———. "The Negro in Art." *The Crisis* Mar. 1926: 219.

5 Adult Learners, Autobiography, and Educational Planning: Reflections on Pedagogy, Andragogy, and Power

Michael J. Kiskis
Elmira College

This essay began as a celebration of the potential that autobiographical writing holds for adult students as they struggle with their decision to return to college and as they work to compose a clear plan of study. Because I experienced the tension as my adult students moved into new intellectual territory, I was intrigued by the relationship between the act of writing first-person narrative and the process of identifying learning as a means toward intellectual growth. I felt that writing autobiography was one tool to foster the critical reflection necessary if students are to understand the knowledge they already possess as they plan future coursework. While writing this essay, however, I have had to reflect on my own assumptions about learning and writing and to come to terms with how those assumptions have affected my relationships with students and colleagues. Writing has helped me understand the increasingly complex struggle we experience as we are asked to become more reflective about pedagogy and power. And the complexity of that struggle has muted the celebration that characterized my earlier drafts.

Adult students were rarely mentioned during my study of composition theory and pedagogy as a graduate student at the State University of New York at Albany. While there, I became familiar with the writing process movement and a follower of James Moffett and Peter Elbow. I discovered Janet Emig's research into the composing process, Nancy Sommers's work on revision, Mina Shaughnessy's portrait of error, Linda Flower and John Hayes's cognitive schemas, the rhetorics of E. D. Hirsch and James Kinneavy. Most important, for me, were James Britton and his colleagues' study of audience and William Perry's scheme of intellectual and ethical development.[1] In essence, I was introduced to writing theories and pedagogies developed by theorists and practitioners who focused on students eighteen or younger, and I developed course syllabi and writing tasks with their concepts as the background for my teaching. Adult and returning students figured infrequently within the graduate curriculum.

At Empire State College[2] I consult with new and established faculty as they evolve strategies for working with adults, and I teach adult students. My students are my contemporaries: their average age is thirty-seven. Some are older than I am; few are younger. These students are returning to college after years in the work force or in the home; many have considerable work experience; some hold major corporate responsibilities. A decade ago, Lynn Troyka offered a generic description that is still valid: returning students are older, are often the first generation to go on to college, are often parents. Most have full-time jobs and many are women now returning to the academy (253). While K. Patricia Cross reminds us of the hazards of generic descriptions, because of the diversity at work within this broad category, my own experience suggests that the majority have had some contact with the academy after high school (many have completed a series of courses but have not been able to complete degree requirements) and have long looked for a way to continue their studies that offers the least interference with their daily lives. Increasing numbers of women among my students (many of whom are single parents with primary responsibility for their children's welfare) are unable to take time out to go to class once or twice a week. These students are drawn to the individualized instruction and the philosophy of guided independent learning that characterize Empire's program. All of them are apprehensive about the changes they are about to face.

When I started at Empire, the one-to-one instruction that is at the heart of the academic program did not seem much different from the work I had done in Albany's writing center, and I felt comfortable relying on my background. That background included an appreciation for and some knowledge of autobiography and the potential to be found in reflective writing (I had designed and taught a course in autobiography at SUNYA, had completed my dissertation on Mark Twain's autobiography, and had repeatedly used autobiography to focus courses I taught.) At first, I did not think much about whether adult students faced different demands or about how their lives were affected by the studies they were taking. I did not consider how thirty-seven-year-old students would be different from a population of seventeen-to-twenty-one-year-olds. Still, I seemed to be successful. My students worked through their course projects and many felt the study worth the time and effort. I realize now that their success had more to do with their motivation than with my sensitivity.

As I became more deeply connected with adult students as a tutor, a mentor (a mix of teacher, academic advisor, and confidant), and an administrator, however, I began to understand that power—who holds it and how it is shared within the teacher-student relationship—is central: it affects how we see students and how we choose to work with them. It affects our approach to students who are academically superior and in need of little more than a guiding touch; it affects our approach to students who are not prepared to meet the academy's demands. It also affects whether we are able to break from the traditional emphases on structured class time and lectures and move toward new roles as guides to individualized, independent learning.

Adult students are especially sensitive to questions of power because they are directly and swiftly affected by our expectations (they are also well acquainted with the power relationships they face each day at work or within their families). And because they are "adults," we often unthinkingly and unfairly raise our expectations; for example, we think them automatically capable of advanced work in literature because they are older and more experienced, have read extensively and have highly developed oral skills; we think them capable of advanced study of management because they have years of successful business experience. We are tempted to equate chronological age with intellectual awareness and sophistication. Perry's *Forms of Intellectual and Ethical Development in the College Years: A Scheme* helped turn our attention away from a focus on chronological, unconscious natural development (based on Piaget's work with children[3]) to a model that insists that intellectual development is chosen, consciously attempted, and teachable.

The idea of a conscious intellectual development led many of us to develop syllabi aimed at leading students through the various positions in Perry's scheme. We fell into this practice not only because the design offers the potential for ethical growth through the humanities (a focus that is very clear throughout Perry's discussion) but because it gives us a means to categorize and understand our students as they are repeatedly challenged by the various sets of values displayed within the academy. Patricia Bizzell, however, has offered us a clear warning: "The whole thrust of [Perry's] developmental scheme," she notes, " is toward an increasing distance on the beliefs of one's childhood. These beliefs can no longer be accepted uncritically as Absolutes, once we realize that well-intentioned people may hold beliefs different from our own. As the pedagogical pluralism which Perry recommends widens the students' perspectives, it also fosters relativism by casting their beliefs into comparative relations with those of others" (453). A little later, Bizzell concludes:

> Perry's quasi-spiritual tone should remind us that we tend to invest teaching with moral fervor. . . . Given that we do have this moral investment in the objects of knowledge and the ways of thinking that we teach, it seems hypocritical to pretend that academic activity is value-neutral, that we are merely teaching "thinking," not thinking in a certain way. And it seems more respectful to our students to see what we are doing when we teach as attempting to persuade them to accept our values, not simply inculcating our values. (454)

Bizzell's comments are especially important for our work with adult students. She emphasizes our need to admit that what we teach comes with a complete set of values attached. But it is not enough to admit this to ourselves. We must be open with our students so that they can account for the dissonance that may appear as their previous ideas and beliefs are called into question. We must show that their values are in play against other (our?) values and that the learning they gain will allow them to choose between and among the variety of perspectives.

The debate that began with John Dewey's progressive movement to tie experience and education closely together is directly related to Bizzell's reading of Perry and our continued work with adults. In *Experience and Education* Dewey described standard education practices:

> The main purpose or objective is to prepare the young for future responsibilities and for success in life, by means of acquisition of the organized bodies of information and prepared forms of skill which comprehend the material of instruction. Since the subject-matter as well as standards of proper conduct are handed down from the past, the attitude of pupils must, upon the whole, be one of docility, receptivity, and obedience. Books, especially textbooks, are the chief representative of the lore and wisdom of the past, while teachers are the organs through which pupils are brought into effective connection with the material. *Teachers are the agents through which knowledge and skills are communicated and rules of conduct enforced.* (18; my emphasis)

Dewey felt that this static form of education led to disconnection and alienation. Paulo Freire, too, criticized this traditional approach as the "banking concept of education," in which "knowledge is a gift bestowed by those who consider themselves knowledgeable upon those whom they consider know nothing" (58). Education thus becomes "an act of depositing, in which the students are the depositories and the teacher is the depositor. Instead of communicating, the teacher issues communiqués and makes deposits which the students patiently receive, memorize, and repeat." Both Dewey and Freire scorn traditional notions of the student as empty vessel, a notion that is exploded by students themselves when we begin to talk with adults who have come back to the academy.

Significantly, Dewey advanced the theory that learning could become integrative only if tied to experience: "The beginning of instruction shall be made with the experience learners already have" (74). While Dewey spoke to the education of children, his ideas fold neatly into the general concerns of adult learners: prior learning is especially important when working with students who have already accumulated some thirty years of learning. As a group, these students are interested in finding connections between their past experience and the lessons to be gained by entering the academy. In literature, for example, adult students often look for connections between their reading and their own lives. Literature comes alive for them as they consider the choices that characters make and listen to stories with one ear tuned to echoes of their own past encounters. Business students, similarly, often have extensive experience with how to get things done within organizational structures. They find the variety of management theories useful because such theories often address immediate work situations. The same can be said of studies in economics, human resources, human services, law, and communications. Most adult students, in fact, seek out and find material within their studies that can be transported back to their home or work environments to help them make better sense out of experiences they face. Their practice is clearly tied to Dewey's theory.

How, then, do we work with adult students? What can we offer them as a strategy for breaking out of traditional student roles? How do we break our own pedagogical bonds? Malcolm Knowles uses the term "andragogy" to describe the basic processes at work in self-directed learning (19). His contrast between pedagogy (the teaching of children) and andragogy (helping adults learn) is compatible within Dewey's progressive tradition. Laurent Daloz expands on Knowles's definition: "In the end, good teaching rests neither in accumulating a shelf-full of knowledge nor in developing a repertoire of skills. In the end, good teaching lies in a willingness to attend and care for what happens in our students, ourselves, and the space between us. Good teaching is a certain kind of stance. . . . It is a stance of receptivity, of attunement, of listening" (244). This, for Daloz, is the centerpiece of a mentor's responsibility.

Traditionally, our being receptive, being attuned, and listening also requires students to adopt a mode of discourse that allows us to converse more clearly. The challenge is to help students and mentors create a shared discourse, a discourse that makes it more likely that they will discover and tune their voices, a discourse in which we become active partners in a conversation rather than stolid announcers of the Truth. The varieties of autobiographical writing establish the broad boundaries for such discourse. They also allow students to develop a sense of voice.

Matching autobiographical writing—the telling of one's story—to Dewey's emphasis on the integration of past and new learning—the very act of reflection itself—is one of the guiding principles of Empire State College's program. As students develop learning contracts (see Knowles 26–28), they work with a mentor to determine what learning they already have and how that learning can serve as the foundation for continued inquiry.[4] That exploration is the starting point for the writing we ask our students to attempt. In its purest form, this process allows students to shape each piece of their programs. But the whole process can be both helped and hindered by faculty and student perceptions of power—of who has control, of whose image of the relationship of past to present will prevail.[5] Writing is at the heart of that struggle. Reflective writing—autobiographical writing—is key.

Support for the use of autobiography has grown during the past few years. Elaine Maimon's "Some Uses of Autobiography: Private Writing in Public Places" and Donald Murray's "All Writing Is Autobiography" propose autobiographical writing as a valuable first step in helping writers see their own interest and awareness as the starting point for public writing.[6] Maimon distinguishes autobiography as a literary genre from its use as a "private way to find ideas" (131). She sees the expressive nature of autobiography as a starting point in a continuum that runs to the transactional prose of public writing. Murray is more strident in his support because he sees autobiography as one way all writers find their subjects and as one way we allow ourselves "to explore the questions that itch our lives" (73). That itch is vital for Murray, who goes on to argue that "we should [not] make our students write on many different subjects, but . . . write and rewrite in pursuit of those few subjects which obsess them" (73).

Exploring obsessions is, in fact, a useful way to think about autobiography as a form of general academic discourse.[7] In "Reflections on Academic Discourse: How It Relates to Freshmen and Colleagues," Peter Elbow has argued for a greater emphasis on nonacademic discourse, on "discourse that tries to render experience rather than explain it" (136). Though focusing on traditional students, Elbow's comments are important to our work with adults, especially when he emphasizes how stories allow students to begin to develop their own voices: "We need nonacademic discourse even for the sake of helping students produce good academic discourse. . . . That is, many students can repeat and explain a principle in physics or economics in the academic discourse of the textbook but cannot simply tell a story of what is going on in the room or the country around them on account of that principle—or what the room or the country would look like if that principle were different" (137). While a basic problem is that there is no one definition of academic discourse, Elbow opens up a larger issue as he makes a case for a general definition of academic discourse that focuses on the writer's responsibility to be "clear about claims and assertions rather than just implying or insinuating: getting thinking to stand on its own two feet rather than leaning on the authority of who advances it or the fit with who hears it" (140). This emphasis is becoming more and more the focus for discussion about writing, as theorists and practitioners explore autobiography as a tool not only for their students but for themselves as they attempt to break the barriers against self-reference in scholarly discussion.[8] It is also a way to clarify the obsessions we have with learning.

But just what does "obsess" adult students? Often, re-entry into the academy. Focusing on that transition, in the spring of 1990 we enrolled first-time students in a study that emphasized autobiographical writing. Five tutors delivered the study to fifty students. Groups were intentionally kept small (the maximum was fifteen, and no group grew even that large), and tutors were given the freedom to improvise. Our intention was to offer autobiography as a tool students could use to explore issues that would arise as they continued their studies. We hoped students would begin to reflect upon their reasons for coming back into the academy, would consider how that choice affected and was affected by other aspects of their lives, and would be exposed to and begin to think about multicultural perspectives. We saw this study as an opportunity for students to reflect upon the personal and cultural contexts within which they would be spending their coming year or years. In the spirit of Rogers and Maslow, we hoped to stimulate our students' sense of self.[9] Playing off the developmental stages identified by Erikson and Levinson, we also hoped to introduce students to the advantage of finding and maintaining a clear, personal voice.[10]

While we concentrated on the discovery of voice more than on the characteristics of the genre, we asked students to read Donald Murray's *Write to Learn* and Robert Lyons's *Autobiography: A Reader for Writers*.

They also read other autobiographies (suggestions included Benjamin Franklin's *Autobiography*, Frederick Douglass's *My Bondage and My Freedom*, Harriet Jacobs's *Incidents in the Life of a Slave Girl*, and Maxine Hong Kingston's *The Woman Warrior*). Students kept a journal of their reactions to the readings and their thoughts on returning to college. As their final assignment, we asked students to offer selections from their journals. We asked them to act as their own editors to preserve their control over the writing and to show how their voice would gain strength if they exercised strict editorial control. Students shared entries that called attention to both the excitement and the risk of writing:

> As I read through Murray's *Write to Learn*, my mind was racing. He reminded me of the reason I am going back to school. It's mostly because I feel like I have been standing still for too long. I have lost having a time and space of my own through the years of working, raising children, and having a husband and home. I used to do a lot of writing when I was younger, either through correspondence or writing poems and keeping diaries. I miss it.

> What is scaring me is, almost everything I look at or think about is something I could write about. It's overwhelming! If I let myself start to write, I will never get anything else done! If I look at a "big" picture, there are so many "little" pictures that make up that big picture. It becomes more complicated because there are so many parts to the whole story. Or one story makes you think of another. I just can't write fast enough to keep up with what my mind is telling me.

> Dear Journal:
> There comes a point in writing, like other things in life, when the decision must be made whether you can do it, and if you can, do you want to do it, or do you want to watch someone else do it. . . . When I get to Heaven, there will be pc's, pens, paper, many erasers, the ocean, my loved ones, peace and time to enjoy them all. There will be no ironing, no death or hurt. There will be great writings and time to read them, create them or both.

While each of these writers had his or her own agenda—getting reacquainted with writing, exploring the possibility for innovation, trying to control the idea of story, working past intimidation to speculate about an afterlife that is more friendly toward writing—they are united by an obsession with their uncertainty of their own potential. Those who felt they wrote well remained anxious about their reintroduction to writing and the alien demands of the academy. But the freedom to choose topics out of their own experience gave them a sense of comfort and control. It also showed that individual interest is the basis of all successful writing, even writing that is done to meet the demands of an academic community.

Individual interests shape our academic community: we tell stories to mark the trail, to chart our intellectual journey. "When I was in school" becomes much more than an empty introduction—it gives students a taste of the experience that stretches ahead. Our students already know how to tell stories about themselves, their families, their interests. They have simply stopped telling them to us—to the evaluators—because the academy discourages first-person narrative; it prefers and rewards the cool stance of the "objective" researcher. Adult students rely on their memories of the academic prose they learned in previous school experiences and remain suspicious of personal narrative because it is so often not considered, or even actively discouraged, in the writing they do on the job.[11] They silence their energy and wit; they use formal diction and stilted prose to drown out their natural voices. Our reintroduction of personal narrative in an academic context, then, reinserts students into the center of their own educations. By reading and listening to their stories, we acknowledge them and extend the franchise by including them in the learning process.

I want to point out, however, that our acknowledgment begets both success and failure. Our students do gain the strength and confidence to offer their own ideas in their own words. But our celebration of their success must be tempered by the realization that students may encounter a barrier similar to the submerged "bluff reef" that waited to tear the bottom from Mark Twain's steamboat in *Life on the Mississippi*: in our case our lack of attention to relationships between gender and students' intellectual development.[12]

This problem became increasingly clear to me as I reflected on Educational Planning—a study at Empire State that sharpens the focus on autobiography—and on one student's experience with that study. Educational Planning is the only study required of all matriculating students. During the study, mentors ask students to reflect on their past experience and learning. Using that reflection, students and mentors collaborate as they explore options for future studies and design an individualized, academically sound degree program. Throughout this process, students keep records of their explorations as they collect and analyze evidence of their prior learning, design degrees that grow out of their specific goals and plans, and reflect on the impact their education may have on their lives. Educational Planning is thus a potent and rhetorically complex mix of autobiography, research, and persuasive writing—potent because students work to recognize and then remain sensitive to the often conflicting roles they play in a variety of contexts (citizen, worker, spouse, parent, friend, lover, child, student), and rhetorically complex because students submit their plan of study to the faculty and to the college for review. Students are asked to describe the context that informs their choices and within which they will come to understand the prospect of a lifelong process of education—a herculean task for even those of us who are in the habit of explaining ourselves to the "experts." The need to convince faculty to accept the study plan adds to the pressure of composing and can sometimes lead students to stick with simple narrative or chronological listings of topics. Some give up and refuse to file their programs. The whole process often becomes an exercise in applied politics because of the negotiations and compromises that may, in fact, become necessary as the review goes forward.

Jane, a coordinator of information systems in an office of employee relations, came to Empire State with an associate's degree in business. She was returning to college because of her desire for a bachelor's degree. I tell her story here because I think it illustrates how even the most careful planning can go awry if we fail to take into account relationships of gender to intellectual development and academic discourse.

Jane's and my initial meetings went well. Jane was a voracious reader, and her reading had led her down a variety of paths. As we talked our way toward a clearer sense of her personal goals, she expressed interest in the relationship between her job in the technology field and the impact technology has had on her life and on the lives of people she knows. She was especially intrigued by the relationship between technology and society, the ways technology can put emotional blinders on people—"dehumanize" them. She wanted to explore this subject in considerable depth. Jane also liked to write. She wanted to explore a variety of topics and to get more experience writing. With that in mind, we prepared a reading list for her learning contract: Bill Moyers's *World of Ideas*, Robert Coles's *The Call of Stories*, Robert Lyons's *Autobiography: A Reader for Writers*, Eudora Welty's *One Writer's Beginnings*. We also identified shorter pieces including excerpts from Thoreau's *Walden*, Virginia Woolf's *A Room of One's Own*, and even E. B. White's "The Death of a Pig." This reading list established the basic design of her contract, and autobiography became the primary focus.

By looking to her past, Jane began to take notice of the range of her experience and the variety of school-based and experiential learning she had accumulated. This was the first step—looking backward in order to begin to look forward. She reflected on that learning as she shaped a degree program: her transcripts allowed her to see her formal education from a distance; her learning contracts turned her toward what she would study in the future so that she could both earn her degree and take away a substantial amount of learning. Eventually, we trimmed away the myriad topics and course titles that she found and began to focus on a "doable" program of study. Throughout the process, Jane remained energized by her reading and thinking. She was so taken with the idea of designing her own program that she requested only 19 credits of advanced standing, whereas she could have brought in the equivalent of two years' credit from her earlier study. She would have to complete 109 credits in contract studies. She titled her program Technology and Society.

An essay Jane wrote explaining the rationale for her study displayed the energy of her thinking and the range of learning she had acquired outside the academy. She was neither afraid of the personal pronoun nor squeamish about calling attention to her own ideas and her own processes for arriving at an integration of her past experience and present interests. She was not afraid to admit that she thought a great deal about the social implications of technology and that she wanted to spend more time reading and thinking about them. Jane went on to write about each of her areas in great depth.

Yet, for all our careful focus on Jane's initiation into the discourse of the academy and into the disciplinary approach to her program (notions based in Perry's developmental scheme), she wavered in her attention to the demands of discipline-based academic writing. Her work in Educational Planning was strong because of the focus on her own voice; her contract studies in comparative democratic systems undertaken in tandem with Educational Planning was more problematic because she was asked to conform to the conventions of political science. She disliked the reading and rebelled against the demands for analysis. At the halfway point of her contract, it was clear that Jane would not complete her work. Although she talked about completing it, she had effectively halted her work, and she soon announced her intention to drop the contract, saying she would come back once she was more settled. That was one year ago. I have not heard from her since.

As I reflect on my work with Jane and consider what role I played in her decision to break away from the academy, I begin to realize that a portion of blame can be allotted to a reliance on schemes of adult development that have little in common with Jane's approach to reading and writing. After all, Perry and Levinson focus their attention on young males' reactions to intellectual challenge. Even Daloz's sensitive portrait of mentoring focuses heavily on Perry's male-dominated scheme. Those schemes do not address the developmental cycles and spans common to women's experience. Faculty need to become familiar with the full range of developmental schemes, a range that includes the theory and research of Carol Gilligan, Mary Belenky and her colleagues, and Ruthellen Josselson. The work of all of these scholars argues for a more complex vision of the ways in which women find their way through the intellectual thickets that are so much a part of the academy. It argues for an awareness of the variety of voices that women use to express their connection to or alienation from the academy. It also argues for a realization that the impetus for intellectual development does not always reside within the academy, and that changes in personal lives are potent with possibilities for shifting attitudes and perspectives.

I think Jane finally decided to set aside her work at Empire because we were not listening to *her* voice or, put another way, because we decided that the voice we heard needed to change, to conform, if she was to succeed in the program. In this respect, Jane had much in common with the student in our autobiography study who wrote that she had "lost having a time and space of my own," and perhaps even more in common with the student who put her choices in the stark terms of a hoped-for afterlife. We asked Jane to make those choices, but we did not allow her the time to find her own answers. We were too concerned with getting her to tune her voice to be one of the choir. We should have taken the time to celebrate her ability as a soloist and then showed her the possibilities that present themselves when we blend our voices with others within the academy to take part in the disciplinary conversation. I keep hoping that Jane will find her way back. I suspect, however, that wherever she is, she continues to read and to write and to learn.

Mary Belenky comments that "teachers have to start with who students are—including their perspectives on the world—and, from that start, help students articulate what their driving questions are." From that initial inquiry, we can next show them how to "merge their questions with the ongoing questions in their disciplines." Too often, however, we seem to "be engaged in upholding the standards of the field or the institution without ever noticing who students are and what their driving questions are ... an unfortunate imbalance for men as well as women" (Ashton-Jones and Thomas 289). That imbalance is especially threatening to adult students already fearful about their re-entry into the academy. As educators, we must take care to find out their basic questions and use those questions to excite their writing—the reflective writing that uncovers interests and shapes intellectual discourse.

We also have to become better listeners. Daloz argues that we need to become mentors who "can help [our] charges to understand from a greater perspective the forces affecting them, thus enabling them to change direction" (211). Belenky and her colleagues found that many of the women they interviewed were looking for someone to help them discover a knowledge they already possessed: "The kind of teacher they praised and the kind for which they yearned was one who would help them articulate and expand their latent knowledge: a midwife-teacher. . . . While the bankers deposit knowledge in the learner's head, the midwives draw it out. They assist the students in giving birth to their own ideas, in making their own tacit knowledge explicit and elaborating it" (217). Daloz and Belenky, et al., argue for a return to the concepts of education and experience espoused by Dewey, who defined an educator as one who must have "that sympathetic understanding of individuals as individuals which gives him an idea of what is actually going on in the minds of those who are learning" (39). Too often we put students through an intellectual hazing. We, after all, hold power. Instead, we need to share the power and authority that comes from the clear articulation of one's own ideas. Many of us were told that this is not the way to teach. And perhaps it isn't. But it is the way learning happens. And sharing this concept of learning is vital in our work with adult students if they are to see that they are already active and important participants in our culture's conversation.

Notes

1. I mention this series of researchers and their work to establish the beginning point for my own thinking about composition. The articles and studies include James Moffett's *Teaching the Universe of Discourse*, Peter Elbow's *Writing without Teachers*, Janet Emig's *The Composing Processes of Twelfth Graders*, Nancy Sommers's "Revision Strategies of Student Writers and Experienced Adult Writers," Mina Shaughnessy's *Errors and Expectations*, Linda Flower and John Hayes's "Cognitive Process Theory of Writing," Linda Flower's *Problem-solving Strategies for Writing*, E. D. Hirsch's *Philosophy of Composition*, James Kinneavy's *Theory of Discourse*, James Britton and his colleagues' *Development of Writing Abilities (11-18)*, and William Perry's *Forms of Intellectual and Ethical Development in the College Years*.

2. Empire State College is part of the State University of New York. It enrolls some seven thousand students in locations across New York State.

Along with its regional learning centers, the college also serves students through its Center for Distance Learning, Office of International Programs, Graduate Program, and corporate-sponsored programs. The college has just begun a new venture—SUNY by Satellite—that is designed to offer instruction using satellite links to various community-college locations across New York.

3. See Jean Piaget, *The Language and Thought of a Child* (1932) and *The Moral Judgement of the Child* (1932).

4. I am struck by the similarities between Knowles's scheme for independent learning and Elbow's concept of teacherless instruction.

5. Michael Holzman's discussions in "The Social Context of Literacy Education" and "A Post-Freirean Model for Adult Literacy Education" are helpful, as are Janice Neuleib's "The Friendly Stranger: Twenty-Five Years as 'Other'" and Jane Tompkins's "Pedagogy of the Distressed."

6. Several other essays are quite helpful; for example, Lynn Bloom's "Autobiography and Audience," Mary Jane Dickerson's " 'Shades of Deeper Meaning': On Writing Autobiography," and Marilyn Smith's "The Time of Their Lives: Teaching Autobiography to Senior Adults." Jack Mezirow and Associates' *Fostering Critical Reflection in Adulthood: A Guide to Transformative and Emancipatory Learning* is also useful. We might further extend the definition of autobiography within our discussion to include the interviews and case studies that inform the work of theorists such as William Perry, Daniel Levinson, Mary Belenky and her colleagues, and Ruthellen Josselson.

7. See Nicholas Coles and Susan Wall's "Conflict and Power in the Reader-Responses of Adult Basic Writers" and Thomas Kent's "On the Very Idea of a Discourse Community."

8. Nancy Sommers's "Between the Drafts" is an example of personal scholarship.

9. C. R. Rogers and A. H. Maslow theorized that adulthood is marked by continual movement toward self-actualization.

10. Erik Erikson and Daniel Levinson theorized about developmental stages that span an individual life. Erikson focused on the interaction of biological, psychological, and social processes that combined to shape psychosocial development; Levinson built on Erikson's work as he fine-tuned the notion of a life cycle. Levinson's study focused only on the cycle experienced by adult men.

11. For a look at writing on the job, see Lester Faigley and Thomas P. Miller's "What We Learn from Writing on the Job." Several researchers have examined the writing done by engineers; for example, see Jack Selzer's "The Composing Process of an Engineer," and Dorothy Winsor's "Engineering Writing/Writing Engineering."

12. The issue of gender is the basis for studies conducted by Nancy Chodorow, Carol Gilligan, Mary Belenky and her colleagues, and Ruthellen Josselson. Several writers have also looked at the connection between gender and autobiographical writing; see Elizabeth Flynn's "Composing as a Woman" and Linda Peterson's "Gender and the Autobiographical Essay: Research Perspectives, Pedagogical Practices." Alice Gillam's "Returning Students' Ways of Writing: Implications for First-Year College Composition" is also helpful.

Works Cited

Ashton-Jones, Evelyn, and Dene Kay Thomas. "Composition, Collaboration, and Women's Ways of Knowing: A Conversation with Mary Belenky." *Journal of Advanced Composition* 10.2 (Fall 1990): 275–92.

Belenky, Mary Field, Blythe McVicker Clinchy, Nancy Rule Goldberger, and Jill Mattuck Tarule. *Women's Ways of Knowing: The Development of Self, Voice, and Mind.* New York: Basic Books, 1986.

Bizzell, Patricia. "William Perry and Liberal Education." *College English* 46.5 (Sept. 1984): 447–54.

Bloom, Lynn Z. "Autobiography and Audience." *Journal of Advanced Composition* 4 (1983): 119–31.

Britton, James, Tony Burgess, Nancy Martin, Alex McLeod, and Harold Rosen. *The Development of Writing Abilities (11–18).* London: Macmillan Education, 1975; distributed in U.S. by NCTE.

Chodorow, Nancy. *The Reproduction of Mothering: Psychoanalysis and the Sociology of Gender.* Berkeley and Los Angeles: U of California P, 1978.

Coles, Nicholas, and Susan V. Wall. "Conflict and Power in the Reader-Responses of Adult Basic Writers." *College English* 49.3 (Mar. 1987): 298–314.

Coles, Robert. *The Call of Stories: Teaching and the Moral Imagination.* Boston: Houghton Mifflin, 1989.

Cross, K. Patricia. *Adults as Learners: Increasing Participation and Facilitating Learning.* San Francisco: Jossey-Bass, 1981.

Daloz, Laurent A. *Effective Teaching and Mentoring: Realizing the Transformational Power of Adult Learning Experiences.* San Francisco: Jossey-Bass, 1986.

Dewey, John. *Experience and Education.* 1938. New York: Collier, 1963.

Dickerson, Mary Jane. " 'Shades of Deeper Meaning': On Writing Autobiography." *Journal of Advanced Composition* 9 (1989): 135–50.

Douglass, Frederick. *My Bondage and My Freedom.* Ed. William L. Andrews. Urbana: U of Illinois P, 1987.

Elbow, Peter. *Writing without Teachers.* New York: Oxford UP, 1973.

———. "Reflections on Academic Discourse: How It Relates to Freshmen and Colleagues." *College English* 53.2 (Feb. 1991): 135–55.

Emig, Janet. *The Composing Processes of Twelfth Graders.* Urbana, IL: NCTE, 1971.

Erikson, E. H. *Childhood and Society.* New York: Norton, 1950.

———. "Identity and the Life Cycle." *Psychological Issues* 1 (1959): 1–171.

Faigley, Lester, and Thomas P. Miller. "What We Learn from Writing on the Job." *College English* 44.6 (Oct. 1982): 557–74.

Freire, Paulo. *Pedagogy of the Oppressed.* New York: Continuum, 1970.

Flower, Linda. *Problem-solving Strategies for Writing.* New York: Harcourt Brace Jovanovich, 1981.

Flower, Linda, and John Hayes. "A Cognitive Process Theory of Writing." *College Composition and Communication* 37.4 (Dec. 1981): 365–87.

Flynn, Elizabeth A. "Composing as a Woman." *College Composition and Communication* 39.4 (Dec. 1988): 423–35.

Franklin, Benjamin. *Autobiography*. With introduction and notes by R. Jackson Wilson. New York: Modern Library, 1981.

Gillam, Alice M. "Returning Students' Ways of Writing: Implications for First-Year College Composition." *Journal of Teaching Writing* 10.1 (Spring/Summer 1991): 1–20.

Gilligan, Carol. *In a Different Voice: Psychological Theory and Women's Development*. Cambridge: Harvard UP, 1982.

Hirsch, E. D., Jr. *The Philosophy of Composition*. Chicago: U of Chicago P, 1977.

Holzman, Michael. "The Social Context of Literacy Education." *College English* 48.1 (Jan. 1986): 27–33.

———. "A Post-Freirean Model for Adult Literacy Education." *College English* 50.2 (Feb. 1988): 177–89.

Jacobs, Harriet A. *Incidents in the Life of a Slave Girl: Written by Herself*. Ed. Jean Fagan Yellin. Cambridge: Harvard UP, 1987.

Josselson, Ruthellen. *Finding Herself: Pathways to Identify Development in Women*. San Francisco: Jossey-Bass, 1987.

Kent, Thomas. "On the Very Idea of a Discourse Community." *College Composition and Communication* 42.4 (Dec. 1991): 425–45.

Kingston, Maxine Hong. *The Woman Warrior: Memoirs of a Girlhood among Ghosts*. New York: Vintage, 1989.

Kinneavy, James L. *A Theory of Discourse: The Aims of Discourse*. New York: Norton, 1971.

Knowles, Malcolm. *Self-directed Learning: A Guide for Learners and Teachers*. Chicago: Follett, 1975.

Levinson, Daniel J. *The Seasons of a Man's Life*. New York: Knopf, 1985.

Lyons, Robert. *Autobiography: A Reader for Writers*. 2d ed. New York: Oxford UP, 1984.

Maimon, Elaine P. "Some Uses of Autobiography: Private Writing in Public Places." *Journal of Advanced Composition* 5 (1984): 131–38.

Maslow, A. H. *Motivation and Personality*. 2d ed. New York: Harper and Row, 1970.

Mezirow, Jack, and Associates. *Fostering Critical Reflection in Adulthood: A Guide to Transformative and Emancipatory Learning*. San Francisco: Jossey-Bass, 1990.

Moffett, James. *Teaching the Universe of Discourse*. New York: Houghton Mifflin, 1968.

Moyers, Bill. *A World of Ideas*. Ed. Betty Sue Flowers. New York: Doubleday, 1989.

Murray, Donald M. *Write to Learn*. 2d ed. New York: Holt, Rinehart and Winston, 1987.

———. "All Writing Is Autobiography." *College Composition and Communication* 42.1 (Feb. 1991): 66–74.

Neuleib, Janice. "The Friendly Stranger: Twenty-Five Years as 'Other.' " *College Composition and Communication* 43.2 (May 1992): 231–43.

Perry, William G., Jr. *Forms of Intellectual and Ethical Development in the College Years: A Scheme.* New York: Holt, Rinehart and Winston, 1968.

Peterson, Linda H. "Gender and the Autobiographical Essay: Research Perspectives, Pedagogical Practices." *College Composition and Communication* 42.2 (May 1991): 170–83.

Rogers, C. R. *Client-centered Therapy.* New York: Houghton Mifflin, 1951.

Selzer, Jack. "The Composing Process of an Engineer." *College Composition and Communication* 34.2 (May 1983): 178–87.

Shaughnessy, Mina P. *Errors and Expectations.* New York: Oxford UP, 1977.

Smith, Marilyn B. "The Time of Their Lives: Teaching Autobiography to Senior Adults." *College English* 44.7 (Nov. 1982): 692–99.

Sommers, Nancy. "Revision Strategies of Student Writers and Experienced Adult Writers." *College Composition and Communication* 31.4 (Dec. 1980): 378–88.

———. "Between the Drafts." *College Composition and Communication* 43.1 (Feb. 1992): 23–31.

Thoreau, Henry David. *Walden and Civil Disobedience.* New York: Penguin, 1983.

Tompkins, Jane. "Pedagogy of the Distressed." *College English* 52.6 (Oct. 1990): 653–60.

Troyka, Lynn Quitman. "Perspectives on Legacies and Literacy in the 1980s." *College Composition and Communication* 33.3 (Oct. 1982): 252–62.

Twain, Mark. *Life on the Mississippi.* 1883. New York: New American Library, 1980.

Welty, Eudora. *One Writer's Beginnings.* New York: Warner, 1985.

White, E. B. "The Death of a Pig." *Essays of E. B. White.* New York: Harper and Row, 1977.

Winsor, Dorothy A. "Engineering Writing/Writing Engineering." *College Composition and Communication* 41.1 (Feb. 1990): 58–70.

Woolf, Virginia. *A Room of One's Own.* New York: Harcourt, Brace and World, 1929.

6 "Whose Machines Are These?" Politics, Power, and the New Technology

Elizabeth Klem and Charles Moran
University of Massachusetts at Amherst

As the field of computers and composition moves into its second decade of research, we turn from the research questions of the 1980s, which tended to consider the computer and the writer as a closed system, to those of the 1990s, which consider the computer and the writer as part of a larger system. The larger system we speak of here includes at least four interrelated subsystems: the student, the teacher, and the computer; the classroom teaching environment; the received pedagogy of the writing program; and the power relations of the institution within which these systems operate.

As we take this wider, more contextual view of the teaching and learning that occur. in our writing classes, it becomes clear that introducing a computer-equipped classroom into an existing writing program is a change that will cause adjustments in every part of the system. Most of the studies in our field focus on the student writer; here we focus on the teacher. The effect of the new environment on the teacher must, of course, itself have an effect on the students in the teacher's classes, and we think we see the outlines of what such an effect might be. Because what we have found has implications for teacher training programs, we conclude by suggesting that training programs do more than they now do to help teachers in computer-equipped classrooms cope with the change in the "work" of teaching that has been brought about by the new technology.

In attempting to ascertain the effects of the introduction of computer-equipped classrooms into an existing writing program, we have used multiple instruments and perspectives. Charles Moran, a faculty member and a prime mover in the establishment of computer-equipped classrooms, has kept teaching journals that chronicle his experience as teacher, teacher trainer, and administrator in the program. Elizabeth

Klem, a graduate student and teaching assistant who teaches in the computer classrooms under study, has conducted interviews with teachers who teach in the computerized facility and has administered questionnaires to students in these teachers' writing classes. In addition, Klem and Moran have together conducted a semester-long naturalistic study of two teachers teaching for the first time in the new classrooms ("Teachers"). Over two years of studies and discussion, the authors feel that they have begun to develop an understanding of some of the ways in which technological change has affected the larger system they are part of.

We begin with the institutional situation of the writing teacher at the University of Massachusetts/Amherst. It is an old truth, but an important one: that writing teachers are situated on the margin of the profession. Their situation in any given institution of postsecondary education is likely to be one of relative powerlessness. At our particular institution, a "flagship" research campus, this is certainly the case. Practically all of our writing teachers are teaching assistants, or T.A.'s, poorly paid and overworked, teaching "English" courses but without voting rights in department meetings and therefore with little control over curriculum or teaching environment. While English faculty teach five courses per year for full salaries, T.A.'s teach two courses per year, or 40 percent of a faculty load, for 13 percent of the average faculty salary. Further, in their dual roles as graduate students and teaching assistants, T.A.'s are beholden both to those who direct their academic programs and to those who direct the writing program in which they teach. It is these teachers—the least-paid, often the youngest and least experienced—whom we ask to learn the new technology and to adapt their teaching styles to its requirements. These T.A.'s, one might argue, might be more flexible than senior professors, having less invested in prior experience. Yet one can just as forcefully argue that these same teachers, "T.A.'s" with little institutionally granted status, most need to establish their own authority and are therefore most likely to teach as they have been, and are being, taught themselves.

These teachers teach within the university, and within a subset of the university: the University Writing Program. This writing program has a received pedagogical goal: to treat writing students as *writers*. You can hear in this goal echoes of the program's ancestors—James Moffett, Donald Murray, Janet Emig, Peter Elbow, and Roger Garrison— and of the Bay Area Writing Project, and in particular its assumption that teachers are writers too, more experienced, perhaps, than most of their students, but in the same category, or on the same continuum. The syllabus used by all the instructors states:

> The goal of this course is to help you become better able to accomplish the writing you will be asked to do here at the University and, we imagine, in your life generally. We believe that writing is most usefully considered an activity, not a subject—that is, you are more likely to learn by doing, with some coaching, than by listening to lectures about good writing. This writing course is rather like a studio course in dance or music, or like the practice and performance schedule of a varsity sport.

The course has no textbook. The students' own writing is to be the text given greatest importance. To this end, student writing is published regularly, by means of photocopying. Students will write, revise, edit, and publish, adhering to a set of deadlines published in the "Writing Schedule" that makes up the last two pages of the syllabus (see Moran).

So far we are describing a situation that is shared by T.A.'s in many, perhaps all, writing programs. But what happens when a writing program enters the computer age, and asks its teachers to teach in computer-equipped writing classrooms? Given the program's view of writing and the teaching of writing, the computer seemed a "natural" to its director. The program's focus on the student as writer would be sharpened, its director believed, if the students could be given access to the power inherent in this new writing instrument. And the director of the UMass/Amherst Writing Program was not alone in believing that computers would reinforce a particular pedagogy. To Ron Sudol, writing a year after the UMass classrooms were opened, the computer-equipped classroom

> offers an opportunity to re-invent the workshop classroom model in the context of the new technology. The combination of lecture and discussion, of reading assignments and writing assignments allocated to two or three weekly meetings, has been a legacy of the days when composition was indistinguishable from introductory literature, or stylistics, or some other subject-matter course. But inasmuch as composition is a skill requiring more practice than anything else, it is best taught according to a workshop model. . . . (331)

According to Helen Schwartz, writing in 1984, computers will encourage our students to take risks. To Elder, et al., writing in 1989, computers will give students greater authority over texts. Each of these authors would acknowledge, of course, that the new technology, in and of itself, would not force change, but all believe that the new technology has *some* force—and that through its use student writers might be more fully empowered than they would be in a conventional, pencil-and-paper writing classroom.

The Writing Program's computer-equipped classrooms were configured in accordance with the program's received pedagogy. In these rooms there are no teacher-places, no workstation that is more eminent or powerful than the others, and no teacher's desk. The computers are linked in a local area network (LAN), but one designed, in accordance with program pedagogy, to give student writers autonomy. The staff chose not to install the kind of network software which permits the teacher to broadcast to all students, or to read the students' screens without the students' knowledge—what is becoming known in the trade as "snoopware." Instead, a Novell Ethernet LAN was set up in such a way that students had substantial "rights" to files stored on the fileserver. Influenced by Trent Batson's work at Gallaudet and the work of the Daedalus group at the University of Texas at Austin, the staff chose a network that is a relatively open structure, one that students can "use" to write online, send text to one another, peer edit and peer respond online, and edit and publish the biweekly class books. Each writing class has its own set of subdirectories or "boxes," a virtual classroom in which students can "post," store, read, exchange, and modify their own and others' writing. On the network is a powerful word-processing program, so that student writers have access to this power, and a "chat" program, the Daedalus Interchange, to permit and facilitate online discussion. The staff chose not to install style-checkers and workbook-like grammar programs, because these programs had, in their judgment, the potential of becoming online authorities.

So the computer-equipped classrooms took from the teachers traditional modes of authority—the teacher's desk, the blackboard, the rows of chairs facing the teacher. But it made available to the teachers, too, new modes of authority. The teachers had "special" powers in the online environment. They had read-write privileges in all the class subdirectories or "boxes"; students had read-write privileges in four, and read-only in four. So the teacher could put texts online that the students could not change, while all student texts were potentially open to change by the teacher. Further, the staff suggested teacher uses for the read-only boxes: the teachers could leave a "gradebook" file on, say, the "Tallies" box, and also an attendance record—an online equivalent of the gradebook that is such an effective symbol of authority in the conventional classroom. In this "Tallies" box teachers could leave comments on students' writing, schedules for conferences or peer editing, and an online syllabus, with daily activities spelled out in as much detail as the teacher wanted.

The teachers could also create a "greeting" message that students would see automatically when they logged on to the network. The "greeting" message most often contained the agenda for the day—a more powerful exercise of authority, we believe, than the oral "announcement" in the traditional classroom. So the teacher had the ability to construct authority online—but no learned or experienced models for the construction and exercise of such authority.

Our interviews with our teachers, our review of their students' responses to the questionnaire, and our own experiences as teachers in the new facilities suggest that teachers and students are, generally speaking, comfortable and productive in the computer-equipped classrooms. So the Writing Program's decision to spend the time and resources necessary to establish these two computer-equipped writing classes seems a good decision, at least from the perspective of a program director. But in our studies, our interviews, and our surveys, we see that the effects of this decision have not been simple or straightforward. We are seeing teachers who, having chosen to teach in the new facility, resist the computers and the design of the classroom and try to lecture, or to lead long, full-class discussions. We don't know, of course, how these same teachers would teach in the regular, "proscenium" classroom—but if they lectured there, or conducted full-class discussions, they would succeed: the layout of the conventional classroom encourages, or is at least amenable to, these activities. In the Writing Program's computer classrooms, on the other hand, attempts to lecture or to lead offline, full-group discussions are much less likely to be successful. And yet the teachers, some of them, still try. What we now understand is that these teachers have been placed in a position where their previous experiences of teaching and learning will not be useful as models. To a degree, their heritage has been canceled. And this has happened without overt resistance, in part because of the prestige associated with the new technology, and in part because of the good nature of everyone involved, but in some degree because of the power relations that obtain between graduate students and their program directors.

Further, working successfully in the new classrooms requires a knowledge of complex and powerful word-processing software and an ability to navigate and manipulate the network. Teachers, older than their students and, as degree candidates in English, humanists and book people, can be less computer-savvy than many of their students—and therein lies a potential threat to their authority in the classroom. This threat, coupled with the teachers' lack of institutional status, their youth, and their inexperience, makes it more likely that the teachers will try to teach against or around the computers. In the training program the staff stresses the fact that student software-experts in the classroom are a blessing, for they can relieve the teacher of a great deal of work and facilitate the smooth functioning of the first few classes of a semester. But here we remember our own early teaching, when our authority was new and tenuous and not strong enough to give away, even in a highly specific domain.

During our 1989 study of two teachers working in the computer-equipped classrooms, we found that both of them subtly and often unconsciously fought against the kind of class privileged by the computer-equipped classrooms. In the follow-up studies we report on here, we have tried to learn more about this resistance. What did the teachers say about the computer-equipped classrooms? What was their attitude toward the facility and their work in it? In talking about their teaching, might they reveal the kinds of resistance we had seen in our earlier study? How might this resistance be related to the teachers' prior teaching experience? To their prior experience as online writers? And, to the extent that we could discover this, how might the teachers' relationship to the new environment affect their students' attitudes toward the class and the classroom environment? Toward writing and the relationship of computers to that writing? Our objective here was to use what we learned to alter and improve the teacher-training program that we offered to the teachers who worked in the computer-equipped classrooms.

The "answers" we've come to most recently are from half- hour interviews with the instructors of these classes, conducted during the spring and fall semesters of 1990. In the interviews we asked sixteen teachers to describe the aspects of teaching in that setting that they felt were most positive, the features of that setting they would change if they could, and the advice they would give to teachers just beginning to work in the networked classroom. In addition, we administered a questionnaire to 150 students in ten spring sections and 115 in eight fall sections to discover these students' reactions to their new teaching/learning environment. The fifteen-question survey, given at the end of each semester, asked students to detail their past history with computers or word processors, to describe their use of the computers in the class, and to examine their use of the computers as writing tools.[1]

The interviews reveal different teacher-responses to the new classroom environment—not absolute differences, but differences ranged along a continuum. On one end of this continuum were the teachers who give the impression of being most at odds with the landscape of

the computer classroom. On the other were those who, by acknowledging the different context in which they were operating, matched
more amicably their own pedagogical goals with the capabilities of
the environment.

The teachers who seemed most at odds with the environment
frequently pointed to the room's tendency to decenter the classroom
activity and draw the students' attention away from the teacher. These
teachers saw the decentering as a problem. In an interview one teacher
noted,

> It was hard to keep the attention of the large group in that lab
> setting, and the computers were a magnet for people's attention,
> so it was hard to get people physically away from the computers,
> which is why I would insist that people move away from them.

Another teacher said that he would "choose a button that would sink
the screens . . . that would take away the distraction." And another
said,

> The room seems a little cold, everyone seems spread out, they're
> all hiding behind these boxes. It's like having a bunch of TV
> addicts in the room or something. . . . And you have to be pretty
> insistent if you want not to let that get the best of you. You have
> to be able to work the room real well, and to use your voice well.

Here the computer has joined with television to become the English
teacher's enemy, the enemy of the written word. Later, this instructor
carried the performance image further, as he asserted that the screens
really were "too hard to compete with." Another instructor did not
use on-screen messages to give assignments or directions to students

> because I liked getting their attention away from their computers
> at the beginning of class and getting them all focused on the
> board, eyes to the front of the class, so that I could give them all
> explanations and instructions and make sure they understood the
> assignments.

This teacher is doing what we've termed "fighting" the environment:
all students will turn away from the screens and will look at the board
and will follow what the teacher does there. Here it is interesting and
perhaps significant that, on their responses to the student questionnaires, five of this teacher's students—after noting that they did not
receive on-screen messages—commented that these messages would
have granted them more autonomy, would have allowed them to work
at their own speed, and would not have taken up class time with
directions. In these student responses we hear an awareness that the
teacher is working against the environment—resulting in what these

students see as inefficiency—and against their desire to manage their own affairs.

These teachers were uncomfortable with the decentered, activity-based character of the new classrooms. They often felt, too, that online interactions with their students were somehow less real or legitimate than face-to-face interactions would have been. One teacher noted that, if given a chance to redesign the facility,

> I would place all of the computers around the periphery of the room so that I could have a real, legitimate circle of human beings. . . . I have never had a complete circle of people in a quiet space without the hum of computers.

We can also hear a teacher's sense that human contact has somehow been lost in the comment we cited earlier, "The room seems a little cold. . . . It's like having a bunch of TV addicts in the room," and in another instructor's feeling that only in face-to-face interaction could she "make sure they understood the assignments." Even when an asynchronous, online discussion program was introduced and gained in popularity and use, the change from "live" to online discussion required adjustment, and teachers reported feeling distanced from their students. According to one, "I did feel less close to my students. This time I feel I got to know them *through their writing more than as real people*" (emphasis added).

Additionally, even though the network could be used quite easily and effectively for peer editing and responding, these teachers preferred having the students do this work offline. As one teacher put it, when students met face-to-face, they were "responding directly to each other rather than to a screen." This same teacher believed that face-to-face conversation "built more of a sense of community." The preference for face- to-face, offline interaction comes through again in this teacher's decision not to use the class greetings function.

We turn now to the teachers who seemed to accept more completely the new classroom environment, working with it, rather than against it. The teachers who seemed most at ease in the changed setting were not the most, nor the least, experienced teachers. Nor were they necessarily the most experienced computer writers. What these teachers did share was a commitment to adapting their teaching practices to a changed teaching environment.

The following comments of one instructor are typical of this group. In an interview, this instructor noted that the new classroom environment "has really changed the way I teach . . . the class is completely different than when I taught in a standard classroom." Although he owned his own computer, and had felt prepared from the beginning to "make the transition from classroom teaching to computer-classroom teaching," he remembered that he used to fight the computer environment. Now, however, he no longer distributes printed prompts and assignments but puts them online, because using online text saves time. He also noted that for him the most positive feature of the computer classroom is that it fosters one-to-one editorial conferences. In the past, he said, "I used to have this thing about discussion." But he goes on to describe how his class slowly evolved and became more like the workshop privileged by the classroom architecture. "Why fight it?" he says, adding "Once I relaxed, [the students] on their own found a community" without his intervention.

A second instructor in this group noted that she had been uncomfortable at first but, she said,

> I got used to it, got used to not having to have their attention all the time . . . I think what switched me was . . . realizing that I sort of liked not having to conduct. That I liked being able to put my stuff on the screen and have them come in and start whenever they can. . . . Ultimately it's less work. At least less sort of emotional work.

This teacher did notice that she missed the "usual" kinds of contact, but acknowledged that the students "don't miss it"; she says she adapted when she "stopped needing to talk to them so much" because, unlike the conventional class where students would talk about revision, here they *did* the revising. Her comments are echoed by another instructor, who found that it was "really burdensome to always be the center. So if you can free yourself of that, then you can pop your head up where you need to."

Another of the teachers who became comfortable with the new environment noted, paradoxically, that the aspect of the new classrooms he found most positive was "the difficulty I have in getting their attention, if that makes sense. When I'm talking and half of them are still typing, I realize I'm in this other land." He concluded that when he wanted to speak, he had to interrupt the students' own work—and that in this way the new setting granted additional dignity and value to the students' writing and thereby put pressure on him to be useful. In this comment, the instructor attends to the interacting elements: the computers, his own reactions to the changed teaching environment, the students' reactions to the changed writing context, and the increased autonomy granted them by the setting.

Another of these instructors describes her teaching in the new classroom in these terms:

> I think that [the students] write a little bit better... they spend
> more time on it ... write more. I think they just get more writing
> done, and if you buy into the theory that more writing makes
> you a better writer period, then that's that. And I do buy that.

For this teacher, the change was worth the increased effort to become
a less-than-center-stage persona. She noted that discussion "just didn't
work" in the computer-equipped classrooms: "I couldn't get them
away from the screen and when I did they looked bored and resentful."
As advice to teachers, she "would emphasize that it is a big change
in some ways," adding, "If you really like class discussion, if that's
really important to you, you might not like [the setting] very much."

When we turn to the student questionnaires, we see what seems to
us to be a pattern. For the students in classes in which the teacher
resisted the imperatives of the new environment, knowledge of the
computer and its software became an issue to a much greater degree
than it was for students whose instructors did not battle the setting
so vigorously. Further, students in the classes of the "resisting" teachers
tended to see the computers as fancy typewriters, machines that helped
them edit and print a clean final product. Students in the classes of
the "adapting" teachers were more likely to see the computer as an
aid in the full process of composing.

Students in the classes taught by the resisting teachers often indicated
that they were less than comfortable with the introduction they had
been given to the computers and their software. Here are typical
comments gleaned from the questionnaires:

> —Without any prior knowledge of word processors, I felt that I
> knew more than my professor did. It was discouraging, and so I
> simply bypassed her when I had a question and went directly to
> the student lab attendant.

> —It's awkward to get into a class and feel you know more about
> the subject than the teacher. I think more emphasis should be
> placed on learning how to use the program, at least on finding
> out how to do things you might want to.

> —It is really confusing. Have someone who knows what they are
> doing go with you. Good luck.

And students in these classes, when asked if there were any word-
processing techniques they thought should have been taught more
thoroughly, responded in this way:

> —I never learned how to move paragraphs or sentences.

> —Just little things like how to use italics and underlining and
> centering

—Learning to copy a section of text to another part of an essay

—Yes, how to delete or move a block

Some go as far as to comment, at the end of the semester, "I still feel somewhat lost," or "I still do not know how to manipulate all the commands." One student—at the end of the semester!—says, "It was pretty confusing but a couple days ago I finally got the hang of it." For these students, knowledge of the computers' software became an issue. It seems that they, perhaps more than their teachers, understood the potential that was not being used.

On the other hand, the students taught by the instructors who seemed more at ease with the new teaching environment did not report feeling that they had been shortchanged in their introduction to, and knowledge of, the powers of the word-processing software. All but the most die-hard computer-anxious students of these instructors used the survey as an occasion to sound off about other, non-computer-related issues—the most frequent of which was, significantly, their wish that the computer-equipped classrooms be available to them for more hours during the week.

The second difference between the two sets of classes is the students' own perception of the computer and its relation to their writing. In the questionnaire we asked them the following:

> In what ways has working with the word processor changed any of your habits as a writer? Please explain how working with the word processor has affected your approach to each of these activities:
>
> 1. initial notes/brainstorming,
> 2. drafting/composing,
> 3. revising, and
> 4. final editing.

The majority of the students in the classes whose teachers resisted the new classroom environment most often indicated "no change" in their writing habits for "a" and "b," the brainstorming and drafting, and gave positive responses only to "c" and "d," revising and editing. For these students, the computers most often remained "easy," "convenient" transcription devices, contrary to the process-focused aim of the computer classroom as envisioned by the writing program. Comments like these are the norm: "[It is an] electronic typewriter that lets you write and edit huge amounts of text before printing it out." "You see the text on a screen before printing it."

On the other hand, the students in the classes of the teachers who adapted more readily to the new environment more often noted that the computers had affected all aspects of their writing. Here are typical comments from these students:

> —When I brainstorm, my thoughts are able to flow right out of my fingertips and onto the screen instead of scribbling and crossing out on paper.

> —I seem to write in spurts, and then stop and come back later to finish.

> —I have much more of a broader scope of topics then I would with writing with pen and paper. I am able to clear anything I don't want to write about and then quickly rewrite what I would like to write about.

> —I can just let the ideas out instead of pondering over a piece of paper.

This appreciation of the word processor as a tool for thinking, as well as for transcribing thought, was echoed by these students in their responses to the question which asked them to "describe the word processor to someone who was interested in using it for writing but wasn't too familiar with it."

> —It's a fantastic tool for writing, and it lets you compose in a more natural way with its ability to let you go back and insert and change ideas without having to rewrite.

> —The word processor helps you better convey and structure your thoughts without the mess of a pen and paper. It facilitates the writing process.

What becomes clear to us as we listen to the interviews and review the questionnaires is the extent to which the decision to establish computer-equipped classrooms has redefined the "work" of teaching for those who elect to teach in the new facilities. As we think of our teachers as "workers" in a new "workplace," we are reminded of Shoshana Zuboff's study of the effects of technological change in the industrial workplace. Zuboff's study focused on workers in a pulp mill and in a steel foundry. These workers had change imposed on them from above, by an administrative decision to computerize the factories they worked in. While our teachers volunteered to teach in the computer-equipped classrooms, and Zuboff's workers had no choice, still we wonder if our teachers would have been as willing volunteers had they been professors of English, with all the power that comes along with tenure and full membership in the profession.

We've noted that our "resisting" teachers often saw the decentering of their classrooms as an obstacle to be overcome. We've also noted their sense that these classrooms threaten to change the nature of fundamentally important teacher-student interactions. In a chapter titled "The Dissociation of Sentience and Knowledge," Zuboff documents the discomfort felt by plant workers as they replaced what she terms "felt knowledge" with digitized information read from a computer screen. As she describes the workers, who used to judge how wet the wood-pulp was by squeezing it with their hands or by popping a bit of it into their mouths and chewing it, but who now sit in air-conditioned booths to read the moisture content of the pulp on computer screens, their disorientation reminds us of our own teachers' impulses to recreate the classrooms they knew before. Zuboff draws this conclusion: "It is as if one's job had vanished into a two-dimensional space of abstractions, where digital symbols replace a concrete reality. Workers reiterated a spontaneous emotional response countless times—defined by feelings of loss of control, of vulnerability, and of frustration" (62-63).

Our teachers' reactions to the computer-equipped classrooms suggest that these classrooms fundamentally change the kind of "work" being performed by our writing teachers. In the computer classroom, it is possible to spend the hour communicating with students online, despite the fact that they are in the same room with us. As we work in this classroom, we do not necessarily "know" these students in the same way that we would know them in a conventional class space. As our "resisting" teachers repeatedly noted, online communication, at least for the time being, does not seem "real."

Our research suggests to us that writing programs need to account for the change in "work" that accompanies this new classroom environment—both the decentering of the classroom and the move from "live" to "online" tuition. We could deal with the first of these issues—decentering—by making the new environment as much like the old as possible: installing the computer work-stations in rows, facing a teacher-station; installing a projection facility so that the teacher can conduct demonstrations; and installing software that makes it possible for the teacher to control students' screens.

Because we've decided not to take this route, we need to think about changes in our training program, changes that will encourage teachers to reflect upon their own pedagogical assumptions, to identify the assumptions implicit in the new computer-equipped classrooms, and to work with and around points of dissonance. The teachers' familiarity with the software and an understanding of the network, which is currently the main focus of training, are prerequisites to, but not sufficient conditions for, successful and gratifying teaching in the new workplace. Likewise, giving the teachers experience as computer writers (Hawisher) will not prepare them for the discomfort they may feel at the changes in their workplace. Nor will simple exhortation to embrace the online classroom (Kiefer) get all of the teachers smoothly through the transition. The teachers need to understand, and be trained in the use of, techniques for constructing an online presence. The teachers might, for example, be asked to read essays by Andrew Feenberg and Lynn Davie which explore the kinds of authority, or teacher "presence," that might be appropriate to an online teaching environment and to the goals of the "course" being taught. Further, the training program should include excerpts from Zuboff's study, which would foreground the teachers' own discomfort. The reading list would also include studies by researchers who have looked at the effects on students of courses delivered entirely online (Harasim; Hiltz; Mason and Kaye, "Toward"). These would suggest that the online environment need not be less real, human, or pedagogically effective than the environment of the conventional classroom.

In such a training program, teachers would be encouraged to see themselves teaching in their new context, and to accept and reflect upon the discomfort and dislocation they may feel. An overt subject in these training sessions would be the change in the teachers' workplace and the ways in which one might fruitfully respond to the change. The teachers in our study who really used the dissonance they felt as a creative force seemed most comfortable with their own teaching. Further, the students of these teachers seemed to have understood and exploited most fully the potential of the computer as a writing instrument.

Note

We thank Marcia Curtis, Anne Herrington, and James Garman, who have helped us in designing and carrying out the research reported on in this study. We want to thank, too, the teachers who volunteered their time for interviews and written questionnaires, and the students who took the time to answer our survey questions.

Works Cited

Batson, Trent. "Teaching in Networked Classrooms." *Computers in English and the Language Arts: The Challenge of Teacher Education.* Ed. Cynthia Selfe, Dawn Rodrigues, and William R. Oates. Urbana, IL: NCTE, 1989. 247–55.

Davie, Lynn. "Facilitation Techniques for the On-Line Tutor." Mason and Kaye, *Mindweave* 74–85.

Elder, John, et al. *Word Processing in a Community of Writers*. New York: Garland, 1989.

Feenberg, Andrew. "The Written World: On the Theory and Practice of Computer Conferencing." Mason and Kaye, *Mindweave* 22–39.

Harasim, Linda M. "Online Education: An Environment for Collaboration and Intellectual Amplification." In *Online Education: Perspectives on a New Environment*. Ed. Linda M. Harasim. New York: Praeger, 1990. 39–64.

Hawisher, Gail E. "Reading and Writing Connections: Composition Pedagogy and Word Processing." In *Computers and Writing*. Ed. Deborah H. Holdstein and Cynthia L. Selfe. New York: MLA, 1990. 71–83.

Hiltz, Starr Roxanne. "Evaluating the Virtual Classroom." In *Online Education: Perspectives on a New Environment*. Ed. Linda M. Harasim. New York: Praeger, 1990. 133–84.

Kiefer, Kathleen. "Computers and Teacher Education in the 1990s and Beyond." In *Evolving Perspectives in Computers and Composition Studies: Questions for the 1990s*. Ed. Gail E. Hawisher and Cynthia L. Selfe. Urbana, IL: NCTE, 1991. 117–31.

Klem, Elizabeth, and Charles Moran. "Teachers in a Strange LANd." *Computers and Composition* 9.3 (Aug. 1992): 5–22.

Mason, Robin, and Tony Kaye. "Toward a New Paradigm for Distance Education." In *Online Education: Perspectives on a New Environment*. Ed. Linda M. Harasim. New York: Praeger, 1990. 15–38.

Mason, Robin D., and Anthony R. Kaye, eds. *Mindweave: Communication, Computers, and Distance Education*. New York: Pergamon, 1989.

Moran, Charles. "University of Massachusetts, Amherst: University Writing Program." *New Methods in College Writing Programs*. Ed. Paul Connolly and Teresa Vilardi. New York: MLA, 1986. 111–16.

Schwartz, Helen J. "Teaching Writing with Computer Aids." *College English* 46.3 (Mar. 1984): 239–47.

Sudol, Ronald A. "Applied Word Processing: Notes on Authority, Responsibility, and Revision in a Workshop Model." *College Composition and Communication* 36.3 (Oct. 1985): 331–35.

Zuboff, Shoshana. *In the Age of the Smart Machine: The Future of Work and Power*. New York: Basic Books, 1988.

7 Pedagogy and the Academy: "The Divine Skill of the Born Teacher's Instincts"

Mariolina Salvatori
University of Pittsburgh

In this paper I intend to focus on a particular understanding of pedagogy that was constructed and inscribed in the academy at the end of the nineteenth century: i.e., pedagogy as an "art," the effective performance of which ultimately depends on a teacher's act of divination. I wish to suggest that this construction of pedagogy can be seen as a determining factor for certain seizures of power within universities that served *then* and continue to serve *now* as a pretext to relegate pedagogy to an ancillary position.

The quotation in my title comes from an 1891 essay written by Josiah Royce, a philosopher and professor of philosophy at Harvard University. Royce wrote the essay—which he titled "Is There a Science of Education?"—at the request of Nicholas Murray Butler for the first issue of *Educational Review* (1891). The answer Royce gave his own question, a resounding "no," represents one of the two opposing positions in the "teaching as an art" versus "teaching as a science" dispute. The dispute was carried on with particular intensity in the last decade of the nineteenth century, when the education of teachers moved from academies and normal schools to colleges and universities, necessitating—as some argued, while others contested it—the establishment first of chairs, then of departments of pedagogy.

As I have suggested elsewhere ("Contribution"), the dispute itself—teaching as an art versus teaching as a science—can be read as the result of a reductive construction of pedagogy, one that planted the seeds of its devaluation within the university, the very culture that supposedly was to rescue it from the "subculture" of the normal school and grant it disciplinary status. Let me offer a brief narrative of what I think happened.

Before pedagogy was inducted into the university, the sites where it had originally been theorized and practiced with considerable thoughtfulness were the early normal schools. The first private normal school was started in 1823 by the Reverend Samuel R. Hall in his home at Concord, Vermont. In 1838 James C. Carter opened the first public normal school in Massachusetts. The writings of Carter (1826) and Hall (1829) still read today as contributions of considerable sophistication. What I find particularly interesting about these early treatises on pedagogy is their understanding of pedagogy as a *reflective praxis*. The material conditions of the early normal schools might have made it possible for the theory and the practice to be—literally and figuratively—*connected*.[1] Ironically, and unfortunately, as the common schools experienced incredible growth and the demand for normal school teachers increased accordingly, the theory and practice of pedagogy began to suffer, mainly because theory and practice drew apart. Since there were not enough American educators involved in the preparation of teachers, and those who were involved did not have sufficient leisure and theoretical sophistication to produce the necessary texts, people like Horace Mann and Henry Barnard and Coit Gilman traveled and sent other educational envoys to Europe, especially to Germany, in search of appropriate models. Too often, however, the imported models proved to be simply too difficult for the young normal school students as well as for many of their teachers.

One of the first texts to be offered for study to American students and practitioners of pedagogy was Karl Rosenkranz's *Die Paedagogik als System* (1848). Its author was a doctor of theology and professor of philosophy at the University of Königsberg. A translation by Anna C. Brackett appeared in the *Journal of Speculative Philosophy*, 1872–74, under the title "Pedagogics as a System" (an edition of which was also published separately). Four years later, the *Journal* began printing a paraphrase, also by Brackett, in an attempt to make the concepts more accessible. To further aid readers who encountered difficulty with Rosenkranz's metaphysical language, William Torrey Harris wrote an analysis and commentary to accompany Brackett's paraphrase. In 1886, a second edition of the translation, under the title, *The Philosophy of Education* (note the terminological shift) was published as the first volume in Appleton's International Education Series, which was edited by Harris (Chambliss 52-54). As the need for teachers increased, then, more and more American teachers gained access to texts on pedagogy through various intermediary layers—the translators, the paraphrasers, the commentators, the editors, and later the textbook writers.[2] These layers separated theory from practice in a process of progressive estrangement, and often reduced teaching to simplistic, arbitrary, and questionable practices.

Given the particular historical circumstances, that layering might have been an inevitable compromise. However, it does not logically follow that by the end of the nineteenth century (and since) the simplification, the reduction, should have come to be used as an automatic and blanket indictment of the normal schools (Clifford and Guthrie 54); nor that the progressive simplification and reduction of pedagogy, which had enervated its practice within the normal schools, should have been reproduced and indelibly inscribed at the university level as the "art" (practice) versus "science" (theory) dispute.

In the rest of this paper, I intend to analyze the "art" side of that dispute as articulated at Harvard University. In 1891 Harvard, quite reluctantly, opened its doors to pedagogy. That was the year that Paul Hanus, a professor of pedagogy at the State Normal School in Greeley, Colorado, was appointed by President Charles W. Eliot and the Fellows of Harvard College as "Assistant Professor of the History and Art of Teaching." Hanus's appointment marked the establishment of the Department of Education at Harvard University, which was later to develop into the Graduate School of Education. (Hanus's appointment was apparently engineered by President Eliot "to preclude the appearance of a coeducational 'high normal school' in Massachusetts to train college graduates as high school teachers" [Clifford and Guthrie 131].)

In *Adventuring in Education,* an autobiographical account of his "ascent" from normal school to university, Hanus records, without apparent bitterness, his increasing realization of the pervasive skepticism and contempt that characterized most academics' view of pedagogy. He noted that the title he was given limited the activities of the department to considering the *art of teaching.* The broader and more fundamental problems of education were not covered by the title; and, indeed, I doubt if they occurred to the members of the faculty as falling legitimately within the province of the new department (109-10).

According to Hanus, most college and university professors of that day objected to the elevation of pedagogy to university status. What I consider significant is that what they objected to was *their own* construction of pedagogy. What they thought, wrote Hanus, was that pedagogy

> consisted *of necessity* of instruction in methods of teaching; and most of them did not believe that such instruction had any value. The dictum, 'Teachers are born, not made,' was both implicit and explicit in their consideration of the subject. They ignored the fact that 'born' teachers do not happen more frequently than 'born'

lawyers or doctors or college professors or members of any profession, and that, human beings being what they are and the choice of profession being free to all, men and women of every profession must develop by training what native ability they have for the work they elect to do. (111)

At Harvard, among the proponents of the "art" view of pedagogy were such illustrious and influential colleagues of Hanus as Josiah Royce and William James. During the hiring process and at least in the first few years Hanus spent at Harvard, President Eliot had apparently entrusted Royce and James with the responsibility to define pedagogy *for* their younger colleague. Though, as I will demonstrate, they were among those who maintained that "teachers are born, not made," Hanus never explicitly criticized them. Neither did it ever occur to him to speculate why Royce and James defined pedagogy in those terms.

Because I am interested in disrupting the "tradition" that Royce's and James's views of pedagogy can be said to have institutionalized— one that has limited and continues to limit the function of pedagogy— I wish to raise some of the questions that Hanus could or would not raise. (One can well imagine the precariousness and powerlessness of his position vis-à-vis Eliot, James, Royce, et al.)

In "Is There a Science of Education?" which was written the same year that Hanus was hired at Harvard, Royce asserted that he longed to "strengthen the interest of teachers in the theoretical aspects of their profession" (102). At the same time, however, by valorizing the natural, the instinctive, the artistic knowledge of a teacher, he helped disseminate a conception of pedagogy that invalidated both the need for and the possibility of the theoretical. In his definition of pedagogy, Royce relied entirely on Wilhelm Dilthey's argument, which rejected not so much the feasibility of a "science of education" as a science of education based on the assumptions of *uniformity* (universality) of "human nature" and of the end of education ("the highest moral perfection" of the child). As valid arguments *against* the "science of education," Royce deployed Dilthey's insistence on the variability of human nature and on the impossibility of reaching an agreement in regard to a moral system that would define the end of education.

Royce's lead essay in that inaugural issue of *Educational Review* established the terms of the debate about the status of pedagogy in the academy, although the conception of pedagogy as an art that it helped disseminate was much more complex than the catchy quotation I used in my title. Royce clearly valued reflexivity and theoretical understanding. Yet the reductive ways in which the debate was cast prevented him from being heard as advocating and theorizing a fruitful dialectical relationship between "art" and "science." So, in spite of himself, he helped to hypostatize the two as two competing and irreconcilable systems.

"Both parties in such a controversy as that between these pedants [that is, the pedagogues] and their unlearned opponents [that is, the born teachers] are in the wrong," Royce said (22).[3] He recognized that teachers needed "scientific training for their calling," because their instincts, if unchastened by science, could lead them to blind self-confidence. Nevertheless, what he is mostly remembered *for*—and why this should be so is an important question to raise—are a few catchy phrases that have been deployed to *contain* pedagogy: "True pedagogy is an art"; "There is no 'science of education'"; "the divine skill of the born teacher's instincts." In truth, his objection to *a* science of education was qualified in the following terms:

> There is no "science of education" that will not need constant and vast adaptation to the needs of this teacher or of that, constant modification in the presence of the live pupil, constant supplementing by *the divine skill of the born teacher's instincts.* (22; emphasis added)

But even granting that his objection to pedagogy as a science was qualified, it is still appropriate to ask: What becomes of instruction in a system like Royce's, which sets up the difference between a good and a not-so-good teacher in terms of the amount of "divine intervention"?

I would suggest that what prevented the reciprocal interrogation of theory and practice in Royce's system was precisely his reliance on instinct. This was in tune with, in fact it was the foundation of, his naturalistic philosophy. On the one hand, then, his view of pedagogy as art can be read as a sign of intellectual consistency. But on the other hand, that view can be read as a necessary stratagem to hold his philosophical system intact. Had Royce imagined teaching as the testing, let alone the contesting, ground for theory, his reliance on "instinct" might have had to be called into question.

If Royce was heard, William James had an even larger audience, both inside and outside the university. His book, *Talks to Teachers on Psychology and to Students on Some of Life's Ideals,* (1889, reprinted 1900, 1915, 1925) is a collection of public lectures on psychology that James had been asked to give to Cambridge teachers by the Harvard corporation. In these talks he powerfully contributed to advancing the "art" view of pedagogy among future normal school students and their teachers.

As he talked to them, James carefully and repeatedly asserted that psychology, or any other science for that matter, did not "contain" pedagogical formulas:

> I say . . . that you make a great, a very great mistake, if you think that psychology, being the science of the mind's laws, is something from which you can deduce definite programs and schemes and methods of instruction for *immediate* schoolroom use. Psychology is a science, and teaching is an art; and sciences never generate art *directly out* of themselves. An intermediary inventive mind must make the application, by using its originality. (7-8; emphasis added)

James's didactic tone here covers over a number of assumptions that beg to be questioned. Why should one expect to deduce from psychology (or any other science) "definite programs and schemes and methods of instruction for *immediate* schoolroom use?" What does this assumption reveal about what James believed teachers needed? I said earlier that there had been times when the normal school teachers needed "something definite and of immediate use"—often a set of simplified procedures, of rules divorced from the theory in which they were grounded. But why did this "need" come to be institutionalized when somebody of James's caliber was given the responsibility to teach future teachers? As to the "intermediary inventive mind," it is not clear to me whose mind James means it to be: a master teacher's? a textbook writer's? the mind of somebody who interprets for the benefit of others, and disseminates a simplified version of theory? To what extent do such pronouncements contribute to justifying the various intermediary layers that in the past (and still in the present) have set up barriers between the "theory" of pedagogy and its "practice," between theorists and literary critics and teachers?

Given the fact that within James's philosophical system "teaching" could not be taught, something was needed to justify teaching and the professional preparation of teachers that he had been entrusted with. Predictably, that something had to be an "additional endowment" that no theory or method could foster. For Royce, the additional endowment came from divine intervention. James constructs a secular version of it.

> A science only lays down lines within which the rules of the art must fall, laws which the follower of the art must not transgress; but what particular thing he shall positively do within those lines is left exclusively to his own *genius.* . . . To know psychology . . . is absolutely no guarantee that we shall be good teachers. To advance to that result, we must have an *additional endowment* altogether,

a *happy tact* and *ingenuity* to tell us what definite things to say
and do when the pupil is before us. The science of psychology,
and whatever science of general pedagogics may be based on it,
are . . . much like the science of war. Nothing is simpler or more
definite than the principles of either. In war, all you have to do
is to work your enemy into a position from which the natural
obstacles prevent him from escaping if he tries to; then to fall on
him in numbers superior to his own, at a moment when you have
led him to think you far away; and so, with a minimum of
exposure of your own troops, to hack his force to pieces, and take
the remainder prisoners. . . . *Divination* and *perception*, not psychological pedagogics or theoretic strategy, are the only helpers
here. (8–11; emphasis added)

James's theory of learning is a brilliant investigation of the faculties
of imitation and emulation, interest, repetition, and memory. His theory,
however, presupposes a groundedness in a cultural milieu where these
faculties have been *socially* cultivated for so long as to appear natural
"habits."[4] Outside of such a milieu, that theory of learning leads to a
theory of teaching that can be highly problematic insofar as it can
release a teacher from the responsibility to teach those who have not
been *socialized* into these "habits" and are therefore arbitrarily deemed
"unteachable." James uses the metaphor of war to expose the intrinsic
powerlessness of the "science of pedagogy." His "divination/percep-
tion" theory, however, is powerless as well, unless the seeds of what
makes an individual's act of divination and perception possible are
already there. (This is the pivotal point in Mike Rose's *Lives on the
Boundary: The Struggles and Achievements of America's Underprepared*.)

Without a student's "interest," (an interest that is, in this view, as
much natural as it is culturally constructed and socially/instructionally
induced) such a theory has limited power, and James's own experience
as a teacher seems to intimate this. Persuaded to lecture to teachers
as a source of extra income, he wrote privately to his wife about the
lack of stimulation or pleasure this offered. "I have never seen," he
wrote, "more women and less beauty, heard more voices and less
sweetness, perceived more earnestness and less triumph than I ever
supposed possible" (quoted in Clifford and Guthrie 154).[5] I want to
call attention to James's remarks about women to expose the consequences of institutional politics that devalue teaching, and in this
particular case the teaching of women who were used within departments of pedagogy both to populate the classrooms and to be contained
within those classrooms. But I also want to call attention to James's
awareness of his audience's listlessness, and to his *private* despondency
about it. Publicly, however, and addressing the very audience for whom

he had written his "talks," he sounded anything but despondent. In fact, he expressed a very optimistic view about the future of American education. He considered the "outward organization of education" in the United States "the best organization that exists in any country." As proof he cited the diversity and flexibility of the state school systems, the independence of many colleges and universities, the give and take of students and instructors, their emulation, their happy organic relation to the lower schools, and the traditions of instruction.

James's war metaphor suggested that a science of pedagogy would turn *teaching* into *conquering* and *learning* into *being vanquished*. As an alternative, he offered his view of an art of pedagogy that would rely on "perception" and "divination." The question is, how are perception and divination to be taught? When he describes in apparently optimistic terms the future of the American educational system, James uses a metaphor that provides an answer. With so favorable an organization, he says, "All we need is to impregnate it with geniuses . . . for America to lead the education of the world in a generation or two."

Sadly, a number of generations later, the prophesy has not been realized, and certainly not for lack of geniuses. I am fully aware of how insidiously seductive Royce's and James's pronouncements can be, particularly for those who, for various reasons, lean toward the separation of theory from practice. But I am also aware of the problems they can generate. We face these problems day in and day out, in the undergraduate as well as in the graduate classes we teach. We face them within the departments where we do our work and without, inside and outside the academy. And I wonder whether the extent to which Royce's appeal to "divine intervention" and James's reliance on "divination and perception" were passively and uncritically axiomatized might have to bear responsibility for the educational problems with which we are still trying to cope.

In the course of my investigation, I have noticed that one of the most often cited reasons for the academy's aversion to pedagogy has been its association with the normal school, seen as the epitome of the practical, the vocational, the non-liberal, the anti-intellectual. It could be argued, however, that James's and Royce's views of pedagogy have fostered this anti-intellectualism in the teaching profession.

"All too often . . . in the history of the United States," says Richard Hofstadter, "the schoolteacher has been in no position to serve as a model for an introduction to the intellectual life. Too often he has not only no claims to an intellectual life of his own, but not even an adequate workmanlike competence in the skills he is supposed to impart" (310). I cannot completely side with Hofstadter's scathing critique of American life, particularly in the light of the materials that my investigation of pedagogy has uncovered. I think he is right, however, when he points out the paradox of many Americans' reverence for and at the same time disregard for or suspicion of education. But I'd like to get to a possible source of that paradox, and suggest that, rather than locating it *only* in the frame of mind of the man in the street, the businesswoman, the bureaucrat, we should locate it also in the university. More specifically, we should engage in a critique of the institutional moves that, by containing the function of certain disciplines while promoting the expansion of others, establish hierarchies that we need to call into question. I want to suggest that the dysfunctional divisions between reading and writing, literature and composition, theory and practice that continue to affect our profession might be seen as another manifestation of the prejudices about pedagogy that in the 1890s were so indelibly inscribed in the academy.

Of American universities' interest in pedagogy at the turn of the last century, Geraldine Joncich Clifford and James Guthrie have this to say:

> American universities established chairs of pedagogy not in deference to the idea of a science of education nor in imitation of a few German universities that had pioneered chairs in education. It was not to create a discipline of education nor because such noted German intellectuals as Immanuel Kant and Wilhelm Dilthey taught courses on "Paedagogik" in international centers of learning. Rather they launched their initially modest ventures in professional education because it directly served their *own* interests. (123)

Among the self-interests they cite are public relations; competition for enrollments; the ambition of colleges to become universities by adding professional and graduate work; the necessity to populate traditional liberal arts courses, which were being depleted by the elective system, by both attracting and containing female students; and the delegation of onerous responsibilities like high school accreditation. President Eliot's, James's, and Royce's attempts to contain pedagogy at Harvard support Clifford and Guthrie's judgment that "to gain admittance [into the academy] was not to be vouchsafed a welcome."

In spite of the fact that pedagogy has recently become the subject of important conferences and reputable books, that writers like Freire, Foucault, and Derrida have made it legitimate, even faddish, to use the term, and that theorists like David Bartholomae, Ann E. Berthoff, David Bleich, Henry Giroux, Robert Scholes, Ira Shor and others address pedagogy in different and important ways, I fear things have not changed enough to invalidate Hofstadter's indictment.

Clifford and Guthrie construct a cogent critique of the political, ideological, and institutional reasons that made pedagogy such an unwelcome guest on university campuses. I think that critique is essential. But I want to stress something that they do not explicitly address—and they are not unique in this: We must face the realization that it was the trivialized understanding of pedagogy either as "only theory" or as "only practice" that made it possible for many of pedagogy's proponents to become pawns in the exclusionary and divisive games of their opponents. Unfortunately, as I read some current radical critiques of the educational system (Giroux, Aronowitz, Shor) I am struck by the fact that the conception of pedagogy that is their foundation has not been yet *radically* revised. Whereas early theorists of pedagogy turned to the power of divine intervention, of genius-like inspiration, and of intellectual impregnation when confronted with the intractable intricacies of teaching, some contemporary theorists tend to invoke the power of whichever correct political creed they believe in and live by. I make this comment not to expose the shortcomings of past and present pedagogues, but to point out the insidious traps that pedagogy's resistance to being simplified can set up even for its proponents.

This paper is part of a larger study that began several years ago as a philological exercise. Puzzled at first, then deeply disturbed, by the way in which my professed interest in pedagogy led certain people to construct me in ways that I thought were inaccurate, I began to trace the etymological roots of the term "pedagogy." I wanted to detail the origins of its negative connotations, hoping to reveal in the process that to continue to dismiss pedagogy for those reasons would have been both anachronistic and counterproductive. I only wanted to prove *this* point. That's all. My *real, professional* challenge at the time was to call into crisis the division between reading and writing, literature and composition, theory and practice.

Several years later, my real, professional challenge is *still* to invalidate those divisions and to demonstrate that they are dysfunctional. But what had begun as a philological exercise has now become a theoretical framework within which the etymological exegesis is slowly and laboriously turning into a *re*visionary history of pedagogy as an "invisible" but *not* "inexistent" discipline and subject of study. The most rewarding aspect of my current investigation is the realization that American pedagogy has a past that is worth knowing and reactivating. Let me suggest, if I may, that we return to that past and that with both rigor and generosity we try to understand the complex reasons for those singular and collective acts of forgetfulness that have relegated it to dusty library shelves, library basements, and little-known archives.

Notes

1. Normal school–model school; for an early description and theorization of the model school's function, see Stowe 127.

2. For an early critique of the uses and abuses of textbooks, see Baynard Hall 84–114.

3. I am currently exploring the almost automatic association, within North American culture, between pedagogues and pedants.

4. For a thoughtful, though brief, discussion of the complex relation between "habit" and "instruction," see Stowe 123–50.

5. See also Jacques Barzun's comments on James's genius-like teaching in *A Stroll with William James*, 262–302.

Works Cited

Barzun, Jacques. *A Stroll with William James.* New York: Harper and Row, 1983.

Brackett, Anna, trans. "Pedagogics as a System." *The Journal of Speculative Philosophy*, 1872, 1873, 1874.

———, trans. *The Philosophy of Education.* 2d ed., revised. New York: Appleton, 1907.

Carter, James G. "Outline of an Instruction for the Education of Teachers." *Essays upon Popular Education*, Boston, 1829. Rpt. Manchester, NH: Ayer, 1969.

Chambliss, Joseph J. *The Origins of American Philosophy of Education. Its Development as a Distinct Discipline, 1808–1913.* The Hague: Martinus Nijhoff, 1968.

Clifford, Geraldine Joncich, and James W. Guthrie. *Ed School: A Brief for Professional Education.* Chicago: U of Chicago P, 1990.

Hall, Rev. Baynard R. *Teaching: a Science; Teacher: an Artist.* New York: Baker and Scribner, 1848.

Hall, Samuel R. *Lectures on School-Keeping.* Boston: Richardson, Lord and Holbrook, 1929. Rpt. Arthur D. Wright, George E. Gardner, eds. *Hall's Lectures on School-Keeping.* Hanover, NH: Dartmouth P, 1929.

Hanus, Paul. *Adventuring in Education.* Cambridge: Harvard UP, 1937.

Hofstadter, Richard. *Anti-intellectualism in American Life.* New York: Knopf, 1963.

James, William. *Talks to Teachers on Psychology and to Students on Some of Life's Ideals.* 1899. New York: Henry Holt, 1925.

Rose, Mike. *Lives on the Boundary: The Struggles and Achievements of America's Underprepared.* New York: Free Press, 1989.

Royce, Josiah. "Is There a Science of Education?" *Educational Review*, 1 (Jan.–Feb.) 1891, 15–25; 121–32.

Salvatori, Mariolina. "The Contribution of Normal Schools to the Discipline of Pedagogy: Disturbing History." Conference on College Composition and Communication. Chicago, 23 Mar. 1990.

———. "Pedagogy as Reflexive Praxis." Conference on College Composition and Communication. Seattle, 17 Mar. 1989.

Stowe, Calvin. "Normal Schools and Teachers' Seminaries." *Normal Schools, and Other Institutions, Agencies, and Means Designed for the Professional Education of Teachers.* Ed. Henry Barnard. Vol 1. Hartford: Case, 1851. 2 vols.

8 Representations of Literacy and Region: Narrating "Another America"

Peter Mortensen
University of Kentucky

In late autumn 1989, CBS News dispatched its *48 Hours* production crew to the mountains of eastern Kentucky. The crew spent several days there documenting life in a remote Floyd County hollow, a place that maps call Muddy Gut and that CBS labeled "another America." A damning recital of statistics punctuated the *48 Hours* broadcast: among other social ills, unemployment and teenage marriage were said to exceed national averages. And the adult illiteracy rate, too, warranted attention for supposedly being abnormally high. "Forty-six percent of the people in Floyd County . . . cannot read," frowned correspondent Doug Tunnell, his tone implicating illiteracy as a chief source of the hollow's woes. The narrative logic is clear here: No wonder Muddy Gut suffers such economic and moral privation. If only its people could read and write, they might get real jobs, earn a little self-respect, and stop marrying so young.

No doubt economic times are tough in Muddy Gut. The same can be said for communities throughout central and southern Appalachia. Coal has gone bust again, perhaps for the last time. And the regional infrastructure coal built cannot now support the service economy that has kept afloat many a rural town throughout America—though often at the expense of distinctive local culture. More and better literacy cannot single-handedly forestall the economic crisis facing eastern Kentucky and places like it. Yet public discourse (witness *48 Hours*) again and again points to literacy as the particular technology that can restore all other technologies: better reading, better writing, better roads, better paycheck, better life. The consequences of this logic are subtle, and such subtleties are what I wish to explore in this essay.

Henry Giroux, after Gramsci, argues persuasively that literacy is "a double-edged sword" that can be "wielded for the purpose of self and social empowerment or for the perpetuation of relations of repression and domination" (Introduction 2). I would suggest that narrative representations of literacy contend similarly on this "terrain of struggle" (2). That is, the way people talk and write about literacy concerns not only "basic" reading and writing skills, but also serves as

> a cultural marker for naming forms of difference within the logic of cultural deprivation theory. What is important here is that the notion of cultural deprivation serves to designate in the negative sense forms of cultural currency that appear disturbingly unfamiliar and threatening when measured against the dominant culture's ideological standard regarding what is to be valorized as history, linguistic proficiency, lived experience, and standards of community life. (3)

The people of Muddy Gut are different, CBS tells us. That nearly half of Floyd Countians are illiterate would seem to explain that difference conveniently, if not precisely. The assessment of literacy, then, provides a framework within which to evaluate cultural practices. And such evaluation—to extend Giroux's argument—may yield occasions for intervention calculated to conceal or, alternatively, to stigmatize cultural difference.

This process of narrating assessment, evaluation, and intervention necessarily constructs particular versions of reality that serve, innocently or not, the ends of those authorizing the narrative. Thus, CBS promotes a story of illiterate America that is startling—but somehow reassuring—to its middle-class audience. The values of this audience are reaffirmed by images of a place that apparently lacks its values, especially its values pertaining to literacy. The moral of the story is plain enough: failure to attend to literacy and literate institutions has unhappy consequences; there is much to be lost if the middle class succumbs to the creeping illiteracy that claimed Muddy Gut.

This is an old story, and it is instructive to think about where old stories have been before we repeat them. The story of illiteracy in Muddy Gut is the residue of a much more complex discourse on literacy, coupled with a discourse on place, that reached its influential zenith about a century ago. Drawing from texts that circulated in a variety of overlapping public spheres, I will sketch how the discourse on literacy and place exhibited its double-edged potential—to mark difference and to resist such marking.

Difference and Resistance

Narratives of the South as Other are staple in American experience and tradition. The force of these narratives in the popular realm seems to have been amplified in the late nineteenth century as postbellum "redemption" faltered. Addressing the "Southern problem" in 1880, E. L. Godkin noted the difficulty of converting "Southern whites to the ways and ideas of what is called the industrial stage in social progress" (qtd. in Woodward 142). But Godkin, observes one commentator, was saying nothing especially new (142). He merely echoed the sentiments of antebellum voices such as Emerson's and Lincoln's, voices which had garnered authority by figuring the South as Other in their speaking to (and for) a growing northern middle class. This middle class, according to Burton Bledstein, was made extremely anxious by southern difference—difference assessed tangibly in terms of education and literacy:

> The South both stifled the emergence of a class with professional skills and was burdened by the highest illiteracy rate in the nation. An illiterate people, lacking the discipline necessary to avoid promiscuous sex and illicit orgies, was insensitive to the sanctity of the nuclear family with its example of control, planning, and management. (28)

Thus, even before the Civil War, the stage was set for measuring southern difference in terms of literacy: no literacy, no middle class, no progress.[1]

After 1880, as in northern states, a professional middle class was emerging in the central Kentucky "Bluegrass." These "self-made" men and women did not appreciate the implication that they lacked literacy—and more important, the cultural sophistication literacy supposedly affords.[2] James Lane Allen's popular sketches of the genteel Bluegrass might be read in this light as an attempt to assert, against northern critics, that southern living was indeed sophisticated. Wrote Allen in 1886, "The highest mark of the gentleman is not cultivation of the mind, not intellect, not knowledge, but elegant living" (40). Certainly Allen meant not to disparage reading and writing, but rather simply to situate literacy as subordinate in value to "elegant" manners and taste. Of course, in Allen's Bluegrass, relatively few could attain the status of gentleman, so not everyone required the foundation of literacy upon which the gentleman stood. But these few literate gentlemen were charged with providing for the best interests of the many—interests defined clearly in terms of race, class, and gender. In advancing this argument, Allen echoed the dying, distorted strains of a Jeffersonian ideal: some people needed basic literacy to labor, others needed more advanced literacy to govern. But in neither case did being literate mean being cultured. In Allen's world literacy may well have regulated the acquisition of cultural capital, but literacy itself did not constitute such capital.

Thus Allen defended Kentucky culture by inverting contemporary middle-class values, by appealing to the elitist tradition those new values opposed. So even as school reform dramatically reduced the number of illiterate Kentuckians and contributed to the growth of a middle class, Allen insisted on promoting manners, not literacy, as the cultural capital which Kentuckians should aspire to acquire. Had Allen's attitude prevailed in his day, measures of literacy would have continued to mark all of turn-of-the-century Kentucky as problematically different.

Allen's popularity surged at century's end, but as the twentieth century commenced, his vision of Kentucky and the Old South lost its national appeal (Bottorff 86). Before that happened, however, while Allen was still considered "the Hawthorne of his day," a young Harvard graduate returned to his Bluegrass home desirous of winning fame as an author, and a gracious Allen was there to boost John Fox, Jr., toward his goal. Even in Fox's earliest short stories, he exhibited sympathy for Allen's impulse to defend Kentucky from aspersions cast from the North upon the South. But Fox's fictional Bluegrass differed from Allen's in significant ways. Unlike Allen, Fox figured Bluegrass culture as drawing its intellectual wealth from books and its financial strength from a modern industrial economy. Further, in modish "local color," Fox juxtaposed his idea of the Bluegrass with an invented culture that conspicuously lacked both literacy and modernity.[3] He situated this invented culture in the eastern mountains of Kentucky, where he had spent some time traveling in connection with a family coal-mining venture (see Moore 80–82).

Although today it seldom reaches more than a regional audience, Fox's fiction commanded a national readership at the time of its publication. Collections of his stories and the appearance of his first novel, *The Kentuckians* (1898), secured for him recognition as an important figure in the local color movement. Just after the turn of the century, two novels, *The Little Shepherd of Kingdom Come* (1903) and *The Trail of the Lonesome Pine* (1908), became bestsellers and prompted successful Broadway and Hollywood adaptations. Each of these works contrasts mountain and Bluegrass culture; each measures progress toward modernity—or distance from it—in terms of literacy.[4]

That Fox's work attained such immediate and widespread notice enabled him to advance a theory of southern improvement measured against the low mark of supposedly primitive, illiterate conditions in the southern mountains. Over time, Fox's particular narratives have faded from national memory. What is remembered, though, is an idea of a culturally impoverished region within a region: an eastern Kentucky in which the spectacle of CBS's Muddy Gut is tragic, but not surprising.[5]

In Fox's narratives, the power to mark so-called "Appalachian difference" derived, in part, from his privileged position at the confluence of conservative and liberal intellectual currents. Fox received a classical education at his father's academy near Lexington, and at Harvard he continued to excel in classical studies. But at Harvard, Fox also showed interest in contemporary scholarship. The vogue of Spencer's Social Darwinism peaked during Fox's upper-class years in Cambridge, 1881–83; exposure to American strains of Spencer's philosophy was unavoidable (see Cremin 90–100). Thus was Fox equipped to speak of mountain and Bluegrass difference as at once a traditional problem of cultural refinement and a scientific question of societal evolution.

For Fox, the logic of cultural refinement validated *class* hierarchy. Mountaineers were different, then, because they had always been too poor to benefit from the influence of the middle- and upper-class Bluegrass. Fox's notions about social evolution, however, had to do more with *race* than with class.[6] He held fairly steadily to the view that if allowed a place in Bluegrass culture, the mountaineer would adapt to its civility, if not its gentility. This adaptation was possible, Fox explained in his novels, because the mountaineers descended from solid Scotch-Irish and Anglo-Saxon stock, the same as their Bluegrass cousins. (It should be noted that for Fox, as for many of his contemporaries, certain peoples could not hope for "racial improvement"— namely, African Americans and southern Europeans.) These themes of race and class assume a special clarity in Fox's first novel, *The Kentuckians*, wherein they infuse a narrative of literacy with dramatic tension.[7]

The Kentuckians plots the lives of three characters: Randolph Marshall, a young legislator from the Bluegrass; Anne Bruce, daughter of the governor; and Boone Stallard, the newest state representative in the mountain delegation. The novel initially concerns itself with the romantic interests of these three characters, but as the narrative progresses, romance yields to politics in the relationship between Marshall and Stallard, between embodiments of Bluegrass and mountain cultures. Marshall emerges as thoroughly, classically literate: his speeches before the house are meticulously composed and then memorized; he keeps a journal which serves on occasion as an important aid to memory; and he is shown writing, as well as paralyzed by writer's block. Stallard, on the other hand, is a fresh arrival on the scene of literacy—that is, the sort of literacy Marshall exhibits. Although he reads the law voraciously, he rarely writes; he never composes more than a few notes to prompt the "cyclonic" oratory that earns him notice in the legislature. Perhaps James Lane Allen or Thomas Jefferson might have appreciated Stallard's literacy as appropriate to his agrarian station, but Fox's narrator betrays no such sympathy.

The Marshall-Stallard dialogue remains tense throughout the novel, in large part because Marshall continually articulates a "degeneracy" theory to explain human conditions in the mountains, and because Stallard never adequately rebuts him. Stallard does, however, recognize a counterargument. He wonders aloud whether anything more than "the slipping of a linchpin in a wagon on the Wilderness Road had not made the difference between his own family and the proudest in the State" (16).

Fox does not permit Marshall and Stallard the agency to resolve their own conflict. Instead, he calls in experts to do the job—experts who voice then-popular discourses on race and class politics. Fox introduces a northern newspaper reporter and a southern geologist, two experts whose various professional experiences have led them to form opposing theories of literacy and region. The northern reporter speaks first, articulating a class- and race-based theory of degeneracy:

> The accepted theory of the origin of the mountaineer, particularly the Kentucky mountaineer, is that he is the descendant . . . of exported paupers and convicts, indents, and "pore white trash". . . . (75–76)

This argument resonates with claims made by Henry Cabot Lodge in his *Short History of the English Colonies in America* (1881), and, at about that time, by John Fiske in public lectures that eventually became *Old Virginia and Her Neighbours* (1897). The theories of Lodge, Fiske, and others committed to Social Darwinism were very much in the air at Harvard during Fox's undergraduate career there. In his narrative, Fox neither explicitly embraces nor rejects Lodge's and Fiske's "scientific racism" (Batteau 61). Instead, Fox nods to the validity of their theories, then claims an exemption for the Kentucky mountaineer. He does so by insisting that eastern Kentuckians are not descended from the racially "weak" populations of the Virginia commonwealth, and so are not prone to the degenerate potential of those peoples. Extending this argument, Fox establishes that the "primitive" nature of mountain people cannot be explained by prevailing theories of racial difference. Fox lets the southern geologist explain:

> Some of them [mountaineers] are the descendants of those people ["pore white trash"], of course. There are more of them in the mountains than in the blue-grass, naturally; but the chief differences between them and us come from the fact that they have been shut off from the world absolutely for more than a hundred years. Take out the cavalier element, and, in rank and file, we were originally the same people. Until a man has lived a year at a time in the mountains he doesn't know what a thin veneer civilization is. It goes on and off like a glove, especially off. Put twenty *average* blue-grass families down in the mountains half a dozen miles from one another, take away their books, keep them there, with no schools and no churches, for a hundred years, and they will be as ignorant and lawless as the mountaineer. (76–77)

From the perspective of Fox's geologist, the absence of literacy and literate institutions arrests the development of culture. Such institutions once civilized *"average"*—that is, middle-class—Bluegrass families and, presumably, could do the same again for the mountaineer. In this view, literacy is an instrument for instilling cultural refinement, as well as a tool for assessing it. That Stallard, the mountaineer, is reformed by literacy finally sways Marshall to see that the boundary between mountains and Bluegrass amounts to a class distinction—a distinction marked by literacy.

But Fox's theory of literacy and difference falls short when we consider the following statistics on "illiteracy" drawn from the 1900 U.S. Census.[8] In the county of Fox's birth and childhood, 23 percent of all persons aged ten years and older could neither read nor write. In the Tennessee and Virginia counties where Fox became familiar with mountain life while on coal-mining business, the illiteracy rate was 23 and 21 percent, respectively. In Franklin County, Kentucky, seat of the state capital and setting for *The Kentuckians*, 22 percent of those ten or older could not read and write. In Rowan County, site of the "feud" fictionalized in *The Kentuckians*, only 18 percent of those ten and up were considered illiterate.[9] That same figure, 18 percent, also applied to Fayette County, of which Lexington has always made up the largest part. Put succinctly, comparing numbers from Fox's Bluegrass and his mountains, one finds a relatively consistent rate of basic, self-reported literacy—about 80 percent.

Fox clearly misrepresents literacy in the mountains. In addition to census statistics, numerous documents testify to the presence of literate behavior where, according to Fox, none was to be found.[10] But perhaps Fox's mountains are bereft of literacy because he could not sense it there; the seeming absence of "modern" literate institutions in the mountains—public libraries, daily newspapers—made it difficult for

Fox to imagine the presence of literacy sponsored and valorized by local culture. In *The Kentuckians*, Boone Stallard fails to defend his mountain constituents against charges of illiteracy and ignorance because he is unable to invoke the sign of a single literate institution serving that constituency. Indeed, his own literate career begins only after he leaves the mountains for the Bluegrass, where his literate potential is cultivated at college. Even on the issue of literate potential, Stallard remains silent. Only the expert, the geologist, has the authority to speak to the mountaineers' dormant capacity for reading and writing.

Like Fox's man of science, and so many other educated folk in his writing, Fox himself came to be acknowledged as an expert on mountain life.[11] So compelling were Fox's observations that contemporary scholars in a variety of disciplines cited him as an authority in their treatises on Appalachian difference. In fact, the literature on Appalachian difference contains many more references to Fox than to the professionals, Lodge and Fiske among them, from whom Fox's thinking about mountain life derived (Batteau 61).

For example, the Southern Education Board issued a report in 1902 on "Educational Conditions in the Southern Appalachian Region" which begins by tracing the ancestry of the region's inhabitants back to northern European origins:

> These mountaineers come . . . of a noble stock. There are no facts whatever to support the old theory that they are the descendants of indentured servants or renegades from the old colonies. John Fox, Jr., suggests the right theory when he says that the "axle broke" and the pioneer and his little family had to stop and go into camp, with the result that their descendants remain in the mountains today. (3)

Here Fox's name lends credibility to a particular notion of race classification. A decade earlier, with a younger Fox looking on, Lodge and Fiske had injected their science of race into public debate about southern European immigration—immigration they saw as a threat to "American democracy in the purity of the Anglo-Saxon race" (Batteau 61). The Southern Education Board seized upon the public perception that this threat had not abated in ten years' time. Consequently, using Fox's name, the board promoted Appalachia as the "home and training ground of the southern whites" who might stave off the genetic (i.e., racial) and moral degradation of American culture (3). But, the board pointed out, to be useful in cultural preservation, mountaineers would have to become literate.

The twelfth decennial census in 1900 announced distressing news: the South remained the nation's most illiterate section. U.S. Census

Office enumerations placed "native white" southern illiteracy at 16.44 percent, as compared to a national average of 7.7 percent. Andrew Sledd, professor of Latin at Emory College, wrote that "no explanation of Southern illiteracy can . . . be based on the generally accredited statement that our large and almost wholly illiterate negro population lowers the percentage of our section" (2471). The problem, Sledd argued, was with "poor whites," that "body of Southern lawlessness and Southern illiteracy . . . almost wholly responsible for some features of Southern life that bring odium (not undeserved) on all the section" (2473). Like Sledd, the Southern Education Board measured this odium in terms of illiteracy. While it found adult illiteracy in the southern mountains to be roughly the same as throughout the South, the board did notice several exceptions. It declared excessive Kentucky's illiteracy rate of 21.65 percent and implied that in the eastern mountains illiteracy in "the white population over 10 years of age" might range between 50 and 65 percent (5). This, of course, was hardly the case. As already mentioned, most mountain counties—just like most Blue-grass counties—posted an illiteracy rate of around 20 percent at the turn of the century. At that time, Kentucky's highest illiteracy rates were near 30 percent in its far southeastern counties.

Three of these southeastern counties—Breathitt, Perry, and Knott—were featured in an influential 1898 study by George Vincent, a prominent University of Chicago sociologist. Vincent noted that in the Kentucky mountains "the frontier has survived in practical isolation until this very day," a condition "made vivid" for Vincent by Fox's writing (1). But later, perhaps indirectly referring to Fox, Vincent comments, "We had heard so many stories of the ignorance of the mountaineers that we were somewhat disappointed by their familiarity with a good many things we had expected them not to know" (15–16). What these mountaineers knew, apparently, derived from an array of literate activity. Among other pursuits, Vincent mentions seeing evidence of letter writing, newspaper reading, and organized schooling. Clearly, the conditions Vincent reports do not square with those that Fox and the Southern Education Board characterize in their texts. Yet in spite of his observations, Vincent keeps to the view that illiteracy held back modernity in what had become the southern mountain *region*—its boundaries mapped firmly in both popular and scientific discourse.[12]

Consequences: Intervention

As Raymond Williams reminds us, regional boundaries are at once physical *and* cultural ("Region" 232). And he argues that cultural boundaries manifest themselves primarily in discursive forms—the regional novel, for example. Such forms of discourse mark the "contrast between refined or sophisticated tastes or manners, and relatively crude and limited manners and ideas" (*Keywords* 265). As we have seen, Fox's writing helped create regional difference of the sort Williams describes. Trading on middle-class preoccupations with tastes, manners, and intellect—the elements of cultural capital—Fox found audiences for a narrative which dramatically juxtaposed Bluegrass progress and mountain decline. Scholarly experts then validated this narrative by working it into the discourse of the middle-class academic professions (e.g., education and sociology).

In this way, the mountains of eastern Kentucky were rather rapidly established as culturally inferior, with this inferiority defined partly in terms of illiteracy. Consequently, by century's end, Appalachia was vulnerable to an onslaught of social reform efforts. One such effort is memorable for its ostensible concern with literacy: the opening of "settlement schools" for mountain children. Most successful among these institutions was the Hindman Settlement School in Knott County, Kentucky, which enrolled its first students in 1902. Founded as a project of the Kentucky Federation of Women's Clubs, Hindman's initial mission "consisted in teaching students how to read and write effectively, and in equipping them with good habits and practical training" (Jim Wayne Miller, "Madly" 239). Historian David Whisnant points out that Hindman's curriculum focused more on practical training—cooking and sewing, for example—than it did on literacy education (51–68).[13] It is not clear whether literacy education took second place to training in practical arts at Hindman, or whether literacy was viewed as a prerequisite to advanced work in these arts. But in any event literacy instruction at Hindman emerged tangled within often conflicting gestures to improve local culture while somehow preserving it.

The production of handicrafts, for example, provided the school with a healthy income, while supposedly affording students the opportunity to conserve their mountain heritage. But many of the handicrafts produced at Hindman were quite unlike local crafts. For example, most weaving and furniture making at Hindman reflected practices imported (along with instructors) from urban settlement houses, industrial schools, and universities (Whisnant 61). Like Fox's mountain tales, Hindman's woven and wooden artifacts of "genuine" mountain life reached a national audience, and thereby confirmed the notion that traditional, if backward, American culture remained unspoiled within the fastness of the southern mountains.

In the process of learning to read and write effectively, then, early Hindman students may have been led to embrace as their own a culture invented for them by middle-class reformers from the Bluegrass. Yet it would be a mistake to dismiss this imposed culture as fraudulent or even inauthentic. As Whisnant argues, "One of the paradoxes of intervention-induced cultural change is its very durability and the degree to which imported forms and styles are accepted and defended by local people whose actual cultural traditions they altered or displaced" (100). Thus, rather than impugning the cultural traditions imposed at Hindman, critique should center on the very act of imposition, of intervention. Necessarily, then, attention must also be paid to the enabling role of literacy in such cultural intervention.[14] In this light, we can see the problem posed by Hindman's initial approach to literacy education: Hindman, like schools involved in literacy campaigns nationwide, restricted "the ability to read to learning a particular text or doctrine" (Arnove and Graff 7).

That "particular text," or rather its narrative, is the very one celebrated in Fox's popular novels. It is, too, the single narrative repeated at the turn of the century by academics with a professional interest in mountain life. As we have seen, this narrative, whether popular or scientific, figures the Appalachian region and native as Other. And as reform efforts worked this narrative back into the mountains, the proverbial circle was closed. Children and adults throughout the southern mountains, like those at Hindman, were schooled to accept their otherness precisely as it was understood by those who had invented it. Such is the double-edged nature of representations of literacy.

Conclusions

The turn-of-the-century "literacy crisis" that reshaped Kentucky's cultural geography was far from an isolated phenomenon. Indeed, the discourse of that crisis permeated public discussions of modernity and progress throughout the country, particularly with regard to the threat illiteracy was thought to present to higher education (Susan Miller; Trimbur). Against this backdrop, bringing literacy to the mountains continued to be the goal of many reformers throughout the early part of the century. On occasion, this "mountain work" extended beyond regional boundaries. In the 1920s, for instance, a national "crusade" against illiteracy sponsored by the National Education Association grew out of attempts to teach reading and writing to adults in eastern Kentucky.[15]

The discourse of literacy in crisis did not unify those acting against illiteracy. If students entering Harvard in the 1890s were illiterate, as E. L. Godkin lamented in the *Nation* and elsewhere, it remained that southerners were much more illiterate, and southern mountaineers and African Americans even worse off (cf. Klotter). Redeeming Godkin's illiterate "boys" nationwide demanded that "preparation of the schools should be made sterner than ever, and the standards of the college higher than ever, so that everybody who [was] meant to go to college should" (285). This was not, however, the remedy generally proposed for southern mountaineers and others of rural circumstance.

In 1910, Theodore Roosevelt's Commission on Country Life argued that rural schools should concentrate on teaching "farm and home subjects," not the curriculum of urban schools (123). Rural education that followed the urban model allegedly contributed to "ineffective farming, lack of ideals, and the drift to town" (121). The commission in effect called for "relevant" education such that, as Godkin might have put it, everybody who was meant to live a rural life would do so. Following the commission's advice, the government developed domestic policy that in practice directed educators to ignore illiteracy where it was supposedly the worst. Intentionally or not, then, "country life" policy helped inject the myth of Appalachian illiteracy into the durable mold of federal law.

That myth persists today, having been articulated variously and repeatedly throughout this century. It persists largely because the conditions that first gave it shape have changed so little. There remain economic and ideological tensions between the northern and southern sections. The middle class in the Bluegrass (and elsewhere throughout the South) aims always, if subtly, to resist James Lane Allen's old suggestion that Southerners put elegant living ahead of knowledge and intellect. And still quite useful in that resistance are comparisons to mountain life, portrayed to be as different, as alien, and as illiterate as ever.

Yet in eastern Kentucky, generations of voices have contested the invention of an illiterate Appalachia. Following a public reading by John Fox, Jr., for example, one observer wrote that "the mountain boys were ready to mob him." The boys claimed that if Fox's "Cumberland tales" were true, "he was 'no gentleman' for telling all the family affairs of people who had entertained him with their best." And if his stories were false, "they were libelous upon the mountain people." But such complaints were not taken seriously. President William Goodell Frost of Berea College, who related this incident, wrote that the boys simply had "no comprehension of the nature of fiction" (102).

Voices of resistance are better heard today, and better received— but mostly locally, and only occasionally. When CBS aired its *48 Hours* program on Muddy Gut Hollow, daily newspapers in Lexington and Louisville covered negative reaction to the broadcast for several days. Over the next month, the papers published letters and opinion pieces critical of CBS. Objections were also heard on local television. An hourlong panel discussion aired just after *48 Hours* on the CBS affiliate serving southeastern Kentucky. The panelists included the governor and various community leaders in eastern Kentucky, who agreed that "the program exaggerated the incidence of teen-age marriages and illiteracy, [and] made spouse abuse appear an accepted practice" (Keesler A13). But the *48 Hours* staff never took a full turn in this conversation. A CBS spokesperson would say only that the network had covered Kentucky fairly over the years, "including shows about the Kentucky Derby and bluegrass music" (qtd. in Keesler A13). More telling, however, are informal comments made by Phil Jones, a *48 Hours* correspondent, upon his return to New York from eastern Kentucky. "It's foreign," he told a television critic for the Lexington daily. "It's awful. It's filthy. They're not educated" (qtd. in White D1).

People in Appalachia struggle every day to resist such damaging representations of life and literacy. It is an especially frustrating struggle: these representations have long been sanctioned by those who control the very forums in which resistance must be registered to have rhetorical effect. Regrettably, the noise generated by the current literacy crisis too often drowns out alternative representations of literacy in Appalachia. Given this situation, how might formal literacy instruction intervene in this discourse of crisis, how might it create a space for representations of literacy that respect the experience of people in the region?

Of course, this question cannot be answered here. Instead, meaningful answers must emerge from dialogue on literacy, dialogue centered on voices heretofore unheard or dismissed in debates about literacy instruction. We can, however, briefly consider elements essential to such dialogue, especially those relevant to the preceding analysis that implicates notions of literacy in the invention of Appalachian difference, of the Appalachian Other.

First, we must recognize that traditional literacy instruction continues—whether by design or by accident—to mistakenly equate a narrow range of literacies with intelligence, even humanity. With this in mind, Giroux urges us to view curriculum as a historically specific narrative and pedagogy as a form of cultural politics that either enables or silences the differentiated human capacities which allow students to speak from their own experiences, locate themselves in history, and act so as to create social forms that expand the possibility of democratic public life. ("Liberal Arts Education" 119–20)

If we begin with these assumptions about the nature of literacy curriculum and pedagogy, then, a range of possible initiatives follows. Such initiatives aim to challenge restrictive definitions of literacy and to upset oppressive representations of difference authorized by such definitions.

The pedagogy of difference Giroux theorizes speaks directly to problems of literacy education that arise wherever borders—regional, cultural—are negotiated. At its core, a pedagogy of difference addresses "the important question of how representations and practices that name, marginalize, and define difference as the devalued Other are actively learned, internalized, challenged, or transformed" (136). Most schools and colleges choose not to support this sort of pedagogy. But in many institutions, by looking beyond bland course descriptions and into classrooms we can find teachers committed to literacy pedagogies that interrogate cultural difference. At the University of Kentucky, for example, Mary Winslow recently taught a first-year writing course that brought together students from the mountains and the Bluegrass to investigate various representations of Appalachia. Winslow's students analyzed and criticized photographs, broadsides, and short stories that narrate life in the mountains of eastern Kentucky, with particular attention to the economic, political, and cultural consequences that coal mining has had for the region. On a modest scale, courses like Winslow's prompt students to understand how representations of cultural differences between mountains and Bluegrass are rooted in the relations of power that, historically, form the border between the two regions.

Giroux reminds us, too, that a pedagogy of difference must "not only . . . unravel the ways in which the voices of the Other are colonized and repressed," it must help us "understand how the experience of marginality at the level of everyday life lends itself to forms of oppositional and transformative consciousness" (136). A growing body of work in Appalachian studies models how such transformations of consciousness might be inferred from a variety of texts, "literary" and otherwise (see, for example, Cunningham). But actually raising oppositional and transformative consciousness in the English classroom is quite another matter. Teachers who commit themselves and their students to the sort of critical pedagogy Giroux describes can easily document the myriad difficulties they daily face. Members of the Eastern Kentucky Teachers' Network, for example, tell of successes and failures in their efforts to challenge traditional forms of literacy instruction that perpetuate "powerlessness" in Appalachia, as Rebecca Eller describes (76). In an ethnographic study of the network, Eller writes that while some teachers achieve "autonomous empower-ment"—control over their own professional lives—others are able to attain the "transformative empowerment that would enable them to work for social change." It is these teachers, Eller reports, who attempt "to educate their students for power—power to define their own identities, and power to challenge the status quo." In so doing, these teachers struggle "to provide their students with a more proper, critical literacy" and strive "to fashion a new leadership in the region—leaders who have an understanding of the problems of Appalachia, and who have both the confidence and the ability to confront those problems" (328).

Other stories of reinventing Appalachia by reinventing literacy do not abound, but they do exist. Eliot Wigginton's "Foxfire" pedagogy, in a public school setting, links literacy instruction with the retrieval and preservation of cultural memory in the southern mountains. And the Highlander Research and Education Center in Tennessee has for years immersed students in the discourse of civil rights and radical democracy (see Horton and Freire). But what is most important about Foxfire and Highlander may not be the work they accomplish *in* the mountains. Rather, the specific pedagogy they model, and the attitude about Appalachia they promote, lay the groundwork for an inclusive dialogue *with* Appalachia, dialogue consistent with a "politics of difference and [a] border pedagogy responsive to the imperatives of a critical democracy" (Giroux, "Post-Colonial Ruptures" 13).

If we as scholars and teachers participate in dialogues about the role of literacy in the creation and perpetuation of Appalachian otherness—indeed, any kind of otherness—what should we expect? We should expect, above all else, to be confronted with hard choices: "To write and to teach writing—to teach literacy—is to exercise a choice," argues J. Elspeth Stuckey. "Literacy is an idea with a violent history. We can continue that history or we can divert it. The signs are mostly discouraging" (112). There is hope, but only if we can divert our attention from what seem normal and natural ways of talking about literacy and literates, illiteracy and illiterates.

Maxine Greene locates this hope in "the capacity to unveil and disclose." She observes that "these are dark and shadowed times, and we need to live them, standing before one another, open to the world" (248). We must seek to unveil the historical complexity of literacy and to disclose how literacy can subjugate as well as liberate. Only then can we begin to understand how a place like Muddy Gut, how Appalachia, might come to be viewed as "another America." Only then can we begin to imagine yet another America, one in which the manifold literacies of a plural culture mark regional boundaries as open places that invite us to learn carefully and teach patiently.

Notes

1. Indeed, such measurement predates the Civil War. As early as 1840, the U.S. Census Bureau attempted to measure the nation's illiteracy, and found the South wanting. By 1880, the year Godkin lodged his complaint against the South, the Census Bureau had gathered data that purportedly confirmed, prima facie, that southern states, some fifteen years after reunion, still had the highest illiteracy rates in the nation. Over the next twenty years, assessments of literacy in the South returned the same results. (See decennial censuses for years 1840–1900 for the government's ongoing commentary on illiteracy in the South.)

2. Note, for example, that Barrett Wendell passed over Kentucky letters in his *Literary History of America* (1900). Wendell's gesture merely continued a tradition that dates back to antebellum years, during which certain abolitionist writers contended that investment in slavery was responsible for the "literary pauperism of the South" (Helper 404).

3. In *Appalachia on Our Minds*, Henry Shapiro discusses at length the development of the "idea" of Appalachia—and how that idea served the interests of those who invented and disseminated it. A good explanation of the economic pressures that have influenced perceptions of Appalachia appears in Ronald D. Eller's *Miners, Millhands, and Mountaineers*.

4. According to William S. Ward, Fox's *Little Shepherd of Kingdom Come* was the nation's tenth-best seller in 1903 and seventh-best seller in 1904. *The Trail of the Lonesome Pine* appeared as the nation's third-best seller in 1908 and fifth-best seller in 1909. In 1913, Fox's *Heart of the Hills* was the fifth-best-selling book in the nation (139). A silent cinematic treatment of *The Little Shepherd of Kingdom Come* was released in the 1920s, and three film versions of *The Trail of the Lonesome Pine* were made, all by Cecil B. De Mille. The 1936 production featured Fred MacMurray, Henry Fonda, and Sylvia Sydney (Titus 70, 95).

5. Numerous other "local colorists" situated their fictions in central and southern Appalachia. See Lorise C. Boger's *The Southern Mountaineer in Literature* for an extensive listing of relevant titles.

6. Alexander Saxton identifies "two thrusts" of Social Darwinism. He argues that in the 1890s a race-linked theory of social evolution came to dominate, supplanting an earlier class-linked theory. The class-linked theory facilitated mass industrialization and justified unequal distribution of wealth;

the race-linked theory warranted resistance to immigration and the forced opening of economic markets abroad (369–77).

7. Like *The Kentuckians* (1898) published before them, *The Little Shepherd of Kingdom Come* (1903), *The Trail of the Lonesome Pine* (1908), and *The Heart of the Hills* (1913) invoke literacy as a primary measure of character and intelligence. Also, two essays in Fox's *Blue-grass and Rhododendron*, "The Kentucky Mountaineer" and "The Southern Mountaineer," discuss literacy and culture in metaphors quite similar to those appearing in *The Kentuckians*. Both essays were first published in *Scribner's*, April–May 1901.

8. Harvey Graff makes a good argument for the careful use of census reports on literacy (329–33). He suggests that around the turn of the century people complied in high number with requests for accurate census information. They did so, Graff says, because powerful social institutions—the church, for example—encouraged compliance, and because federal penalties for noncompliance were considerable. Still, we must learn more about the politics of census taking if we are to have an adequate sense of census reliability. Margo J. Anderson's *The American Census: A Social History* (1988) discusses the politics of population enumeration, but more remains to be written about census questions pertaining to literacy.

9. Details of the "feud" portrayed in *The Kentuckians* resemble those of the Martin-Tolliver conflict which beset Rowan County in the 1870s and 1880s. Fox's fictional Roland County is threatened with abolition if law and order are not restored by county officials. In 1887, Rowan County received a similar order from the state legislature after the commonwealth militia, instructed to arrest unruly "feudists," acted to put down a "fantastic melée in the county seat" (Channing 154).

10. S. S. MacClintock, a University of Chicago sociologist, followed Fox's lead when he observed that in eastern Kentucky "newspapers and daily mails do not exist." He allowed that "[a] few denominational and agricultural papers, mostly weeklies, may be found in the more prosperous homes, but there are many that never see a paper of any kind" (14). In fact, the number of commercial weekly newspapers published in eastern Kentucky before 1900 attests to the presence of considerable literate activity in the mountains. The roster of weeklies active in the late nineteenth century includes the *Kentuckian* (Ashland, c. 1856), the *Mountain Echo* (Barbourville, 1873), the *Sentinel* (Catlettsburg, 1875), the *Times* (Williamsburg, 1885), the *Big Sandy News* (Louisa, 1885), and the *Inquirer* (Ewing, 1897).

11. Even today Fox's authority stands in some quarters. A widely read history of Kentucky states that "in John Fox, Jr., the mountaineers found an understanding chronicler who recorded in his novels their loves, hatreds, and philosophies" (Clark 275). A similar sentiment appears in the most current literary history of the commonwealth (Ward 76). And a new high school social studies text celebrates an "immensely popular" Fox as one who "gained a national reputation as an interpreter of mountain culture" with writing that "contrasts the life of the mountains and the Bluegrass" (Hall 222).

12. The emergence of twentieth-century regionalism is discussed from a geographical perspective by Fulmer Mood and Vernon Carstensen in chapters in *Regionalism in America*. The conventional formulation of sections and regions they summarize is questioned by John Alexander Williams in "A

Regionalism within Regionalisms: Three Frameworks for Appalachian Studies," and is challenged and revised by Edward Soja in *Postmodern Geographies* (163–65). The relationship between region and literature is considered by Jim Wayne Miller in a chapter in *Geography and Literature*.

13. In *The Heart of the Hills*, Fox characterizes a mountain settlement school teacher from the Bluegrass: "She taught the girls to cook, sew, wash and iron, clean house, and make baskets, and the boys to use tools, to farm, make garden, and take care of animals; and she taught them all to keep clean" (64).

14. Rhonda George England argues that Whisnant assesses only the "cultural losses" brought about by the founding of the settlement school at Hindman. She tallies the "cultural gains," among them what "the teachers learned from the mountain people" (6). Harry Robie takes an opposing view, insisting "that on balance the settlement schools were harmful to the culture of the southern mountains" (6). Several readers of Robie's argument responded to his "fallacious indictment" of settlement schools with observations drawn from experiences as students at such schools (Deaton, Flannery-Dees, and Hobgood 45).

15. Cora Wilson Stewart, a native Kentuckian, headed the NEA's Illiteracy Commission after steering a similar body in Kentucky. A former school superintendent in Rowan County, Stewart founded the "moonlight schools" for "adult illiterates" (see Stewart). News of Stewart's schools spread outside Kentucky after they were featured in a 1913 Bureau of Education bulletin, *Illiteracy in the United States and an Experiment for Its Elimination.*

Works Cited

Allen, James Lane. *The Blue-grass Region of Kentucky and Other Kentucky Articles.* New York: Harper and Brothers, 1892.

Anderson, Margo J. *The American Census: A Social History.* New Haven: Yale UP, 1988.

"Another America." *48 Hours.* CBS. WKYT, Lexington, KY. 14 Dec. 1989.

Arnove, Robert F., and Harvey J. Graff. Introduction. *National Literacy Campaigns: Historical and Comparative Perspectives.* Ed. Robert F. Arnove and Harvey J. Graff. New York: Plenum, 1987. 1–28.

Batteau, Allen W. *The Invention of Appalachia.* Tucson: U of Arizona P, 1990.

Bledstein, Burton J. *The Culture of Professionalism: The Middle Class and the Development of Higher Education in America.* 1976. New York: Norton, 1978.

Boger, Lorise C. *The Southern Mountaineer in Literature: An Annotated Bibliography.* Morgantown: West Virginia U Library, 1964.

Bottorff, William K. *James Lane Allen.* Twayne's United States Authors Series 56. New York: Twayne, 1964.

Carstensen, Vernon. "The Development and Application of Regional-Sectional Concepts, 1900–1950." In *Regionalism in America.* Ed. Merrill Jensen. Madison: U of Wisconsin P, 1951. 99–118.

Channing, Steven A. *Kentucky: A Bicentennial History.* New York: Norton, 1977.

Clark, Thomas D. *A History of Kentucky.* 6th ed. Lexington, KY: John Bradford, 1960.

Cremin, Lawrence A. *The Transformation of the School: Progressivism in American Education, 1876–1957.* 1961. New York: Vintage–Random House, 1964.

Cunningham, Rodger. "Appalachianism and Orientalism: Reflections on Reading Edward Said." *Journal of the Appalachian Studies Association* 1 (1989): 125–40.

Deaton, John H., Vivian Sexton Flannery-Dees, and Jane Bishop Hobgood. "Those Settlement Schools: Harmful or Benign? Three Responses to Harry Robie." *Appalachian Heritage* 19.3 (1991): 45–52.

Eller, Rebecca Gaeth. "Teacher Resistance and Educational Change: Toward a Critical Theory of Literacy in Appalachia." Diss. U of Kentucky, 1989.

Eller, Ronald D. *Miners, Millhands, and Mountaineers: Industrialization of the Appalachian South, 1880–1930.* Knoxville: U of Tennessee P, 1982.

England, Rhonda George. "Voices from the History of Teaching: Katherine Pettit, May Stone, and Elizabeth Watts at Hindman Settlement School, 1899–1956." Diss. U of Kentucky, 1990.

Fiske, John. *Old Virginia and Her Neighbours.* Boston: Houghton Mifflin, 1897.

Fox, John Jr. *The Kentuckians.* New York: Harper and Brothers, 1898.

———. "The Kentucky Mountaineer." *Blue-grass and Rhododendron: Out-doors in Old Kentucky.* New York: Scribner's, 1901. 27–54.

———. "The Southern Mountaineer." *Blue-grass and Rhododendron: Out-doors in Old Kentucky.* New York: Scribner's, 1901. 3–24.

———. *The Little Shepherd of Kingdom Come.* New York: Scribner's, 1903. Lexington, KY: UP of Kentucky, 1987.

———. *The Trail of the Lonesome Pine.* New York: Scribner's, 1908. Lexington, KY: UP of Kentucky, 1984.

———. *The Heart of the Hills.* New York: Scribner's, 1913.

Frost, William Goodell. "Our Contemporary Ancestors in the Southern Mountains." *Atlantic Monthly* Mar. 1899: 311–19. Rpt. in *Appalachian Images in Folk and Popular Culture.* Ed. W. K. McNeil. Ann Arbor: UMI Research P, 1989. 91–106.

Giroux, Henry A. Introduction. *Literacy: Reading the Word and the World.* By Paulo Freire and Donaldo Macedo. South Hadley, MA: Bergin and Garvey, 1987. 1–27.

———. "Liberal Arts Education and the Struggle for Public Life: Dreaming about Democracy." *South Atlantic Quarterly* 89 (1990): 113–38. Rpt. in *The Politics of Liberal Education.* Ed. Darryl J. Gless and Barbara Herrnstein Smith. Durham, NC: Duke UP, 1992. 119–44.

———. "Post-Colonial Ruptures and Democratic Possibilities: Multiculturalism as Anti-Racist Pedagogy." *Cultural Critique* 21 (1992): 5–39.

Godkin, E. L. "The Growing Illiteracy of American Boys." *Nation* 15 Oct. 1896: 284–85.

Graff, Harvey J. *The Literacy Myth: Literacy and Social Structure in the Nineteenth-Century City.* New York: Academic P, 1979. New Brunswick, NJ: Transaction, 1991.

Greene, Maxine. "In Search of a Critical Pedagogy." *Harvard Educational Review* 56 (1986): 427–41. Rpt. in *Teaching, Teachers, and Teacher Education.* Ed. Margo Okazawa-Rey, James Anderson, and Rob Traver. Cambridge: Harvard Educational Review, 1987. 234–48.

Hall, Wade. "Literature." In *Our Kentucky: A Study of the Bluegrass State.* Ed. James C. Klotter. Lexington: UP of Kentucky, 1992. 219–37.

Helper, Hinton Rowan. *The Impending Crisis of the South: How to Meet It.* Ed. George M. Fredrickson. 1857. Cambridge: Belknap–Harvard UP, 1968.

Horton, Myles, and Paulo Freire. *We Make the Road by Walking: Conversations on Education and Social Change.* Ed. Brenda Bell, John Gaventa, and John Peters. Philadelphia: Temple UP, 1990.

Keesler, William. "Show Gripes Governor; He Asks CBS-TV Chief to Visit." *Courier-Journal* [Louisville, KY] 16 Dec. 1989: A11+.

Klotter, James C. "The Black South and White Appalachia." *Journal of American History* 66 (1980): 832–49.

Lodge, Henry Cabot. *A Short History of the English Colonies in America.* New York: Harper and Brothers, 1881.

MacClintock, S. S. "The Kentucky Mountains and Their Feuds." *American Journal of Sociology* 7 (1901): 1–28, 171–87.

Miller, Jim Wayne. "Anytime the Ground Is Uneven: The Outlook for Regional Studies and What to Look Out For." In *Geography and Literature: A Meeting of the Disciplines.* Ed. William E. Mallory and Paul Simpson-Housley. Syracuse, NY: Syracuse UP, 1987. 1–20.

———. "Madly to Learn: James Still, the Teacher." In *From the Fort to the Future: Educating the Children of Kentucky.* Ed. Edwina Ann Doyle, Ruby Layson, and Anne Armstrong Thompson. Lexington: Kentucky Images, 1987. 230–43.

Miller, Susan. "The Feminization of Composition." In *The Politics of Writing Instruction: Postsecondary.* Ed. Richard Bullock and John Trimbur. Portsmouth, NH: Boynton/Cook, 1991. 39–53.

Mood, Fulmer. "The Origin, Evolution, and Application of the Sectional Concept, 1750–1900." In *Regionalism in America.* Ed. Merrill Jensen. Madison: U of Wisconsin P, 1951. 5–98.

Moore, Tyrel G. "Eastern Kentucky as a Model of Appalachia: The Role of Literary Images." *Southeastern Geographer* 31 (1991): 75–89.

Robie, Harry. "Resolved: That on Balance the Settlement Schools Were Harmful to the Culture of the Southern Mountains." *Appalachian Heritage* 19.1 (1991): 6–10.

Saxton, Alexander. *The Rise and Fall of the White Republic: Class Politics and Mass Culture in Nineteenth-Century America.* London: Verso, 1990.

Shapiro, Henry D. *Appalachia on Our Minds: The Southern Mountains and Mountaineers in the American Consciousness, 1870–1920.* Chapel Hill: U of North Carolina P, 1978.

Sledd, Andrew. "Illiteracy in the South." *Independent* 17 Oct. 1901: 2471–74.

Soja, Edward W. *Postmodern Geographies: The Reassertion of Space in Critical Social Theory.* London: Verso, 1989.

Southern Education Board. "Educational Conditions in the Southern Appalachian Region." *Bulletin of the Southern Education Board* 1.1 (1902): 3–12.

Stewart, Cora Wilson. *Moonlight Schools for the Emancipation of Adult Illiterates.* New York: Dutton, 1922.

Stuckey, J. Elspeth. "The Feminization of Literacy." In *Composition and Resistance.* Ed. C. Mark Hurlbert and Michael Blitz. Portsmouth, NH: Boynton/Cook, 1991. 105–13.

Titus, Warren I. *John Fox, Jr.* Twayne's United States Authors Series 174. New York: Twayne, 1971.

Trimbur, John. "Literacy and the Discourse of Crisis." In *The Politics of Writing Instruction: Postsecondary.* Ed. Richard Bullock and John Trimbur. Portsmouth, NH: Boynton/Cook, 1991. 277–95.

U.S. Commission on Country Life. *Report of the Commission on Country Life.* New York: Sturgis and Walton, 1911. Chapel Hill: U of North Carolina P, 1944.

United States. Department of the Interior. Bureau of Education. *Illiteracy in the United States and an Experiment for Its Elimination.* Bulletin 20. Washington: GPO, 1913.

———. ———. Census Office. *Population* Twelfth (1900) Census. Vol. 1, pt. 1. Washington: GPO, 1901.

———. ———. ———. *Population* Twelfth (1900) Census. Vol. 2, pt. 2. Washington: GPO, 1902.

Vincent, George E. "A Retarded Frontier." *American Journal of Sociology* 4 (1898): 1–20.

Ward, William S. *A Literary History of Kentucky.* Knoxville: U of Tennessee P, 1988.

Wendell, Barrett. *A Literary History of America.* 1900. Detroit: Gale, 1968.

Whisnant, David E. *All That Is Native and Fine: The Politics of Culture in an American Region.* Chapel Hill: U of North Carolina P, 1983.

White, Susan. "CBS Puts Floyd County in Unflattering Light." *Lexington Herald-Leader* 14 Dec. 1989: D1+.

Wigginton, Eliot. *Sometimes a Shining Moment: The Foxfire Experience.* Garden City, NY: Doubleday, 1985.

Williams, John Alexander. "A Regionalism within Regionalisms: Three Frameworks for Appalachian Studies." *Journal of the Appalachian Studies Association* 3 (1991): 4–17.

Williams, Raymond. *Keywords: A Vocabulary of Culture and Society.* Rev. ed. New York: Oxford UP, 1983.

———. "Region and Class in the Novel." *Writing in Society.* London: Verso, 1983. 229–38.

Woodward, C. Vann. *Origins of the New South, 1877–1913.* 1951. Baton Rouge: Louisiana State UP, 1971.

9 The Essay Dies in the Academy, circa 1900

Jean Donovan Sanborn
Colby College

The current revival of interest in the essay as a genre (e.g., Anderson; Butrym; Good) has created some confusion in terminology and in context. On the one hand are "literary essays," a form of high culture suitable for study in the classroom; on the other hand are "school essays," a form antithetical to the literary essay but suitable for production by students in the classroom. One pole is unreachable for students, and the other is often unusable for their purposes. The space between is not open for the range of movement that would encourage learning. An understanding of a critical point in the history of the genre may make it possible to open up a field between the two poles and thus resuscitate academic essays.

Since the focus of this chapter is the academic essay, I will refer only briefly to the literary history of the genre. Despite roots in classical genres, the essay in its literary form is usually attributed to Montaigne and defined as a "trying out" of ideas. As Carl Klaus points out, essayists often write essays on the form itself, and he has gathered a stimulating collection of their remarks in "Essayists on the Essay." All of them insist that the essay has no regularized form, that it follows the movements of the mind. In Montaigne's words: "My ideas follow one another, but sometimes it is from a distance, and look at each other, but with a sidelong glance" (qtd. in Klaus 166).

Klaus's survey also shows that essayists have long made a distinction between their form and what Addison called "the Regularity of a Set Discourse" (Klaus 158) and more recently Joseph Wood Krutch has termed the "article" (18; see also Klaus 162). Klaus continues his analysis of the literary essay by examining the creation of the authorial self and concludes: "The essay, far from being a form of nonfiction, is a profoundly fictive kind of writing" (173). As a result he considers it too sophisticated and advanced a form for use by student writers. Such a conclusion reflects the entrenched split in the schools between

121

literature and composition, between reading and writing, between passive reception of knowledge and active creation of knowledge. In *Textual Carnivals* Susan Miller analyzes the "high/low" dichotomy which results in "the tendency to exclude the majority from easy converse with language ideals while containing them in organized spiritual longing for these ideals" (44).

Coming from a perspective on literacy that embraces a world wider than that encased in the academy, Shirley Brice Heath suggests that it "is no accident that the essay, the literary form in which writers *try out* their ideas, became the favourite genre of the English classroom" ("Talking the Text" 111). Talking about a period in the eighteenth and early nineteenth centuries when there were close links between literature and conversation, when people talked about what they read in their parlors and in their periodicals, Heath goes on to say, "Ideally, this form captured the openness of letters and conversations, while also allowing room for including narratives or stories and promoting a particular direction of argument" (111). It has not yet been established, to my knowledge, whether a form matching this description ever in fact did widely dominate classroom discourse, however. The essay in this ideal form is neither the literary essay nor the academic essay as we understand them now. Heath uses the term "literate essay,"[1] a concept that upsets the dichotomy accepted by both essayists and academics between the literary and the learned, both of which essentially exclude students.

Potentially, the ideals of the literate essay—open, conversational, with room for narrative as a part of argument—can mediate between the two unreachable poles and open the doors for an expansion of validated forms of academic essays. Openness in the essay form would allow students to bring their existing literacies into the classroom. Every piece of writing, from friendly letter to dissertation, requires the creation of an authorial self and an imagined audience. The process is not limited to "high" culture. With forms rich in rhetorical possibilities, such as Heath describes, students can engage in a conversation of learning at various levels, in various rhetorical stances.

Of the two existing poles, the ideals of the essay rooted in Montaigne that tried out ideas would be more valuable for learning, but this model has been squeezed out of the classroom in favor of a form still called the essay but antithetical to the intentions of essayists in the Montaigne tradition. The point at which the essay became redirected, I would say misdirected, is reflected in Johnson's 1755 dictionary. His definition of essay is: "A loose sally of the mind; an irregular indigested piece, not a regular and orderly composition." The de-valuation of the essay form is evident in his imagery. The essay does not attack efficiently; it is unfinished and messy, visceral rather than intellectual, ragged rather than symmetrical. In these terms the living and open essay would indeed seem inappropriate for the academy, particularly if the goal of writing instruction is to "clean up" the students (see Miller 57, for example). The "regular and orderly composition," a form rooted in the ancient rhetoric and oratory from which the essayists dissociated themselves, became the model for the academic essay late in the nineteenth century.

Because Fred Newton Scott is a central figure in the discussion that follows, I will use the definition of this academic model offered by Donald Stewart, who has established the important, usually oppositional, role that Scott played in the formation of modern rhetoric. Stewart says, "Most of the writing modern freshmen are encouraged to do is mechanically structured; the five-paragraph essay; the paper split into introduction, body, and conclusion, or beginning, middle, and end; the thesis statement and elaboration" (41).

Although most writing teachers would be horrified to be associated with the "five-paragraph theme," a current and popular text, picked from my shelf at random and even written by a "real" writer rather than an academic, embodies the same relentless, hierarchical, straight-line development:

> We must move in an orderly way, from earlier to later, or from less to more important, or from periphery to center, or from smaller to larger, or from larger to smaller. Sometimes we will want to move from center to periphery, from present to past. But we must not scatter our sequence—from larger to smaller to larger to larger to smaller to largest to larger to smallest to large. We may want ABCDEF. On occasion we may want ZYXWV, but never AQIXLD. (Hall 267)

It would seem that a form so solidly ensconced in academia would have been discussed as composition was establishing a place in the curriculum, its merits extolled, its shortcomings lamented. It may be that such discussions can be found in the archives of colleges and universities all over the country, and such searches would be worth undertaking by those who have access to those records. In the texts, the professional journals, and the popular journals appearing from roughly 1870 to 1920, however, justification for the form of the essay so familiar to us was rarely mentioned. The form slipped into place and has remained largely unchallenged. We complain about it, but it does not abdicate its controlling position.

Histories of rhetoric and composition and English departments offer some clues, nonetheless, in their descriptions of the conditions surrounding the rigidification of the academic essay (see, for example, Berlin, Halloran, Kitzhaber, and Ohmann). Early in the nineteenth century the teaching of writing in the colleges occurred largely in a mentor relationship. Edward Everett Hale, for example, says that Edward T. Channing, Boylston Professor of Rhetoric at Harvard from 1819-51, "read our crude themes, corrected them, and made us sit by his side while he improved them. He laughed at the bombast, struck out the superfluities rigorously and compelled us to say what we really knew and really thought" (qtd. in Bainton 182). Higher education was still mostly for gentlemen of the privileged classes preparing for professions in law, medicine, or the ministry. The prescribed curriculum centered on Greek and Latin, and English was treated as a fine, not a practical, art. Toward the end of the century, however, education changed. The classics were no longer the center, the new sciences were clamoring for a place, increasing numbers of students from a wider socioeconomic spectrum were entering higher education, new colleges and land grant universities were opening, and ideals of meritocracy and Social Darwinism motivated the business world. English was fighting for a place in the new educational order. Two pressures prevailed: the need to be scientific and, from the business world, the demand for efficiency.

Against this background, a look at some of the composition texts and journal conversations of the period will help to illustrate how Montaigne's version of the essay died in the academy and the academic essay fell into place.[2] The squeezing of the exploratory essay into the didactic essay is not, of course, the work of any one person, but it is startlingly evident in a text by Charles Sears Baldwin, Professor of Rhetoric at Columbia. In *Composition: Oral and Written*, published in 1909 as a revision of his earlier *College Manual of Rhetoric* to "serve those colleges who wish more detailed review of elementary applications, and less detailed study of style" (v), Baldwin in seven steps and seven pages redefines the essay from "a trial or a sketch" (341) to "an orderly, logical development by paragraphs" (347). In order to accomplish this transformation, he divides the essay into the *Spectator* type—loose, short, descriptive, sometimes fragmentary—and the *Edinburgh Review* type—logically sustained, descriptive only incidentally, paragraphed in logical units or stages. These types correspond with the two types discussed here: the Montaigne tradition and the academic essay.

Baldwin begins his redefinition by limiting the trial or sketch to explanations rather than representations of life and then goes one step further, from explanations of life to abstract ideas:

Step 1: "a trial or a sketch" (341)

Step 2: "Their common goal is less to suggest or represent life as it comes to us through our five senses than to comment on life, to explain its underlying principles, to set forth the writer's ideas." (341-42)

Step 3: "Its goal is some general, abstract idea, some principle or proposition, in a word, some idea." (342)

Steps 4 through 6 involve some prior assumptions about form, making the connection with oral rhetoric:

Step 4: "This being the object of an essay, its method is generally by paragraphs, as in a speech." (343)

Step 5: "We may revise our general definition, therefore, by calling an essay an exposition of ideas." (343)

Step 6: "Finally, then, an essay may be defined as an exposition by paragraphs of a single controlling idea." (343)

In other words, the very presence of an idea necessitates a proposition, which is of course developed in paragraphs into an exposition no longer of ideas, as in step one, but of one single controlling idea. All possibility of an interplay among ideas, much less of a conversation with the audience, is excluded.

These three steps are taken in a single paragraph and, despite what step 6 suggests, are not yet final. One step remains. At this point Baldwin divides the essay into the stricter and looser categories mentioned earlier on the basis of "the handling of the paragraph" (344). He offers Bacon's "Of Ceremonies and Respects" as his example of the stricter category, and right away his definition is in trouble, as he realizes with a neat sidestep: "This [essay] is clearly systematic; but where are the paragraphs? The answer is in the habit of Bacon's mind. He was content to formulate in concise, suggestive summary. He had none of the public speaker's wish to develop an idea fully. He has very little amplification. Thus for the average man his essays make too hard reading. . . . Bacon's readers are limited to the intellectual" (345). Baldwin's position would exclude the "average man" from intellectual culture. Yet Bacon's own characterization of his aphoristic essay, one among the methods for the transmission of learning that he discusses, is: "Aphorisms, representing a knowledge broken, do invite men to inquire further; whereas methods, carrying the show of a total, do secure men, as if they were at furthest" (173; see also Klaus 157). In opposition to the closure of "method," Bacon values "knowledge that is delivered as a thread to be spun on" (171). Baldwin's need to distort previous essayists to fit his form is apparent when one realizes that the appearance of the modern paragraph in rhetoric texts is usually traced to Alexander Bain, writing in 1866 (see Connors, "Rise and Fall" 448), over two centuries after Bacon wrote his essays. Yet after pointing out one putative paragraph break in the Bacon essay, Baldwin directs his student reader: "Point out the ends of other undeveloped paragraphs" (346).

Hence, according to Baldwin, Bacon, though learned, is not the perfect model for students. Rather than turning to the *Spectator* type of essay, which "aimed to keep the character of good conversation" (346), however, Baldwin moves on to his nineteenth-century model, the *Edinburgh Review*, and its noted contributor, Macaulay. Here he finds essays that "wished to carry a reader through a definite course of thought to a definite conclusion" (347), and he concludes: "This type of essay was followed later by Cardinal Newman, Matthew Arnold, and so many others of recent times that when we hear the word *essay* to-day we think naturally of an orderly, logical development by paragraphs" (347).

Step 7: "an orderly, logical development by paragraphs."

Putting steps 6 and 7 together, Baldwin's definition of the academic essay becomes:

> An essay may be defined as an orderly, logical development by paragraphs of a single controlling idea.

The exploratory essay has been displaced and either demeaned as "loose" or exalted as too intellectual; only the orderly, "scientific," didactic essay is fit for the academy. In the process all of the writing occurring outside of the academic world has been ignored as though the students arrive from a literate vacuum. Their own literacies are negated, denying students access to writing that could be purposeful and effective, could critique and alter the worlds they live in.

In a piece written for the *Educational Review* in 1914 Baldwin states explicitly the educational value he places on the essay form that he has chosen. It embodies "logical methods of structure which constitute an almost unique and indispensable discipline in higher education, and which indubitably stimulate even the average educated intelligence to surer grasp of knowledge and more effective use" ("The College Teaching of Rhetoric" 3). The concept of "mental discipline" is a prevalent theme in nineteenth-century discussions of education at every level. Often the argument for composition as mental discipline is directly linked with the displacement of the classics from the center of the curriculum.[3] Henry Pearson, who was teaching composition at MIT, sums up the position: "The instant and practical value of the study of English is evident; but teachers should realize and remember that besides this it is possible to get from the living tongue much of the training which past generations got from dead ones." He goes on to the specific form of the essay: "The planning of the simplest theme, if done intelligently, is an exercise in ordering thought, and in properly shaping a series of ideas. . . . Even more necessary is it for the learner to perceive that this same literary form is an absolute essential of all clear thinking, and that thought, to be adequate, must be orderly" (xii). The underlying assumption of these claims is that all human thought of any value exists in linear, hierarchical form, that the academic essay is a "natural" reflection and vehicle for transmission of all thinking. The connection with training in classical languages also keeps essay writing linked to the precepts of oral rhetoric.

The need to "scientize" rhetoric in order to ensure its place in the new curriculum must also have influenced Baldwin despite the fact that in the same 1914 article he says, "The large abstract relations, the logic of parts in the whole, might perhaps be inculcated sufficiently by science; but rhetoric asks further the relations to human life"; that is, it should "stir and satisfy the public" (16). If rhetoric does demand not just system but relations to human life, and I certainly would agree, Baldwin would have done better to choose the *Spectator* model of the essay for students. In it they could initiate a conversation between their prior knowledge and the new knowledge they encountered in their classes. Apparently, however, the need to be validated as a worthy scientific subject was stronger than the recognition of the more human and potentially more egalitarian role of rhetoric, a role that could actually include students. Baldwin goes on to say that "for all students [rhetoric] may be the effective *organon* of the sciences" (20), that rhetoric as he presents it embraces the logic of all thought (9).

It could be argued that Baldwin's was just a particularly systematic mind, but the social and cultural forces in ascendancy at the time may be seen perhaps even more clearly in texts written by Fred Newton Scott, which show the same tendency toward increasing rigidity of form in spite of Scott's opposition to much of that tendency. Scott, as Stewart has pointed out on numerous occasions, was a counterforce to the way that composition was developing in the Eastern schools.

Head of the Rhetoric Department at the University of Michigan, Scott was a strong proponent of the growth model as opposed to the manufacturing model, in both composition and education. He kept his eye more on students than on systems. One of his battles was against the uniform college entrance exams which were determining the course of high school curricula. He preferred the certification method whereby schools were visited and certified on the basis of the quality of their preparatory programs. After Harvard published a series of reports on composition and rhetoric between 1892 and 1897 that were damning of the "fitting" schools, as academies and high schools were called, and condescending toward students, Scott in 1909 published a spirited response. He wonders:

> Back of this mess and confusion were genuine individuals with likes and dislikes, with budding ambitions, with tingling senses, with impulses toward right and wrong. Where did these individuals come in when judgement was passed upon their faulty English? What were they trying to do? What motives lay behind these queer antics of the pen? If one could only tear away the swathings, set the imprisoned spirits free, and interrogate them, a strange new light might be thrown upon the causes of bad English.
>
> Another thought occurred to me as I read the reports. Should we not—at least those of us who are pragmatic philosophers—apply to the young offenders the crucial test of pragmatism? Where are they now, the writers of these rejected addresses? Are they in jail? Are they social outcasts? Are they editing yellow journals, or in other ways defiling the well of English? Or are they eloquent preachers, successful lawyers, persuasive insurance agents, leaders of society? ("What the West Wants in Preparatory English" 18; see also Stewart 39)

An essay by Scott is always refreshing in the debates of this era, yet even he was not immune to the pressures of the times which reduced the essay to a predetermined form. With Joseph Villiers Denney of Ohio State University, he published several texts that went through numerous editions and revisions, and a close look at four of these texts, published between 1895 and 1911, illustrates a move away from the view of writing as a growth of ideas and toward a thesis-centered linear model for the essay. The texts under review are: *Paragraph-Writing*, third edition, 1895; *Composition-Rhetoric*, second edition, 1898; *Composition-Literature*, 1902; and *The New Composition-Rhetoric*, 1911. These texts will be referred to below by date of publication.

Led by its focus on the paragraph as a unit, even the first text opens its preface with assembly-line language: "Learning to write well in one's own language means in large part learning to give unity and coherence to one's ideas. It means learning to construct units of discourse which have order and symmetry and coherence of parts" (1895 iii; from 1893 preface). Later in the same text, though, Scott and Denney refer to the new psychology of William James, saying, "the thought-process consists of a series of leaps and pauses," moving toward a central thought, to fill what James calls "an aching gap." Scott and Denney add, "The feeble mind feels only in a vague way the propulsion toward the central idea; the genius often flies toward the goal as unerringly as the armature leaps to the magnet," reflecting their view of the direct linearity of the "best" minds. In composing, say Scott and Denney, the writer "traverses the same ground (though not always necessarily in the same order) that he traversed in his thought. The essay, therefore, is not a fortuitous concourse of ideas. It is a careful record of the mind's activity when exercised in a single direction. This fact it is which gives the essay that striking characteristic known as organic unity." This characterization of the essay mixes elements of the essay that follows the irregular paths of the mind's activity with the ordering principle of "single direction." James's description of the thought process does embody moving toward an end point, yet Scott and Denney feel compelled to straighten out even the leaps and pauses into a linear form: "The essay, with its beginning, its development, and its conclusion, owes its existence to the peculiar way in which writers do their thinking" (1895 94–95). Even though the mind may not have proceeded from beginning to middle to end, the linear essay is considered "a careful record of the mind's activity." Such an essay has no leaps and pauses. Again, the assumption has been made that the orderly, straight-line essay is the perfect reflection of the mind's workings, which allows Scott and Denney to gloss over the contradictions inherent in their incorporation of James's ideas.

The most vivid expression of the organic basis of Scott's and Denney's thought occurs in the 1897 preface to the first edition of *Composition-Rhetoric*, reprinted in the second:

> A composition is regarded not as a dead form, to be analyzed into its component parts, but as a living product of an active, creative mind. The paragraph is compared to a plant, springing up in the soil of the mind from a germinal idea, and in the course of its development assuming naturally a variety of forms. This kinetic conception of discourse, besides being psychologically more correct, has proved to be practically more helpful and inspiring in composition classes than the static conception which it is intended to displace. (iv)

When brought into conjunction later in the text with the already-standard formula item "topic sentence," however, the plant begins to take on a slightly different kind of life: "A general subject narrowed to the point where it expresses just what the paragraph is to contain is called the theme or topic of the paragraph. The theme is to the paragraph what the seed is to the plant; it is the paragraph in embryo" (44). The "active creative mind" is beginning to surrender power to the paragraph.

In the 1902 text, *Composition-Literature*, the preface claims that the book still embodies "the conception of a composition as a growth" (iii), but the metaphor has undergone a subtle alteration:

> The seed is the plant that is to be; the topic statement contains in embryo all that the fully developed paragraph will bring to light. Each seed is the prophecy of a particular kind of growth and the various kinds of plant growth are infinite in number. So it is with the forms in which a growing idea clothes itself as a topic statement and develops into a paragraph. (98)

The plant no longer springs up in the soil of the mind from a germinal idea; now the seed is the topic sentence and it determines the nature of the plant, though apparently the possibilities for form are still various.

In a chapter entitled "How Compositions Grow" another metaphor is introduced which removes the power of forming still further from the mind:

> At the start a composition is merely a vague idea. . . . a luminous fog-bank. . . . The experienced writer . . . knows that this first vague conception is worthless unless it can be made to grow into some definite form. He also knows that the way to make it grow is to reflect upon it long and patiently. Instead of beginning to write, he therefore begins to ponder, turning the idea over and over in his mind and looking at it from all sides and from various angles. As he does so the idea grows clearer. It separates into parts, and these parts again separate, until there are numerous divisions. As he continues to reflect, these divisions link themselves one to another to form natural groups, and these groups arrange themselves in an orderly way. In the end, if he thinks long enough and patiently enough, he finds that the first vague idea has grown into a symmetrical structure. (49–50)

The plant which had sprung up and assumed its natural form, one among the forms that were referred to in 1895 as "infinite in number," is now a "luminous fog-bank" (49) which must be made to reveal a "symmetrical structure." The process of division is still a biological model, but the order is imposed rather than inherent and various. Since the psychology of James suggests that the *mind* does not work symmetrically, the urge for order has transposed the symmetry onto the *idea*, separating it from the mind. Many shapes are potential in a fog-bank, but the implication here is that thought will inevitably discover the symmetrical structure of the idea. In fact, the next sentence reads, "Thinking a vague idea out into its natural and logical divisions and arranging these divisions in an orderly way is called planning" (50). In the texts of this period "plan" is another word for "outline." Although Scott and Denney allow for considerable flexibility in planning and continue to use organic terminology—"groups arrange themselves"—they are heading for imposed form rather than organic growth.

In the 1911 revision, "growth" is mentioned in the table of contents but never in the preface. Instead, "Composition is regarded as a social act, and the student is led to think of himself as writing or speaking for a specified audience." This audience goal has a modern ring to it. The authors go on, though: "Thus not mere expression but communication as well is made the business of composition." So the audience has no part in forming the knowledge; it merely receives the business transaction. Next, Scott and Denney add: "While [the student's] chief purpose is to produce something readable, interesting, and perhaps valuable, he is led to consider questions of form at the same time" (iii). Content may be called the "chief purpose" of writing, but in the syntax of the sentence it is subordinated to form. The authors announce that a new feature in this edition is that "topics are drawn not only from literature and student life, but from the vocations towards which various classes of students are naturally tending" (iv). "Naturally." The predetermined inevitability of the essay form seems to have been extended to the shapes of individual students' lives and to the "natural" classation of society. In this revision the chapter on "How Compositions Grow" introduces the "luminous fog-bank" discussion with a new paragraph: "We have seen that every good composition is a unit made up of smaller units which are closely related. We are now to consider the process by which compositions are produced" (20). The units of composition are becoming more and more detached from thought. Later the "Need for Exposition" is rationalized on the basis of a banking concept of education: "That one age is able to surpass the foregoing in knowledge is due, in large part, to the fact that by means of exposition we pass on the results of study and investigation from one generation to the next" (305). "Business . . . vocations . . . produced . . . classes of students . . . pass on . . .": Scott and Denney have moved students right onto the assembly line.

In the end of this Preface, Scott and Denney come close in both content and tone to the rigidity of form seen in Baldwin's work:

> In the study of the paragraph, attention is called repeatedly to
> the predication made by the topic statement, in order that students
> may learn the difference between general subject and immediate
> topic. This is one of the logical features of composition work that
> can hardly be overemphasized. Other logical aspects of compo-
> sition are not neglected. The laws of association of ideas are
> presented, and practice is afforded in the logical analysis of literary
> wholes into their constituent units. (iv)

In order to arrive at this point they have to go through considerable
metaphorical contortions because of what they know from James about
how the mind works, just as Baldwin has to sidestep around models
of writing because of what he knows about actual essay texts.

I do not want to denigrate Fred Newton Scott in any way. His
educational theories are sound, his attitudes toward students humane.
The flat, tight tone of the above passage does not represent the Fred
Newton Scott who two years earlier worried about the "imprisoned
spirits" of students. To illustrate that even his texts move in the
direction of rigid, hierarchical, linear form for the essay shows how
relentless this development was. Rigor mortis had occurred. The essay
form which could lead students into the conversations of educated
men and women was crushed by what many texts of the time, including
Scott and Denney's, labelled the "didactic essay." It is a one-way
transmission, suitable for expert treatises and apprentice feedback
examinations perhaps. But our students must adopt an utterly sterile
rhetorical stance when we ask them to produce the academic essay as
a matter of course in all stages of their learning.

Exacerbating the limitations of the academic essay in composition
courses at the turn of the century was an emphasis on mechanical
correctness, with its exclusionary intentions (see Connors, "Rhetoric";
Halloran; Miller; Ohmann). A student in Harvard's English A during
this period sums up the effect on him:

> A great weeding out process has been in operation, estimable and
> effective when the Freshman looks properly at the matter. He
> must see that he has been really made over, or rather, that his
> style of composition has been remolded into firmer mate-
> rial. . . . (Copeland and Rideout 81)

Richard Ohmann's analysis of this remaking process that began in
first-year composition a century ago and continues today is worth
quoting at length:

> The things we have traditionally attempted to teach: organizing
> information, drawing conclusions from it, making reports, using
> Standard English (i.e., the language of the bourgeois elites), solving

problems (assignments), keeping one's audience in mind, seeking objectivity and detachment, conducting persuasive arguments, reading either quickly or closely, as circumstances demand, producing work on request and under pressure, valuing the intellect and its achievements. . . . Even if our record of achievement is spotty in these matters—as it certainly is—the mere fact of a student's *having to submit* to our regimen of verbal and logical graces shows him where some of society's values lie. (301–2; emphasis in original)

We have made some progress in recognizing how exclusionary our mania for correctness in language is. We understand more about dialects and, at a level of deeper complexity, more about how students from non-mainstream literacies use language in ways that are different from the "standard" and hence disempowered. Much of what Ohmann says, though, relates to the essay form we impose on students, and we are less aware of how alienating, how damaging, that form can be than we are of the destructiveness of a focus on correctness. In the name of academic discourse we insist on the "rational" linear form to "report" knowledge in a "detached" and "objective" way. Michael Prince has recently pointed out that eighteenth-century thinkers "understood that cultural knowledge was often encased within genres of writing that excluded the vast majority of people eager for education" (731). With our insistence upon the didactic essay, we are excluding from productive academic discourse many of our own students who have made it through the weeding-out process, and we are killing their eagerness for education.

Evidence for the damaging effects of the hegemony of the academic essay comes from pedagogical theory, from cognitive psychology, from feminist studies, and from our own students. Students for whom the academic essay is not congenial are frustrated or blocked or cynical, separated from their learning because their minds do not easily adopt the linear, hierarchical structure that the academic essay assumes is "natural" for all minds (Sanborn). Twenty years ago Keith Fort made a strong argument for the ways in which the thesis-driven essay limits how we can read; if the point of the essay is to prove a thesis, then we can only choose theses which are provable (631). He goes on to say, "To insist on the standard form of the essay is to condition students to think in terms of authority and hierarchy" (635).

By rooting the academic essay in the rhetorical mode of a speaker presenting finished thought to a receptive audience, we are perpetuating a model of learning we no longer espouse and a political homogeneity we no longer experience or even imagine. The parallel tradition of the conversational essay, which assumes community and invites the reader in, gives us a model more appropriate for our world. The canonized models of this essay form we call "literary," but by using Heath's term "literate" we can invite students into the genre.

We are also assuming a single linguistic standard when we privilege the traditional academic essay. Leslie Marmon Silko has offered one example of another mode: "For those of you accustomed to a structure that moves from point A to point B to point C, this presentation may be somewhat difficult to follow because the structure of Pueblo expression resembles something like a spider's web—with many little threads radiating from a center, criss-crossing each other. As with the web, the structure will emerge as it is made and you must simply listen and trust, as the Pueblo people do, that meaning will be made" (54).

In the fields of linguistics and psychology, pluralism is replacing monolithic views of language and mind. A recent article by Vera John-Steiner, "Cognitive Pluralism: A Whorfian Analysis," makes it clear that there is no one "natural" way in which the mind works. Not only is the human mind capable of multiple forms of thought (John-Steiner, *Notebooks*; see also Gardner), but the individual mind is capable of access to various modes, although each of us may have a preferred way of thinking. Rather than the continuum suggested by the concept of multiplicity, ranging, for example, from verbal to visual, John-Steiner's concept of cognitive pluralism moves the possibilities off the line and into a field, where it is impossible to impose polar dichotomies. Now that we have accepted pluralism in dialects, we need to accept pluralism in minds and stop shutting off our students' thinking by attempting to jam it into a single acceptable mode. Such pluralism need not be what Miller calls "benign but finally static" (195); dialogues arising from multiple minds and within the multiple possibilities of each mind would open paths to purposeful and effective written discourse. The monologic essay has its place in expert treatises and inexpert examinations, but it should make room for more dialogic writing, more woven writing, more literate essays to inhabit the field between literary and learned where our students and most of us live.

The work currently being done on women's ways of knowing and writing is becoming well known (e.g., Belenky et al.; Gilligan; Martin). Like discussions of the essay form and like Silko's representation of Pueblo expression, feminist scholarship is full of images of web and tapestry. As an illustration here of how women may approach writing in a less straight-line fashion than the academic essay requires, I will in keeping with my material turn to a writer of the early nineteenth century, Mary Clavers, who wrote under the pen name Caroline

Kirkland.[4] Kirkland wrote of her journey westward in a book published in 1839, and throughout her narrative repeatedly apologizes that "this rambling, gossiping style, this going back to take up the dropped stitches, is not the orthodox way of telling one's story," but she "despair[s] of improvement" (140). Later she says, "I will make an effort to retain the floating end of my broken thread" (189). At the end of her book she is distressed by "a conclusion wherein nothing is concluded" but finds her appropriate last words:

> But such simple and sauntering stories are like Scotch reels, which have no natural ending, save the fatigue of those engaged. So I may as well cut short my mazy dance and resume at once my proper position as a "wall-flower," with an unceremonious adieu to the kind and courteous reader.
> THE END (317)

The language of sewing, weaving, and dance, so frequent in feminist theory, captures the essence of the woven essay, this "mazy dance." Its dropped stitches, the turns of the reel, invite the reader in. These turnings also allow the writing to follow the convolutions of thought. It is a mode far closer to the ways in which we now talk about learning and thinking and collaboration than is the traditional academic essay. It may be a way in which many students, regardless of gender, can enter into academic discourse without being "made over." And it may enlarge academic discourse itself by picking up those threads that have been lopped off in the quest for "an orderly, logical development by paragraphs of a single controlling idea."

The open, woven essay forms allow a student to engage in conversation with texts and other forms of new knowledge. The essay forms proposed as alternatives to the academic essay have no thesis statement, but that does not mean they have no *point*. The meanings are embedded in the journey of the essay, not isolated in the last sentence of the first paragraph. In order to read such essays we have to bypass the template in our heads that is ready to receive a didactic essay and enter instead into the essay in our hands, to take the journey with the writer. This process will bring both our students and ourselves back into the conversations of learning.

Notes

1. Heath's "The Literate Essay: Using Ethnography to Explode Myths" is a multilayered example of the sort of essay she is espousing and includes a metacommentary on what she is doing.

2. The sources cited in this chapter are representative of some 127 texts, rhetorics, and books about writing and 156 periodical articles chosen from the collections of the Green Library and the Cubberley Library at Stanford University. Most of the work consulted is about college composition from 1870 to 1920, but some earlier and later works and some high school texts are included in the sample for comparison. I am indebted to Shirley Brice Heath for her sponsorship of this project and for her conversation throughout its duration.

3. Susan Miller argues that present historians of composition also forge links to classical rhetoric in order to legitimize the field of composition. She suggests that there is a discontinuity between the oral rhetorical tradition and written discourse.

4. I am indebted to Josephine Donovan for suggesting that I look at Caroline Kirkland. For her own use of Kirkland's work see "Sarah Orne Jewett's Critical Theory: Notes Toward a Feminine Literary Mode."

Works Cited

Anderson, Chris, ed. *Literary Nonfiction: Theory, Criticism, Pedagogy.* Carbondale: Southern Illinois UP, 1989.

Bacon, Francis. *The Advancement of Learning.* 1605. Ed. William Aldis Wright. Oxford: Clarendon, 1869.

Bain, Alexander. *English Composition and Rhetoric.* New York: Appleton, 1866.

Bainton, George. *The Art of Authorship.* New York: Appleton, 1866.

Baldwin, Charles Sears. *A College Manual of Rhetoric.* New York: Longmans, Green, 1902.

———. *Composition: Oral and Written.* New York: Longmans, Green, 1909.

———. "The College Teaching of Rhetoric." *Educational Review* 48 (June 1914): 1–20.

Belenky, Mary Field, Blythe McVicker Clinchy, Nancy Rule Goldberger, and Jill Mattuck Tarule. *Women's Ways of Knowing: The Development of Self, Voice, and Mind.* New York: Basic Books, 1986.

Berlin, James. *Writing Instruction in Nineteenth-Century American Colleges.* Carbondale: Southern Illinois UP, 1984.

———. *Rhetoric and Reality: Writing Instruction in American Colleges, 1900–1985.* Carbondale: Southern Illinois UP, 1987.

Butrym, Alexander, ed. *Essays on the Essay: Redefining the Genre.* Athens: U of Georgia P, 1989.

Connors, Robert J. "The Rhetoric of Mechanical Correctness." In *Only Connect: Uniting Reading and Writing.* Ed. Thomas Newkirk. Upper Montclair, NJ: Boynton/Cook, 1986. 27–58.

———. "The Rise and Fall of the Modes of Discourse." *College Composition and Communication* 32.4 (Dec. 1981): 444–55.

Copeland, C. T., and H. M. Rideout. *Freshman English and Theme-Correcting in Harvard College.* New York: Silver, Burdett, 1901.

Donovan, Josephine. "Sarah Orne Jewett's Critical Theory: Notes Toward a Feminine Literary Mode." In *Critical Essays on Sarah Orne Jewett*. Ed. Gwen C. Nagel. Boston: Hall, 1984. 212–25.

Fort, Keith. "Form, Authority, and the Critical Essay." *College English* 33.6 (Mar. 1971): 629–39.

Gardner, Howard. *Frames of Mind: The Theory of Multiple Intelligences*. New York: Basic Books, 1983.

Gilligan, Carol. *In a Different Voice: Psychological Theory and Women's Development*. Cambridge: Harvard UP, 1982.

Good, Graham. *The Observing Self: Rediscovering the Essay*. New York: Routledge, 1988.

Hall, Donald. *Writing Well*. 5th ed. Boston: Little, Brown, 1985.

Halloran, S. Michael. "From Rhetoric to Composition: The Teaching of Writing in America to 1900." In *A Short History of Writing Instruction: From Ancient Greece to Twentieth-century America*. Ed. James J. Murphy. Davis, CA: Hermagoras, 1990. 151–82.

Heath, Shirley Brice. "The Literate Essay: Using Ethnography to Explode Myths." In *Language, Literacy and Culture: Issues of Society and Schooling*. Ed. Judith A. Langer. Norwood, NJ: Ablex, 1987. 89–107.

———. "Talking the Text in Teaching Composition." In *Language, Authority and Criticism: Readings on the School Textbook*. Ed. Suzanne de Castell, Allan Luke, and Carmen Luke. London: Falmer, 1989. 109–22.

John-Steiner, Vera. "Cognitive Pluralism: A Whorfian Analysis." In *The Influence of Language on Culture and Thought*. Ed. Robert L. Cooper and Bernard Spolsky. The Hague: Mouton, 1991. 61–74.

———. *Notebooks of the Mind: Explorations of Thinking*. Albuquerque: U of New Mexico P, 1985.

Kirkland, Caroline. *A New Home—Who'll Follow? Or, Glimpses of Western Life*. 1839. New York: Garrett, 1969.

Kitzhaber, Albert R. *Rhetoric in American Colleges, 1850–1900*. Diss. U of Washington, 1953.

Klaus, Carl H. "Essayists on the Essay." In *Literary Nonfiction*. Ed. Chris Anderson. Carbondale: Southern Illinois UP, 1989. 155–75.

Krutch, Joseph Wood. "No Essays, Please!" *The Saturday Review* 10 Mar. 1951: 18–19; 35.

Martin, Jane Roland. *Reclaiming a Conversation: The Ideal of the Educated Woman*. New Haven: Yale UP, 1985.

Miller, Susan. *Textual Carnivals: The Politics of Composition*. Carbondale: Southern Illinois UP, 1991.

Ohmann, Richard. *English in America: A Radical View of the Profession*. New York: Oxford UP, 1976.

Pearson, Henry G. *The Principles of Composition*. Boston: Heath, 1898.

Prince, Michael B. "Literacy and Genre: Towards a Pedagogy of Mediation." *College English* 51.7 (November 1989): 730–49.

Sanborn, Jean. "The Academic Essay: A Feminist View in Student Voices." In *Gender Issues in the Teaching of English*. Ed. Bruce Appleby and Nancy McCracken. Portsmouth, NH: Boynton/Cook, 1992.

Scott, Fred Newton. "What the West Wants in Preparatory English." *School Review* 17.1 (June 1909): 10–20.

Scott, Fred Newton, and Joseph Villiers Denney. *Paragraph-Writing*. Boston: Allyn and Bacon, 1891. 2d ed. 1893. 3d ed. 1895.

———. *Composition-Rhetoric*. Boston: Allyn and Bacon, 1897. 2d ed. 1898.

———. *Composition-Literature*. Boston: Allyn and Bacon, 1902.

———. *The New Composition-Rhetoric*. Boston: Allyn and Bacon, 1911.

Silko, Leslie Marmon. "Language and Literature from a Pueblo Indian Perspective." In *English Literature: Opening up the Canon*. Ed. Leslie A. Fiedler and Houston Baker, Jr. Baltimore: Johns Hopkins UP, 1981. 54–72.

Stewart, Donald C. "Fred Newton Scott." In *Traditions of Inquiry*. Ed. John Brereton. New York: Oxford UP, 1985. 26–49.

10 Re-envisioning the Journal: Writing the Self into Community

Sharyn Lowenstein
Lesley College

Elizabeth Chiseri-Strater
University of North Carolina at Greensboro

Cinthia Gannett
University of New Hampshire at Manchester

Journals have become increasingly popular in composition pedagogy and writing-across-the-curriculum movements because of their adaptability and their potential to promote individualized learning. At the same time, however, that many institutions and faculty development committees are hiring consultants or offering workshops on the value and pragmatics of journal-based pedagogies, school journal writing is under strong political attack from both inside and outside the academy. Some educators and parent groups opposed to journals view the practice as trivial, a waste of class time; for others journals are seen as so powerfully subversive that lawyers are being hired to sue for the prohibition of all journal writing in those schools (Gannett 34–39). Since it is unlikely that journals are both simultaneously valuable and trivial or simultaneously trivial and dangerous, we can safely assume that the notion "journal" acts primarily as a cover term for a variety of political and pedagogical arguments about writing practices and their functions in schooling.

From the beginning of its current pedagogical incarnation as a part of the writing-process (or expressivist) movement of the 1960s, the journal has been identified as a primary tool for increasing fluency, stimulating creativity, and personalizing learning. Peter Elbow, an important proponent of the journal in composition, testifies in *Writing without Teachers* to the value of freewriting in journals as a way of preventing premature editing while encouraging both creativity and fluency. Don Murray, also closely identified with promoting journaling as a central part of composition pedagogy, explains to students that his journal, which he calls a daybook, "has become the most valuable resource I have" (68).

Ironically, many detractors fault the use of journals in school for precisely these same "personal" and "expressive" qualities. George Will, in an editorial lambasting the current state of affairs in American schools, attributes part of our "educational decline" to the use of journals in college courses, asserting that on certain campuses "writing requirements are reduced to the mere writing of a journal, a virtually standardless exercise in 'self-expression' that 'empowers' students" (8).

Daniel Singal, in a more thorough jeremiad in *The Atlantic Monthly*, also faults school journals for their focus on self-expression and self-reflection, which he sees as displacing what he calls "analytic writing." Singal claims:

> This is a generation whose members may be better equipped to track the progress of their souls in diaries than any group of Americans since the Puritans. But as for writing papers in college, or later, producing the sorts of documents that get the world's work done, that's another story. (67)

Even within the academy, some of those most conversant with the pedagogical applications of the journal have issued their own caveats. In the "NCTE SLATE Guidelines for Using Journals in School Settings" (1987), Toby Fulwiler, the principal author, cautions that private and intimate topics "more properly belong in *personal diaries* than in school journals" (5; emphasis added). A few years earlier, *English Journal* ran a column debating whether the use of personal journals should be abolished in English classes. In this debate, John Hollowell argued against the use of journals, claiming not only that they promote grammatical and mechanical sloppiness, but also that they encourage children to be *self-centered*, and, worst of all, that they "open up a Pandora's box of the child's *personal* experiences" (14; emphasis added).

The tension created by these competing notions of the journal as primarily (or dangerously) "personal" derives from at least two overlapping sources and/or misunderstandings. First, these tensions reflect differences in current conceptions of the self. Some thinkers—implicitly at least—hold the common traditional view of the self as a unique autonomous entity, while others have begun to consider the notion of self as strongly influenced by, located in, or constructed through social domains. Karen Burke LeFevre, for example, in *Invention as a Social Act*, questions the Platonic notion of writing as a solitary act in which the individual searches for innate or individual truths, and instead offers a view of writing in which meaning is built through a "dialectic between the individual and the social realms" (xi). This notion does not deny that individuals construct meaning and identity through writing, but insists that writers are always positioned in relation to larger social discourses.

A second source of misunderstanding is a general lack of awareness of the historical and cultural traditions from which *school* journal practices have developed (Lowenstein, "Personal Journal") and which implicitly inform our current disciplinary practices in complex ways (Gannett). Consider, for example, the philosophical roots of the journal tradition in the British language-across-the-curriculum movement of the 1960s. As Daniel Mahala has reminded us in his recent critique of writing-across-the-curriculum practices, the original purpose of the British effort was to invite the local language and knowledge systems of students—particularly those from culturally diverse or less socio-economically privileged backgrounds—into the British school environment. According to Mahala, the LAC movement attempted to tap into the nonacademic languages of marginalized students in order to develop a classroom "vision of literacy open to the cultural significations that defined the students' lives outside of the classroom" (782). This enlarged notion of literacy and learning would redistribute classroom power to include the active contributions of students, as well as teachers, in the construction of knowledge. As Mahala points out, however, most American scholars and teachers of writing or WAC have ignored the central sociopolitical, educational, and epistemological goals that motivated the British LAC movement, and have thereby fragmented and limited the intellectual empowerment and pedagogical possibilities it offered, possibilities for writing practices—such as the journal—that could transform social inequities. Thus, journal writing across the curriculum has often been reduced either to a tool for recording "egocentric" personal accounts or a vehicle for the socialization of students into specific, often exclusionary, academic discourses. Mahala's critique echoes Joseph Harris's concern over making "mastery" of academic discourse the goal of composition pedagogy, a practice, he suggests, that distorts the complex reality that students and professors are simultaneously both "outsiders and insiders" to multiple, "overlapping" communities or cultures even within the academy. Journal keeping, then, needs to be acknowledged as necessarily composed in and through a polyphony of academic and nonacademic voices, voices from the mainstream and voices from the margins.

We want to re-envision the academic journal as a mediator through which students can engage in larger academic and social conversations both within and outside the academy. We will view the journal not only as a locus for the construction and transformation of the self as learner but also as a means to define, maintain, and transform the writer's connection with discursive and knowledge communities. We will explore our claims about the social and communal nature of journal processes by looking at two quite different journals that nevertheless illustrate a powerful dialectical engagement between self and communities. In the final section, we will consider pedagogical applications of the journal that promote similar conversations among self, the languages of knowing, and multiple discourse communities. This reconception of the journal might help us build a community of learners who, rather than spilling the contents of "Pandora's box" helter skelter, as John Hollowell fears, might keep the discourses of knowledge sufficiently open to release the matter and mind needed to "get the world's work done."

The Journal as Mediator among Communities

> All writers use the language of a community and all must write
> in ways deemed appropriate to and by a community. (Linda
> Brodkey, *Academic Writing as Social Practice*)

The first diary we want to discuss could be categorized as a "personal journal," a genre with a history at least as far back as the tenth century, when Heian court women in Japan kept private "pillow books." This genre encompasses the host of domestic, spiritual, chronicling, and epistolary traditions that have also flourished in a variety of European cultures since the Renaissance (Lowenstein, "Personal Journal"). Working intuitively out of this rich set of traditions, a novice psychology counselor named Marion Milner—who would later become a well-known early-twentieth-century psychotherapist—began a seven-year diary-keeping experiment. The diaries started as a course assignment, but over time they became powerful self-sponsored tools for analysis and reflection. During the fourth year of her journal keeping, she started a second project, a journal on her journal, *A Life of One's Own* (written under the pseudonym Joanna Field), which allowed her to refine and analyze the cumulative insights of her diaries. While her diary work bears the appearance of being "personal" or "expressive," a careful reading readily exposes its social and communal aspects.

Indeed, the first two sentences of the preface to *A Life of One's Own* open it to many of the denigrating epithets, "personal," " trivial," "confessional," or "expressive," with which we have suggested academic journals or diaries are often saddled. Field writes: "This book is the record of seven years' study of living. The aim of the record was to find out what kinds of experience *made me happy*" (11). Yet it is exactly this "expressive," this "personal," language and these simple acts of recording which allow Field to create a self-dialogue to move her beyond expression toward reflection and analysis. One of the most powerful aspects of all journal-keeping practices, both in and out of school, is that the act of recording one's ideas in a text provides distance and objectifies the self, thus creating a dialectic which can open the self to further scrutiny and analysis. Field observes this dialogic interplay, this polyphony of voices among her multiple selves, when she writes:

> It seemed that I was normally only aware of the ripples on the surface of my mind, but the act of writing a thought was a plunge which at once took me into a different element where the past was intensely alive. Although my glimpses of the inhabitants of these deeper waters of the mind were rather disquieting, suggesting creatures whose ways I did not know, I found the act of writing curiously calming.... (60–61)

The reflection caused by the act of writing allowed Field to acknowledge both the transient "ripples" and the multiple layers in the "disquieting deeper waters" of the self, as well as the socially constructed and "calming" nature of language as a means of negotiating and reconstituting her past and present selves. In essence, writing the diary allowed Joanna Field to build a community of selves.

The social nature of Field's journal is also evident in that it functions as a means of trying on the discourses of her profession and allowing her to engage with and reflect on her relationship to the critical voices of her field. During her training in psychoanalytic methods, Field uses her journal to mediate between the authoritative voices of those whose work she is reading (Jung, Freud, Piaget, Descartes) and her own developing habits of thought. The reflexive praxis of rereading her own journals also allows a kind of double empowerment by locating her both within and outside the academy. For example, Field observes that her fear of feminine knowledge and experience, which she calls "subjective intuition," prompts her to overvalue "male objectivity" and the language of authority encoded in much of her formal reading: "So I had for years struggled to talk an intellectual language which for me was barren, struggled to force the feelings of my relation to the universe into terms that would not fit" (15). Clearly, Field writes out of an engagement with—rather than a submission to— the interests, ideas, and epistemological methods of her disciplinary community— psychology—and the great figures in the history of ideas. Her journal-keeping practice allows her to become increasingly aware of alternate systems of producing knowledge based on other parts of her experience, less sanctioned by the academy, but no less valuable.

And sometimes even more valuable. Citing the gap between her own "professional" knowledge and her "personal" understanding as the catalyst for her journal project, Field writes explicitly about the way in which academic knowledge excludes alternate sources of knowing and cultural authority, an experience shared by many mar-ginalized students who feel alienated by academic discourse:

> For instance, I discovered that there is all the difference in the world between knowing something intellectually and knowing it as a 'lived' experience. . . . Actually, it was the uneasy suspicion of this gap between knowing and living that determined the first steps in the development of my method. Remembering Descartes, I set out to doubt everything I had been taught, but I did not try to rebuild my knowledge in a structure of logic and argument. (13)

Field's journal functions as a mediator between the idea-driven world of academia and the world of direct experiences and reflections (the latter often associated with the nonacademic, self-sponsored discourse of mass culture and women's domestic writing and ways of knowing). In fact, the journal actually helps Field write herself *into* her professional community, as she observes: "I suppose it can be said that I was so astonished at what my diary keeping had shown me about the unconscious aspects of one's mind . . . that I eventually became a psychoanalyst" (xx). Ultimately, Field uses the journal both as a way of joining a new academic discipline and eventually as a vehicle for challenging and transforming this community as well.

The Journal as Community: Emmanuel Ringelblum and *Notes from the Warsaw Ghetto*

> Invention becomes explicitly social when writers involve other people as collaborators, or as reviewers whose comments aid invention, or as 'resonators' who nourish the development of ideas. . . . Finally, invention is powerfully influenced by social collectives, such as institutions, bureaucracies, and governments, which transmit expectations and prohibitions, encouraging certain ideas and discouraging others.
>
> —Karen Burke LeFevre, *Invention as a Social Act*

Our second journal has its origins in a much older, but by no means extinct, set of communal journal traditions. Prior to the Renaissance, journals were primarily public documents, written to fulfill community functions, and were frequently composed collaboratively or by multiple authors rather than by a single author. Ancient account books and records, Roman household accounts called *Commentari*, Chinese historical chronicles from A.D. 56, the Anglo-Saxon Chronicles, ships' logs and scientific journals, manorial commonplace books, and records of public bodies like the *Congressional Record* all exemplify this record-keeping and chronicling function (Lowenstein, "Personal Journal"). *The Oxford English Dictionary* notes the following quotation under the entry on *diary*: "In the thirteenth century men never kept journals or diaries but monasteries did." This journal tradition, which has flourished in a variety of forms, was explicitly constructed by and for communities and represents a view that directly contradicts the more limited notion of the journal as "personal" rather than "social." Such journal traditions can help us re-see the dialectical relation between the individual writer and the social domains in which writing happens. Communal journals can also be used as active agents in the construction, maintenance, renewal, and transformation of communities.

Emmanuel Ringelblum's *Notes from the Warsaw Ghetto* is an exemplary journal from this tradition. A powerful day-to-day account of the invasion, occupation, and ultimate annihilation of the Jewish ghetto in Warsaw during World War II, it is not so much the journal of a man as the journal of a community, of a historical period.

Ringelblum started the journal in November 1939 at the age of thirty-nine, two months after the Nazis had invaded Poland. A trained historian and social scientist, Ringelblum was also a social activist committed to popular education and to the relief and welfare of his people. As a staff member of the American Joint Distribution committee, a relief organization which put him in touch with a wide range of workers and officials both inside and outside the ghetto, Ringelblum was well positioned by his access to information as well as by his training and inclination "to record the whole story of the Jewish catastrophe" (ix). Early on, his *Notes* were intended as a possible appeal to humanity to intervene, but later, as hope for rescue or relief dimmed, "the keeping of the records became meaningful as a gesture for posterity—a pure historical act. The future would avenge what the present could not prevent" (xvii).

Applying his professional training—the methods of his academic discourse community—Ringelblum set about the task of gathering, verifying, and assembling data. But he realized immediately that he could not undertake a project of this scope alone; therefore, he recruited, then trained, dozens of ghetto residents to contribute to what would become an impressive one-hundred-volume archive of assembled data, interviews, and summary reports:

> Everyone wrote, journalists and writers, of course, but also teachers, public men, young people, even children. Most of them kept diaries where the tragic events of the day were reflected through the prism of personal experience. A tremendous amount was written; but the vast majority of the writings were destroyed with the annihilation of Warsaw Jewry during the resettlement days. All that has remained is the material we have preserved in our archive project. . . .
>
> And then there were my own notes. They are particularly important for the first year of the war, when other people were not keeping diaries. My weekly and monthly reports not only give the facts about the most important happenings of the time— they also offer an evaluation of them. Because I was active in the community, these evaluations of mine are important as expressions of what the surviving remnant of the Jewish community have thought about their everyday problems. (xxi–xxii)

Ringelblum's *Notes* are drawn from these collective archives. Rarely using the first person, and often disguising the diary as a letter with salutations and closings to prevent discovery, Ringelblum assembles and synthesizes the many archival voices with "epic calm" (xxiii). This collective journal offers several perspectives on the same event (xxii), listing the thousands of facts on the deportations, the beatings, the bribery of officials, the strategies for smuggling supplies in and out of the ghetto, the malicious decrees, the staggering food prices, the war news, and the catalogue of deaths that constitute the horrifying daily reality of this time, as the following excerpt from one entry shows.

> Dear Father, What happened in Wower, outside Warsaw, has been cleared up slightly. It was this way: Some Poles were sitting in a restaurant. Two German policemen came in . . . and began to shout at the Poles. The latter took out revolvers (apparently there was only one) and shot the Germans. Some of the Germans shot were bandits. Nevertheless, They are demanding that the murderers be handed over. Meanwhile, They've ordered the body of the restaurant owner to be exhumed and hanged. He is to hang for all to see for seven days.
>
> The consternation of Friday, December 30, was, it is now said, unfounded. Not a single German was killed. Word has it that this time it was thieves' work. Still another rumor is that a German soldier got into a fist fight at night on Towarowa Street and was knocked out.
>
> The mortality among the Jews in Warsaw is dreadful. There

are fifty to seventy deaths daily. Before the war, the rate used to
be ten. The burial tax rate has been fixed at 50 zlotys in Warsaw
proper and 100 zlotys in the suburb of Prague. In Radom, the
synagogue was burned down, as was the Jewish Council Building.
The same in Torun, where there were 1000 people deported from
Lodz. In Rajsze there are about 6000–7000 refugees from Kalisz,
Lodz, Upper Silesia.... Tonight Dr. Cooperman shot for being
out after eight o'clock. He had a pass.... (8–9)

Fittingly, Ringelblum called this archival project simply O.S., or
"Oneg Sabbath," translated as "Sabbath Celebrants," for those who
had joined together in this collective record-keeping project. The journal
became more than a task set by the community; it became the source
of community itself. Ringelblum himself had several opportunities to
escape, but he refused to leave what he had come to regard as his
life's work. In 1943, "large scale deportation of most of the remaining
Jews in the Warsaw ghetto began. Three hundred thousand Jews were
sent to their death" (xx). But the project went on. The Oneg Sabbath
had become larger than any single person; it had become the collective
voice of the community, the source of meaning and comfort during
chaos, a commemoration through witnessing, a sacred ritual. Ringelblum writes during this time:

The O.S. work was interrupted. Only a handful of our friends
kept pencil in hand and continued to write about what was
happening in Warsaw during those calamitous days. But the work
was too holy for us, it was too deep in our hearts, the O.S. was
too important for the community. We could not stop. (xx)

It is ironic, yet fitting, that Ringelblum, like many of the others, was
executed in 1944 and buried in a collective grave. The work itself is
a stark testament to the power of writing to construct and maintain a
community through a collective act of chronicling, an act of writing
that resisted and ultimately survived the complete physical annihilation
of the community. This writing also has the power to connect and
communicate across time and place to our own communities. *Notes
from the Warsaw Ghetto* not only transforms our sense of history, it
also transforms and empowers each of us as we read the individual
and collective voices that witness and resist hegemony.

Journals and the Academic Community: Pedagogical Implications

Reconceptualizing journal practices through notions of community
within broader social, historical, and political contexts invites educators
to consider new ways to understand and use school-based journals.

We have suggested that the problem is not so much that journal writing is a limited discursive strategy or genre as that our common and outdated notions tend to constrain the power and potential of journals as they are often practiced in school settings. Some of the arguments raised against school journal keeping by those both in and outside of composition studies are then the result of a lack of understanding or a prejudicial view of the history of diary/journal traditions as well as a narrow view of the function of expressive writing.

We propose that school-based journals offer the intellectual and social empowerment that results from harnessing students' expressive languages. Journals can thereby serve as the site of dialogic mediation among students' overlapping literacies, in and out of school (see Chiseri-Strater for a fuller discussion of students' multiple literacies, generally unacknowledged by the academy).

Several articles in *The Journal Book* (Fulwiler) have already helped move composition studies toward this expanded notion of journals and journal keeping as both personal and social constructions. The journal strategies put forth that stimulate heuristic speculation, critical thinking, and reflection within and among discourse communities include the response journal, the dialectic notebook or double-entry journal, the commonplace book, and the writer's apprenticeship journal, just to name a few. Composition researchers and practitioners are coming to understand that the terms "individual" and "social" are not mutually exclusive categories but rather, as LeFevre suggests, "dialectically connected, always co-defining and interdependent" (37). In this final section, we will focus on some further pedagogical implications—which are by no means exhaustive—that follow primarily from our discussion of the Field and Ringelblum journals.

Just as we have discovered important intellectual and social empowerment in reading the journals of Field and Ringelblum, we feel that educators who assign journals might want to familiarize themselves with a range of published journals, diaries, logs, and daybooks in order to imagine new possibilities for using journals in their own curricula. Educators in composition and across the curriculum may find it valuable to give serious attention to the historical traditions of journal writers within their fields and may benefit as well by acquainting themselves with journals and diaries written outside their disciplines. Edited collections of journals and diaries such as Ronald Blythe's *The Pleasures of Diaries*, Margo Culley's *A Day at a Time*, or Thomas Mallon's *A Book of One's Own* provide a useful foundation for looking at journals historically, and at specific types of journals such as the naturalist's diary, the artist's journal, or the explorer's travel log.

Educators within the academy who are part of the writing-across-the-curriculum movement may be receptive to adapting journal practices which come out of the historical and intellectual traditions of their specific disciplines. For example, a nursing educator might want to excerpt nurses' diaries such as Florence Nightingale's personal journals or the accounts of birthing recorded by an early-eighteenth-century Maine midwife in Laurel Ulrich's *Midwife's Tale,* as a means of exploring the central issues of the profession through the real voices, experiences, questions, affirmations, and tensions of specific practitioners through time. Through a discussion and consideration of the ways in which all journals are socially and historically constructed, teachers and learners can start to envision the university as a set of multiple, overlapping discursive knowledge communities. Framing journal assignments within very particular historical, intellectual, and cultural traditions can help students negotiate among multiple discourse communities, to shift between the languages of academia and their own lived experience and local knowledge.

Field's diaries have illustrated the importance of using expressive language to negotiate between the academic language in her reading of Freud and Piaget and her emerging subjective perceptions about the world and thus to position herself in relation to the field of psychology. Student journals in any discipline can be used to mediate between what the students are learning within academic disciplines and the understandings they bring from their own lives and literacies.

Here, for example, is an excerpt from Tricia's journal, assigned in a women's studies course, which illustrates how the journal helps her connect the course material with the larger course of her life:

> This class journal gives me [an] opportunity to document my growth. I know it's supposed to be thoughts related to this class—but this class is so much related to my life, so I can't help letting myself and my life spill over onto these pages . . . I write what I want to write, and I admit some of it—well you'd have to stretch it to really make it relevant to this course. But then, not really. Women are part of life. Their experiences aren't all with children or work or bodily appearance, or "issues." They are—like me, not always getting enough sleep, holding conversations with friends who are in pain, remembering the loss of loved ones. . . .
> But I find that jotting down even far-fetched examples from my personal life helps me understand the class material better and helps me deal with my own life. That's what education means to me. I don't cease being me when I walk into the classroom. (Gannett 177–78)

Tricia's journal documents the need for her to bring different knowledge communities together, the knowledge that she is learning from her course as well as the knowledge of her own personal experiences. Used in this way, a way similar to Field's journal apprenticeship, the academic journal can become a powerful site of negotiation among knowledge communities.

An important pedagogical consideration, also derived from our study of Field's journal practices, is that rereading and reflecting on journal entries is as important as writing them. Students need to be given opportunities to reflect on their journals periodically in order to understand the significance of individual entries or developing patterns and to discover the cumulative insights that journals can provide. For example, whenever Don Murray completes one of his daybooks, he takes the time to reread the entries and pull out the most interesting nuggets, themes, or ideas, which he then uses to start the next daybook. In essence, this reflective reading acts as the yeast to leaven the next text. Taking a cue from Murray, faculty can craft practices which encourage students' reflective and evaluative rereading of their journals and the experience of writing them. Some assignments that encourage students to use their journals as sites of reflective praxis include summarizing the journal entries that best show the student's growth as a writer during the semester; selecting and annotating the entries from a student's journal which display how he or she has tried out different voices (perspectives, models, theories) in the course; evaluating the patterns or themes a student can identify in his or her own thinking over the course of the semester and asking what directions these point to for future growth as a writer, thinker, and learner; and locating one place in the journal where another reader's feedback has helped shape the writer's subsequent entries.

Requiring students to reread, discuss, and evaluate their journals also benefits teachers. Teachers who assign journals sometimes fear that they have insufficient means by which to evaluate them; allowing students to become involved with self-evaluation is one way of addressing this issue. Further, placing the weight of assessment on students circumvents the problem a teacher might have in interpreting individual entries that are not sufficiently contextualized for full understanding by the instructor, although they may be of real significance to the writer.

Composition teachers can ask journal keepers not only to reflect on what they are learning from their entries but to share these insights with the rest of the class as well. One writing student, Jim, said that by rereading and analyzing his journal he was forced to "look back" and to "look deeply" into his own habits of learning. He noted that the act of writing a reflective paper provided him with some insights into the future use of his personal journal, which might best become a "blend of creative writing and research possibilities." Finally, Jim commented on the value of sharing such journal reflections: after listening to the class discuss their own journals, he "finally [came] to a real understanding of how powerful a journal can be." Teachers who are themselves journal keepers can encourage these reflective practices by talking about their own journal-keeping efforts and by sharing their insights from rereading their own journals with their students as well.

A related means of promoting classroom community, while recognizing the polyphony of individual voices, would be through establishing a collaborative class journal. In such a journal, which would be open and available to all, students could be invited to respond to course content or to the events of the class itself; to bring in relevant outside readings, cartoons, jokes, quotations, proverbs; to make suggestions for class activities, speakers, and readings; or to enter passages from their individual journals. Discursive authority is redistributed by this type of journal since the teacher's voice becomes just one among many. Another alternative for constructing a collaborative journal might be for students to create a conversation through a computer network in which their journal entries are read, shared, and responded to online with others in the network. Or, students engaged in collaborative writing projects might be encouraged to keep a journal together which would reflect their research efforts as well as chart the learning connected with their work as a group. Whatever the format or purpose of the school journal, students can always formally acknowledge the power of their individual and collective voices through communal celebrations or group readings in which they create and define themselves as learners by sharing excerpts of their journal writing.

Such deliberate efforts at promoting community through journal writing may result in new practices that help students re-envision the shape of their own self-sponsored literacies and learning while maintaining, sustaining, and even transforming the community of the classroom itself. Socially constructed journal-writing practices should help empower student writers within their own learning communities, assist them in resisting institutionalized language practices, and encourage them to use both expressive and academic writing to get their work *and* "the world's work" done.

Works Cited

Belenky, Mary Field, Blythe McVicker Clinchy, Nancy Rule Goldberger, and Jill Mattuck Tarule. *Women's Ways of Knowing: The Development of Self, Voice, and Mind.* New York: Basic Books, 1986.

Blodgett, Harriet. *Centuries of Female Days: Englishwomen's Private Diaries.* New Brunswick, NJ: Rutgers UP, 1988.

Blythe, Ronald, ed. *The Pleasures of Diaries: Four Centuries of Private Writing.* New York: Pantheon Books, 1989.

Brodkey, Linda. *Academic Writing as Social Practice.* Philadelphia: Temple UP, 1987.

Chiseri-Strater, Elizabeth. *Academic Literacies: The Public and Private Discourse of University Students.* Portsmouth, NH: Boynton/Cook, 1991.

Culley, Margo, ed. *A Day at a Time: The Diary Literature of American Women from 1764 to the Present.* New York: Feminist Press, 1985.

Dobbs, Brian. *Dear Diary . . . Some Studies in Self Interest.* London: Elm Tree, 1974.

Elbow, Peter. *Writing without Teachers.* New York: Oxford UP, 1973.

Field, Joanna. *A Life of One's Own.* 1934. Los Angeles: J. P. Tarcher, 1981.

Fothergill, Robert A. *Private Chronicles: A Study of English Diaries.* London: Oxford UP, 1974.

Fulwiler, Toby, ed. *The Journal Book.* Portsmouth, NH: Boynton/Cook, 1987.

Gannett, Cinthia. *Gender and the Journal: Diaries and Academic Discourse.* Albany: State U of New York P, 1992.

Harris, Joseph. "The Idea of Community in the Study of Writing." *College Composition and Communication* 40.1 (Feb. 1989): 11–22.

Hollowell, John, and G. Lynn Nelson. "Bait: Rebait: We Should Abolish the Use of Personal Journals in English Classes." *English Journal* 71.1 (Jan. 1982): 14–17.

LeFevre, Karen Burke. *Invention as a Social Act.* Edwardsville: Southern Illinois UP, 1987.

Lowenstein, Sharyn. "A Brief History of Journal Keeping." Fulwiler 87–98.

———. "The Personal Journal–Journal Keeper Relationship as Experienced by the Journal Keeper: A Phenomenological and Theoretical Investigation." Diss. Boston U, 1982.

Mahala, Daniel. "Writing Utopias: Writing across the Curriculum and the Promise of Reform." *College English* 53.7 (Nov. 1991): 773–86.

Mallon, Thomas. *A Book of One's Own: People and Their Diaries.* New York: Penguin, 1984.

Murray, Donald. *A Writer Teaches Writing.* 2d ed. Boston: Houghton Mifflin, 1985.

Ringelblum, Emmanuel. *Notes from the Warsaw Ghetto.* Ed. and trans. Jacob Sloan. New York: Schocken, 1975.

Rohman, D. Gordon, and Albert O. Wlecke. *Prewriting: The Construction and Application of Models for Concept Formation.* Health, Education, and Welfare Project No. 2174. East Lansing: Michigan State U, 1964.

Singal, Daniel J. "The Other Crisis in American Education." *The Atlantic* 268.5 (1991): 59–74.

Ulrich, Laurel T. *A Midwife's Tale: The Life of Martha Ballard Based on Her Diary 1785–1812.* New York: Knopf, 1990.

Will, George F. "Political Indoctrination is Supplanting Education." Editorial. *Foster's Daily Democrat* 19 Sept. 1990: 8.

11 Feminism and Power: The Pedagogical Implications of (Acknowledging) Plural Feminist Perspectives

Linda M. LaDuc
University of Massachusetts at Amherst

Feminist scholars have successfully problematized gender in our culture, arguing that classrooms are not apolitical spaces, and adopting teaching stances that foreground feminism. In turn, however, feminism has itself been increasingly problematized by the entrance of black, Hispanic, and blue-collar women's voices, by the influence of postmodern feminist rhetoric with its insistence on the recognition of multiple perspectives, and by the changing needs of our increasingly diverse student populations.

All these perturbations are subject to amplification in classroom settings. Recognition of gender, race, class, and ethnic diversity challenges our teaching and forces us to rethink our practices. Acknowledgment of plural perspectives within feminism complicates the larger feminist project, our curriculum designs, and our interactions within our classroom environments.

For example, in highly student-centered environments, even feminist teachers may find themselves allowing aggressive, dominating students' positions on contested issues to go unchallenged. Acts of complicity, intentional or not, have educational consequences. At other times, ideological abuses are perpetrated by teachers on students, and it is seductively easy for such abuses to go unnoticed or unchallenged when the teacher has both superior knowledge and institutional power. In both of these cases, the negotiation of power is at issue.

Ideological abuse related to professorial power is especially important to address. Considering these issues in conjunction with feminist theory and praxis,[1] I argue, in this essay, that the presentation of feminism as powerful and overwhelming can preclude certain kinds of communicative interactions in classroom settings; however, more effective pedagogical practice can make issues of authority for feminist teachers in general, and feminist writing teachers in particular, both less problematic and more manageable. My intent here is to explore this thorny nexus of feminism, pedagogy, and power, and my efforts are aimed at encouraging "a modal or methodological pluralism" (Booth 479), in alignment with an ongoing effort to include women's voices and multiple perspectives in classroom practice.

While it is widely acknowledged that feminism is not a monolithic endeavor, feminist praxis (and its accommodation in pedagogy) all too often remains unaligned with the theoretical acknowledgment of diversity and of plural feminist perspectives. I believe more effective pedagogical practice can allow us to resist a tendency to univocality in feminist praxis, a univocality that greatly simplifies teaching (and is exceedingly difficult to avoid), but that nevertheless tends to collapse complexity into a feminist "party line."

The collapsing of feminist categories of thought into a unified story has been urged by some who expediently suggest that we wield more power as women by speaking with one voice, or who rationalize that pluralism itself is exclusionary (e.g., Rooney). While there is merit to these arguments (as there is to Booth's disclaimer that we can't teach everything), pressures that lead to an abstracted, universalized feminist voice not only minimize the multiplicity of issues and limit conceptual room within feminism, but also subject feminists in positions of authority to claims of hegemonic leadership. Such claims contribute to backlash against feminist projects.

Yet if united we fall, do divided we stand?

Can feminist projects be successfully enacted in composition classrooms if we encourage multiple, possibly even incommensurable, feminist and other views? If so, how do we negotiate the mined terrain of the classroom opened to plural perspectives, and, increasingly, to racial, ethnic, gender, and class-based diversity, without conflating openness with complicity, without inviting exercises of domination by some members over others, and without abusing the power vested in us as teachers?

Why Our Praxis Is Louder than Our Words

Feminism, whatever else it may be, is a movement for change in social values based on a primary concern for the problems of women *qua* women (Kramarae and Treichler 158–60). Feminist politics include efforts aimed at adding to, changing, or overthrowing current value sets—those philosophies of thought grounding practice, grounding action. But feminists are by no means united as to what might precisely constitute bettering women's lot, nor as to what strategies might be most appropriate in any given case. Though sharing large areas of commonality, various strands of feminist thought do reflect important differences in approaches to issues, in priorities, in methods, and even in the substantive content of the values put forth to extend or replace those predominant in mainstream discourse.

In spite of the existence of these differences, however, as bell hooks has acutely observed, many feminists have only given lip service to diversity. Hooks points out that we need strategies of communication and inclusion that allow for more successful enactments of feminist visions (19–27). Such strategies would assure that African American women's voices would be included in discourse as well as allow us to answer certain critical questions. For example, how do feminists acknowledge, encourage, and enact plural perspectives and aims without initiating fragmentation? Without denying our (individual) conviction(s) that not all perspectives are of equal value or merit, yet without unfairly suppressing resistances that are likely to ensue? And surely these questions are significant when considered in the context of feminist teaching of reading and writing.

In part, whether in an attempt to avoid conflict, or because of reluctance to overstep or abuse pedagogical authority, some feminist scholars have hesitated to foreground feminism in their classrooms. Meanwhile, others deliberately employ highly confrontational tactics. Regardless of either stance, as Jane Tompkins says,

> what we do in the classroom is our politics. No matter what we may say about Third World this or feminist that, our actions and our interactions with our students week in week out prove what we are for and what we are against in the long run. There is no substitute for practice. (660)

Tompkins offers a frustrated account of attempts to improve pedagogy by breaking up and out of traditional teaching patterns. Her frustration is in some ways reminiscent of Dale Bauer's frustration at the reaction of her students to aspects of her teaching. In each case, pedagogy is implicated in the problems faced by the teacher and in any solutions that the teacher devises.

Tompkins points to a belief that the teacher is responsible for setting the classroom agenda. Extending her argument, I might suggest that the feminist teacher needs to set the agenda in some classrooms intentionally so as to bring into cultural dialogue women's voices and concerns for their own sake and as representative of a wider world of cultural difference. Bauer argues that "feminist commitment . . . is a legitimate classroom strategy and rhetorical imperative," and that "the feminist agenda offers a goal toward our students' conversions to emancipatory critical action" (389). But certain key questions arise: Which feminist agenda is "the" feminist agenda? What shall we do about those students who resist our attempts to emancipate them? And even more important, what psychological damage might ensue in the breaking down of a student's foundational beliefs (Bizzell)? These pedagogical concerns lead us to more critical questions: Why does it so often happen that composition teaching gets narrowed to bipolar methodological choices (e.g., between autocratic teacher-centered and expressive student-centered approaches)? Is there never middle ground? Are there not other multiple combinations? Other alternatives?

In order to answer these questions satisfactorily, we need to call pedagogical training and principles into play. Yet despite significant progress in the field of composition pedagogy, there still seems to exist a general denial about how individual teaching expertise can either aid or obstruct our purposes. Persuasively proposed models (however brilliantly executed by their proponents), are not always transportable into every classroom, because students' needs are different, teaching styles, preferences, and skills are different, and/or the frameworks simply do not encompass all the content requirements. It is often difficult to talk about these kinds of issues. If lip service has been paid to diversity in feminism, lip service has also been paid to pedagogy in the academy generally (as Mariolina Salvatori argues in this volume).

Addressing both feminism and pedagogy simultaneously is no small task: it involves a concentrated interweaving of student needs assessment, instructional design, classroom management, feminist theory, knowledge of significant issues, and knowledge of writing and thinking processes. Yet the knowledge of pedagogical principles, approaches, and classroom management methods that would enable teachers to weave this long list of requirements together are all too often the elements missing from the repertoires of teachers in the academy.

Praxis does speak louder than words, and at least part of the problem with infusing feminism into the classroom involves implementation—implementation that even if well-meant is always problematic with respect to the negotiation of power between the teacher and the students.

Foregrounding Pedagogy to Teach Composition . . .
by Practicing Feminism

To assess our feminist praxis systematically, we need to look at how a wiser use of our instructional methodologies may help us achieve an appropriate form of feminist classroom authority, while simultaneously ensuring that students learn to trust the authority of their own and their classmates' voices (and/or acquire the wisdom not to do so when appropriate). Within the context of writing and reading instruction, abundant choices of materials and ways to use materials exist. If our educational objectives for composition teaching include helping students gain authority over their learning as well as their writing, we need to ask what choices are most apt to connect with more of our students (or better yet, each one of our students), and not just a selected, homogenized representation of those students we call a "majority." If we follow this path, assessment of feminist praxis is a customized and personalized reevaluation of specific teaching practices—an assessment process in which we face three professional developmental concerns: knowledge, methodological flexibility, and openness to criticism.

First, we need knowledge. We know that feminism is not reducible to one agenda, but before we introduce feminism(s) into our classrooms as issues and as critical method, there are ranges of perspectives with which we need to familiarize ourselves just as there are with any large body of specialized knowledge. Even more important than familiarity with the literature is a coming to critical self-awareness of our individual, personal positioning with respect to these perspectives on various issues.

Second, in implementing feminist projects we need to adopt a position of methodological flexibility. While clearly some frameworks for teaching writing are aggressively proposed, well-designed, carefully implemented, and thoroughly documented, is it reasonable to expect that a single framework or mode of learning (or teaching) will encompass all the developmental needs students bring into the classroom?

Third, in employing feminist critique as critical method, we will have to be open to, and even encouraging of, criticism of our own feminist perspective(s) and personal positions on specific issues. I am hopeful that we have come far enough within feminism to critique ourselves. However, anticipating criticism is one thing; encouraging it is much more difficult. How do we encourage critique, acknowledge both critique and contradictions gracefully (and concomitantly our student's autonomous thinking), yet not invite attack, or—if attacked—manage attacks professionally? These moves require a high level of communicative expertise, which in the classroom must be translated not only into action, but to action preceded by careful reflection about the consequences for learning and for our integrity as feminist teachers.

Maintaining our integrity as feminist teachers presupposes that we become knowledgeable about the range of feminist positions, locate ourselves with respect to these positions on a number of critical issues, acknowledge in our teaching that contradictions within feminism exist, and adopt and hold tight to an awareness that personal experiences, attitudes, values, and beliefs vary greatly with the issues and persons at hand. Acknowledgment of these concerns in practice means that no one can use the word "feminism" and pretend, however temporarily, to speak for all women, even in light of commonalities that might reasonably be espoused under a single definition of feminism. If we are unable to lump all feminist standpoints into one generalized perspective, we are forced to look for materials and methods that more carefully represent the variation that exists. By refusing to privilege any one framework, including our own, we can focus on demonstrating the kinds of critical thinking that are necessary if students are to write about conflicting cultures, viewpoints, and issues.

Teaching contradictions involves adopting a concomitant willingness to understand the nature of the contradictions and diverge from feminist and other party lines. It means having faith in our students' general goodwill and ability to learn to think critically, and being able to negotiate the terrain between complicity and coercion when students do put forth a position with which we are at serious odds. The acknowledgment of contradictions suggested here is not the same project as Elbow's "embracing contraries" approach to teaching writing, however. Although the stance I'm describing shares the notion of suspending belief with Elbow's model, the balancing act required in the enactment by feminist teachers of these communication strategies is highly complex: knowledge, methodological flexibility, and openness to critique must necessarily be intertwined in the teacher's performance in interactive, self-reflective ways.

Acquiring Knowledge by Practicing Self-Critique

In a research effort I undertook in response to students' questions about definitions of feminism, I discovered Rosemarie Tong's introduction to the topic. Tong classifies feminist thought into liberal,

Marxist-feminist, existentialist, psychoanalytic, socialist, radical, and postmodern feminist approaches (1–9). Her scheme, one of several attempts at classification and description,[2] is a useful heuristic for composition scholars and teachers. After reading it I was able to clarify for myself how liberal, Marxist-feminist, and existentialist feminism(s) root modern feminist thinking, how liberal feminism conflicts with radical feminist thought, in what ways Marxist feminism has been criticized (for failing to account for political patriarchy), and why existential feminism continues to emerge in various forms (including those informing cognitive approaches to reading and writing).

In addition, Tong identifies and positions numerous feminist scholars within her scheme, making it possible for me to think about juxtaposing their writings about issues in ways useful for specific classroom exercises. For example, I could choose radical and liberal feminist readings to bring two trajectories of thought to bear on issues relating to reproduction, or postmodernist and psychoanalytic feminist readings to focus discussion on "otherness" as a means of examining openness and diversity. In short, I could teach from a far more informed stance. However, it was a stance from which I could no longer presume to speak for all women in the name of feminism.

Perhaps not surprisingly, given the historical circumstances of women's entrance to institutions of higher education, many feminist scholars in composition are white, middle-class, liberal feminists interested in pay equity and fairness issues, and in securing more and better opportunities for women in mainstream culture. Increasingly, feminist literary and rhetorical scholars are taking up socialist feminist or postmodern feminist positions, however, and black, radical, and lesbian feminists' discourses, far more confrontational, are more clearly discernible among the historically predominant feminist voices. How this varied feminist positioning emerges in classroom practice surely merits careful study, and it similarly became imperative for me that I be more consciously self-reflective about my own practice.

Using Tong's strategy to analyze similarities and differences, it became clear that basic contradictions existed within liberal feminism, that there existed a far greater range of feminist perspectives than I had previously considered, and that with respect to specific issues, there were sometimes incommensurable differences between and among positions. Thus the next step for me involved locating myself explicitly within the various perspectives on a number of crucial issues.

I explored whether my stance with respect to women and equal opportunity in the workplace was informed by liberal feminism or by radical thought. Do I believe women are equally physiologically endowed and that gender differences are culturally induced and thus remediable by legislative means, or do I assert the existence of physiological and neurophysiological sex differences that are less likely to be appropriately accommodated by passing or revoking laws? With respect to abortion, do I hold that women have a responsibility to the species to avoid abortion as a birth control method, or that women will always be oppressed unless we alone have the right to choose abortion as the sign of final control over our bodies? Regarding pornography, do I stand for free expression, for censorship of depictions of violence against women, men, and children, or for some accommodation, or even celebration of, the erotic? On pay equity issues, do I support gender-equivalent pay schemes for all, including mothers and others performing services typically assigned to women in our culture, or do I bow to the demands of a market economy in which there is no accounting for reproductive and human maintenance labor?

Answering these questions was a long-overdue personal sorting out of the intersections on a very conflicted map. Interestingly, I found that when shared with my students, my attempts to articulate the honest perplexities I encountered in this process offered them a way to explore their own positions and voices, and in some cases motivated them to do so.

This kind of clarification process can help students see that a stance with respect to the first issue or cause may not be contiguous theoretically or personally with a stance on the second one; completing this process on an issue-by-issue basis can make it difficult for us to identify ourselves consistently with any one feminist position, however labeled. It becomes a method, a heuristic, for sorting out knotty thinking problems embedded in writing tasks, like those that students encounter when writing issue papers and when conceptualizing their audiences. Finally, such a process makes concrete our admonitions about the connections between writing and thinking, and about writing as process.

If one critically examines the incommensurable perspectives illuminated in this kind of reflective, dialogic process it is clear that some contradictions are not easily argued away. Nevertheless, denying or transmuting them would misrepresent the varied experiences we have in our individual lives. Further, if we attempt to gloss over differences, we run the risk of representing personal or sectional interests as universal, all moves which critical theorists (e.g., Giddens) would identify as functions of ideology. To paraphrase Tompkins once again, our practice does indeed speak louder than our words (660).

Ideology, Hegemony, and the Feminist Composition Teacher

From a different disciplinary context, Christine di Stefano has articulated the difficulty feminist scholars are faced with in negotiating among a "generic (hu)manism, a reified femininity, and postmodern pluralism" (78). When situated in the writing or literature classroom, this problem is not only one of avoiding universalizing tendencies, but also of navigating between a commitment to our feminist objectives as informed by theory and experience, on the one hand, and our responsibility as teaching professionals, on the other. The former instills in us the desire to infuse feminist issues into the curriculum—as content, in the form of additions to the canon, and as methodology, in the form of critique. Our professional responsibility, however, requires us not to substitute some variety of feminism, or a single agenda, in place of androcentrism, but rather to guide students, to assist them to explore their and our thinking, and to invite them into our conversation. Bauer calls for a highly agentic/activist approach to feminist issues, and in offering a way to bring feminism actively into the classroom she sets before us a notion of identificatory rhetoric and an interpretation of Burke's formulation of education as persuasion. In unskilled or unethical applications, however, Bauer's project of making the student solely responsible for challenging the agenda could become problematic. Students surely are responsible for ethical choices, but the situation could become an unfair imposition of pedagogical power, given the modeling characteristics of teaching and the respective positions of teachers and students. Precisely because many of us have met with student resistance to our agendas, we need to look at strategies that preclude long-term antagonism on the part of students who may be reacting to heavy-handed, coercive practices rather than to a call for critical thinking. The project is further complicated by the fact that we are "disciplined" by our disciplines (in a Foucauldian sense) to teach in certain ways, as Tompkins's soul-searching reminds us.

The premise that our goals must be built on sound teaching practices is exemplified in Elizabeth Flynn's "Composing as a Woman," in which she describes certain specific and self-conscious classroom practices for exploring reading, writing, and speaking behaviors (432). Donald Schon might characterize the teaching practices Flynn employs as demonstrating the building of "a repertoire of story types, interpretive explanations, and psychodynamic patterns" on the part of the teacher, and "a kind of therapeutic reflection-in-action" (125) on the part of the students in interaction with the teacher. More important, the approach Flynn takes is one "which attends to the peculiarities of each situation or case, rather than applying standard theories or techniques" (Schon 129). In effect, her approach is apt to result in the students' having to reframe problematic situations, though not necessarily to identify with any particular frame. This is a method more in the service of exploration than of persuasion, and one in which pluralism can flourish through the introduction of contrasts.

Schon's description of the processes that managers use to reflect in action applies equally well to teachers; if we cannot describe our coming to a perspective ourselves, we cannot teach others to do so. Yet we must do so if, as Freire makes clear, we seek changes in the consciousness of the oppressed as well as in the situation which oppresses them and us (60). Furthermore, Freire argues, if we fail to perceive that our chosen perspectives or methods contain contradictions about reality, and we coerce students into using them, we become oppressors. The form of pedagogical action we adopt can have a very great influence on the way students will perceive themselves in the world. For these reasons, whether in spite of or because of contradictions among feminist perspectives, a stance based on acknowledgment of these contradictions offers an extremely valuable position from which to critique.

There is that very important caveat, however: We need to be willing to have all perspectives equally open to critique by our students if we truly wish to teach effective critical thinking and reading, if we really believe in dialectic as method. The classroom is not value-neutral ground, nor is the teacher-student relationship symmetrical. Normative power exerts itself in the classroom when communication is distorted by the imposition of interests particular to a certain group—feminist or otherwise. And so in asking for identification, we may be asking our students to do something not truly in their or our best interests. Chantal Mouffe argues that hegemony is not merely domination of one group by another; it involves the ability of one class to articulate interests of other groups with its own (183). Although some degree of hegemony seems inevitable, given our power as experts, uncritical selection of content or of a particular critical perspective may easily become overly hegemonic because persuasive power inheres in such actions when performed by teachers who hold coercive, expert, and legitimate power (Raven and French). It follows then that we need to guard against both ineffective and/or deceptively induced identification with feminist critiques or methods, even if (and perhaps especially if) the objective is transformational.

Dennis Mumby suggests that critical theory's pursuit of social reconstruction should involve the ability of social actors to examine and question the process by which meaning structures become accepted as legitimate, to recognize the human social factors in organizational reality, and to engage actively in the process of self-formation through the building of an alternative reality (36). Such a stance would appear to support emancipatory claims for feminist rhetoric as meta-critique, but not as the only form of critique offered, and certainly not in the form of a reductive critique, oblivious to the voices it is refusing to allow into the conversation.

According to Peter Elbow, people who use conflicting models can simply see and think more. "Though contradiction is an itch we naturally seek to remove," he cautions that we need not be in a hurry to remove it (249). He suggests instead the practice of "methodological belief" as an effective way to teach students to be critical thinkers, a practice not based on critically evaluative doubting or tearing down, but rather on description and on active attempts to experience readings of texts. There is a sense of bargain and of temporary consent, rather than of an identification that replaces all other constructs (259). He categorizes doubting as an act of separation and differentiation, whereas methodological belief entails merging and participating, not based on acceptance of authority, but on dialogue within a community—not a rhetoric of propositions or of persuasion, but a rhetoric of experience, of performance (264).

While we clearly need to address its potential problems for feminist teachers,[3] methodological belief is nevertheless effective pedagogy. We need to continue to explore and adapt this and other alternatives and methodologies to achieve our specific objectives—and to strategize, to counterstrategize, and to resist univocalized teaching—as vigorously as we would resist obstacles to our own unfettered thinking. If we do so, we may find students' past resistances were not to our politics, but to abuses of power.

Feminism and pedagogy must go hand in hand. In order to promote wise uses rather than abhorrent uses/abuses of our professional power, it is critical for feminist teachers to attend to a number of developmental skills and to adjust praxis not only to our theoretical biases, but to the coercive, legitimate, and expert power we have as teachers—because we dance always between authority that leads and authority that coerces. For the feminist writing teacher, leadership is not relinquishing authority, but rather professionally managing the meanings it has for our students (and ourselves) in its classroom enactments.

Notes

1. Praxis is taken here to be "free, creative engagement in the world by the individual, who is changed by the experience and who thereby changes the world" (Donovan 70). If authority equals power, we take on power as we author texts and contexts; that is, we "author" our lives with students.

2. All classification systems are arbitrary, even ideological, a factor which ought to be explained to students. Tong's scheme is one of a number of attempts to define and explain feminist thought. I selected it because of its comprehensive explanations and organized presentation (cf. Donovan; Eisenstein; Langston; Marshall).

3. Susan Jarratt finds Elbow's method of teaching methodological belief (in the expressivist composition class) a troubling enterprise for feminist writing teachers. While I agree with her that his rhetoric is silent with respect to social differences and that an attitude of over-receptivity can be inappropriate for the feminist teacher, I see pedagogical expertise as figuring prominently in any solution, as well as in our ability to use Elbow's and other methods.

Works Cited

Bauer, Dale. "The Other 'F' Word: The Feminist in the Classroom." _College English_ 52.4 (Apr. 1990): 385–96.

Bizzell, Patricia. "Beyond Anti-Foundationalism to Rhetorical Authority: Problems Defining 'Cultural Literacy.' " _College English_ 52.6 (Oct. 1990): 661–75.

Booth, Wayne. "Pluralism in the Classroom." _Critical Inquiry_ 12 (1986): 468–79.

di Stefano, Christine. "Dilemmas of Difference: Feminism, Modernity, and Postmodernism." In _Feminism/Postmodernism_. Ed. Linda Nicholson. New York: Routledge, 1990. 134–55.

Donovan, Josephine. _Feminist Theory: The Intellectual Traditions of American Feminism_. New York: Frederick Unger, 1985.

Eisenstein, Hester. _Contemporary Feminist Thought: An Assessment_. Boston: G. K. Hall, 1983.

Elbow, Peter. _Embracing Contraries: Explorations in Learning and Teaching_. New York: Oxford UP, 1986.

Flynn, Elizabeth. "Composing as a Woman." _College Composition and Communication_ 39.4 (Dec. 1988): 423–35.

Freire, Paulo. _Pedagogy of the Oppressed_. Trans. Myra Bergman Ramos. New York: Continuum, 1970.

Giddens, Anthony. _Central Problems in Social Theory: Action, Structure, and Contradiction in Social Analysis_. Berkeley and Los Angeles: U of California P, 1979.

Habermas, Jurgen. _Legitimation Crisis_. Trans. T. McCarthy. Boston: Beacon Press, 1975.

hooks, bell. *Talking Back: Thinking Feminist, Thinking Black*. Boston: South End Press, 1988.

Jarratt, Susan. "Feminism and Competition: The Case for Conflict." *Contending with Words: Composition and Rhetoric in a Postmodern Age*. Ed. Patricia Harkin and John Schilb. New York: MLA, 1991. 105–23.

Kramarae, Cheris, and Paula A. Treichler. *A Feminist Dictionary*. Boston: Pandora, 1985.

LaDuc, Linda. "Infusing Feminist Critiques into the Teaching of Scientific Method: Reasons and Methods." Paper presented at the Penn State Conference on Rhetoric and Composition, State College, Pennsylvania. July, 1990.

Langston, D. "Feminist Theories and the Politics of Difference." *Changing Our Power*. Ed. W. Cochran, D. Langston, and C. Woodward. Dubuque, IA: Kendall/Hunt, 1991. 10–21.

Marshall, J. "Re-visioning Career Concepts: A Feminist Invitation." In *Handbook of Career Theory*. Ed. M. B. Arthur, D. T. Hall, and B. S. Lawrence. Cambridge: Cambridge UP, 1989. 275–91.

Mouffe, Chantal. "Hegemony and Ideology in Gramsci." In *Gramsci and Marxist Theory*. Ed. Chantal Mouffe. Beverly Hills, CA: Sage, 1979. 168–204.

Mumby, Dennis. *Communication and Power in Organizations: Discourse, Ideology, and Domination*. Norwood, NJ: Ablex, 1988.

Raven, Bertram H., and John R. P. French. "Legitimate Power, Coercive Power, and Observability in Social Influence." *Sociometry* 21 (1958): 83–97.

Rooney, Ellen. "Who's Left Out? A Rose by Any Other Name is Still Red; or the Politics of Pluralism." *Critical Inquiry* 12 (1986): 550–63.

Schon, Donald. *The Reflective Practitioner: How Professionals Think in Action*. New York: Basic Books, 1983.

Tompkins, Jane. "Pedagogy of the Distressed." *College English* 52.6 (Oct. 1990): 653–60.

Tong, Rosemarie. *Feminist Thought*. Boulder, CO: Westview Press, 1989.

12 Rereading the Discourses of Gender in Composition: A Cautionary Tale

Susan V. Wall
Northeastern University

> Re-vision—the act of looking back, of seeing with fresh eyes, of entering an old text from a new critical direction—is for women more than a chapter in cultural history: it is an act of survival. Unless we can understand the assumptions in which we are drenched we cannot know ourselves.
>
> —Adrienne Rich, "When We Dead Awaken"

Adrienne Rich, of course, meant literary texts, especially the canon and its role in shaping our cultural history and our lives. Those of us who work in composition studies cannot claim a canon in that sense; but we too have old texts that need the kind of critique Rich calls for—the texts of our scholarship and teaching. One of the most influential statements of such an agenda is Elizabeth Flynn's 1988 essay, "Composing as a Woman," which defines the issues before us in the following terms:

> For the most part . . . the fields of feminist studies and composition studies have not engaged each other in a serious or systematic way. . . . As a result, the parallels between feminist studies and composition studies have not been delineated, and the feminist critique that has enriched such diverse fields as linguistics, reading, literary criticism, psychology, sociology, anthropology, religion, and science has had little impact on our models of the composing process. We have not examined our research methods or research samples to see if they are androcentric. Nor have we attempted to determine just what it means to compose as a woman. (425)

In 1988, Flynn was essentially right: there was a striking absence of feminist critique in composition studies, at least in what might be termed the mainstream publishing of the discipline. But her essay also raises two issues of *how* we might both understand that absence and establish a feminist critique to remedy it. First, how do we construct the relationship between feminist studies and composition studies? Is it a dialogue, perhaps even a dialectic, as in, "Feminist studies and composition studies have not engaged each other"? Or is it a matter of unilateral influence, as in, "The feminist critique that has enriched such diverse fields . . . has had little impact . . . "? The second issue is a matter of method: If feminist studies in other fields offer ways to frame our re-visions, how, first, should we read them? Flynn suggests that we might "usefully" draw on two works that address women's moral and intellectual development, Carol Gilligan's *In a Different Voice* and Mary Belenky, Blythe Clinchy, Nancy Goldberger, and Jill Tarule's *Women's Ways of Knowing*. How might we understand the relationship between these works as they apply to ours?

The two issues are related: I want to argue in this essay that it makes a great deal of difference how we connect Gilligan's work to that of Belenky and her colleagues, and it makes a difference for us *because* composition studies by 1988 already had in place a critical frame through which we need to read such feminist work. I am making, in other words, the same point about borrowing theory that I take Louise Phelps to be arguing when she says that

> the principle is not to select Theory *because* it is valid in its own terms, but *in view of* those terms and the claims they support, so that application is critical rather than naive. The horizon for pragmatic decisions includes not simply method in the original field, but the placement of Theory in the full context of disciplinary issues, arguments, and beliefs as they play out within a socio-historical frame. (224)

More specifically, I want in this essay to argue that we need to be cautious about how we work with feminist developmental theory, given the particular history of composition studies over the last decade. We have changed, often radically, our collective ability to contextualize our work; but this shift has been uneven and incomplete, prompting an internal critique within the discipline that has strong implications for how we proceed.

Rather than develop my points abstractly, however, I want to locate them in a case study that I completed almost ten years ago. I'll present first a very brief version of that story as I originally told it, and then, after considering what has changed for me over time, I'll return to a re-vision of that study in terms of what I think feminist developmental theory enables me to say about it now. What I say here might best be read as a kind of "blurred genre"—autobiography, history, essay—an attempt to suggest that my history is also in some ways representative of the history of the discipline, without presenting my discussion of "the full context of disciplinary issues, arguments, and beliefs" as something other than the product of my reading.

Dianne

"Dianne" (not her real name) was a student at a large city university who participated in a case study with me while she took the course she'd chosen for first-year composition, a section of critical writing cross-listed with the women's studies program. The purpose of the course, the instructor explained, was to explore connections among gender, language, and power: "By comparing the ways in which men and women write about such topics as work, love, creativity, and sexual identity, we will study how language can be used to affect an audience, how it affects the writer, and how the English language can be construed to either enforce or disrupt sexual stereotypes and institutional sexism in our culture." Students in the course read a selection of essays on these topics, and wrote twelve papers, most of them a mixture of expressive and persuasive discourse.

Dianne welcomed the challenge. Bright, lively, and highly verbal, she had been encouraged to excel in speaking, reading, and writing at home, in the college preparatory program at her Catholic high school, and (coached by her warmly supportive father) in the National Forensics League. I saw this education as a mixed blessing: Dianne had learned to produce a kind of academic discourse that was analytical, highly structured, and assertive; but she had also learned to focus on techniques to bring a speech or paper to closure rather than on writing as a way to develop and reflect on ideas, values, or feelings. The result in her early papers was a rhetorical strategy familiar to many of us who have taught such students: argue "both sides" of an issue, then declare that any tensions or conflicts such discussion has raised can be transcended by people of goodwill. Responding, for example, to a request to define what she took to be the meaning of such terms as "feminism," "male supremacy," and "institutional sexism in American culture," Dianne argued that while men and women can never be truly equal because they are too "complex" and physically "different," they can "share the powers and privileges which they are capable of, while both can appreciate their uniqueness."

Dianne's papers came back from her teacher with such comments to her conclusions as: "Easy to say... You've got a good *beginning* here . . . You've put yourself in a position to do some important thinking about what criticism means in this context. Don't blow it with a cutoff sentence like this." In conference, the teacher characterized the unqualified, unexamined expression of opinion in Dianne's essays as, metaphorically, like "marching around with a flag," and explained what she saw as the epistemological consequences of writing that way: "It's the cutoff sentence that stops all thought." Dianne was shocked: nothing in her education had prepared her for such a response. She had been coached in the approved format, corrected when she wrote in the first person, and admired for "great form"; no one had critiqued her conclusions, which (she admitted) "all came real quick—I didn't even have to think hardly." At first she tried to translate her teacher's challenge into yet another set of procedures "to get the style of writing she really wants," but this strategy, she was beginning to realize, conflicted with her desire not to censor herself—a desire encouraged by her teacher's focus on the development of her own thinking through writing: "I think if I got a set thing on, even if my set definition of a conclusion was that there *was* no set definition of a conclusion, I would be better off because I could at least sit down and write what I felt."

Dianne's struggles came to a head with the fourth assignment, which asked students first to describe the social structure of some organization they'd been part of—a school, group, job situation—using as a model the analysis of gender roles in one of their readings, and then to go on to argue for or against "the sociologists' argument that social roles and organizational structures go further in accounting for sex differences in behavior and status than global personality traits of individuals." As we talked about the assignment, Dianne began to develop a perceptive analysis of the overt and covert power structures in her Catholic all-girls high school. The analysis was in two parts, one concerning the overall school hierarchy, the other the power relationships in the school's forensics club. Concerning the first, she told me that

> coming from that school as a student and looking at it now, in perspective of who really runs it, everyone tells me the pastor runs it. But when I was there I never saw him as running it. He would come in a big meeting or orientation or something and say, 'I'm Father So-and-So and I back _____ High,' and all this. But then he just left. And I wouldn't see him till the next major meeting with the principal and vice-principal, who were always females—would look like they were running everything. But then they would have to go to him for approval . . . it was

necessary for them to be under a male, whether he did anything
or not.

Given the further development of this promising beginning in
Dianne's first draft, I was baffled when I saw her revision, the final
draft she gave her teacher. Here is the first part of her paper:

> I went to a parochial, all-girls' high school. There was a definite
> distribution of power within its entire educational system. The
> head of the school was the pastor of its parish, Father X. Next in
> line of authority was the principal, a rather young nun Sr. Y. The
> vice-principal was also a nun, although she was somewhat older
> than the principal. The school's faculty consisted of several nuns,
> married and single female teachers, and seven male teachers,
> three of whom were priests. Looking at the overall hierarchical
> structure of the school, females presided, but only under male
> domination. Father X controlled the school. He made all the major
> decisions. All other authorities went through him for the final
> approval on all school matters.

Instead of the play of perspectives offered in her first two accounts,
Dianne's final draft was a stereotyped, monological picture of men
controlling women through what her conclusion calls "male domination." Any counterlanguage suggesting resistance to the "official
story" had been entirely deleted. What had happened?

Originally, Dianne explained in our next interview, she and her
friends had thought Father X's power was a sham, that going to him
was "useless" and "stupid." But in rereading her draft she'd realized
that a reader would see evidence that "he actually *did* things; he had
to have that authoritative thing where he had to see the stuff and
they had to go to him because he is the top." The rules of academic
discourse as she understood them meant that her own claims would
have no credibility in the face of such evidence: "I feel like I can't
just say something without having any thought of a type of proof or
something." And these restrictions were, she felt, being reinforced by
her reading of her teacher: "What I did was, I went on two totally
different tracks. So I couldn't save anything from the first track because
then I figured that I'd start on that big rampage . . . on how that's
wrong, that women should run it if they can. So I had to take that
out, 'cause it sounded too—like I was going to go marching around,
like she said. So I cut that whole thing."

This explanation was complicated, however, by evidence that Dianne
was actually trying to change her *own* thinking so as to conform not
just to a particular way of constructing "academic discourse" but to
the official, male-controlled account of reality at her school:

> When I looked at [the draft] and I saw examples of when [Father X] actually did do things, I saw that the whole thing was wrong, even though that was my opinion. . . . But the experience was, you know, totally different. . . . By writing about it, I think I thought it would make me change on the whole way I looked at him. And it didn't. I still felt the way I felt in the beginning. And that's frustrating to me because I didn't change anything at all. And if I didn't really feel it, then I really shouldn't have wrote it.

That extraordinary effort at self-censorship also seemed to carry over into the second half of her paper, the story of Dianne's forensics group. In our first conversation she'd said:

> The whole [group], it was all women, all girls, it was run by one woman teacher. And a male assistant came into the group, and he, him and the moderator, they were real close; they were having an affair that everyone knew about. And he wanted to dominate the group. He worked through her in so many ways that even whenever she'd give us a decision, or tell us something, or really moderate her job, it was like him speaking through her. So now that I look at it, there was a kind of parallel where even if women *looked* like they were in charge, they really weren't. They were always being controlled in one way or another by a male.

When Dianne wrote this out and then reread her draft, she'd realized that the two situations in her high school were *not* parallel; instead, the second example, in which a woman seemed to be in control but the real power was exercised behind the scenes by a man, "totally contradicted" the first. So she'd rewritten the whole paper to eliminate contradictions and make it "flow easily."

Here is a section of that revision, with Dianne's deletions in brackets and added text in italics. These changes dramatize how much messier the actual situation seems to have been than anything she had said at first. They suggest (as the final text does not) the power struggle that Dianne had been engaged in not only with the male moderator but with her female teacher and peers, and they illustrate her continuing struggle as a writer over issues of gender, power, and representation:

> I was the *voted* head of the organization and [had the control over all of the group's activities] worked hard to make the group cohesive. [The male assistant wanted *tried* to control the group and by working through our female moderator. He tried] *The male moderator tried* to exercise control over the other members of the group by [sexual manipulation] flaunting his masculine authority. He would flirt with the members and *try to* control their behavior. He did not succeed in gaining total control because I refused to relinquish my power *to him.* . . .

In my situation, the [sexual] distribution of power between the
sexes were never reversed. In every [way possible] instance the
male was in control one way or another. *My example supports the
sociological category of stereotyped male dominated authority over
females.*

Further discussion revealed just how much Dianne's example "sup-
ported" a stereotypical view of gender and authority precisely because
she had revised the situation to fit the stereotype. The male assistant,
she said, had actually been more sexually manipulative than this draft
suggests; he would "pinch" the girls and "weasel his way through
situations with all that physical garbage." Dianne had resisted, but her
classmates had not backed her; she remembered how she "went from
loving the group to hating it to loving it to hating it." And so she'd
deleted the part about her control over the group's activities because
it only "fit what *should* have happened. . . . If I *had* all the control, I
would never have let him do what he did." Most significantly in this
draft, she has omitted any mention of the complicity of the female
moderator in what she clearly saw as professionally and sexually
inappropriate—even threatening—behavior.

What Dianne did do (she finally told me) was to confront the
principal and vice-principal and her female forensics teacher with her
story—only to find that they accused her of "going to extremes,"
"conjuring up" a fiction, trying to get her teacher fired. In this final
version of the story that her revision so thoroughly evades, it was the
women who actually wielded the power in the school and betrayed
her trust and ideals. And Dianne had internalized their blame, turning
it against the credibility of her own voice: "The way I had to deal
with everything was to try to tone down everything that was actually
happening . . . I would say, 'Oh no, maybe it wasn't that, maybe it
wasn't that. It wasn't meant to mean this or it wasn't supposed to
look like that.' " No wonder, then, that revision was such a struggle:
"I still feel like I'm holding back and I shouldn't."

Dianne wrote many more papers before the term was out, and I
continued to see in them a struggle between her desire to express
strong ideas and values and her resistance to exploring complex and
ambiguous topics. We discussed these struggles at length in our
interviews, and she also discussed them with her teacher, who now
seemed more understanding and supportive than Dianne had first
believed. All these discussions heightened Dianne's awareness of her
struggles with self-censorship, and some of the readings and class
discussions provided her a way to connect her struggle to those of
other women. Yet I found her work wildly uneven: she would write

some papers that seemed to me to take great risks, only to write a revision or another paper that would show no evidence that the insights she'd come to about self-censorship had any impact on her writing.

At the same time, however, Dianne began to defend her work in class discussions, feeling that when a "whole person is involved in something" it is legitimate to defend a "conviction" even if its expression lacked objective "proof." She revised, too, her way of talking about the powerful women in her life, especially her mother, a professional with a Ph.D. who had died a few years earlier; whereas early in the term she'd praised her mother's "clarity, organization, and academic-sounding" vocabulary but portrayed her father as the model for her writing, now Dianne spoke of her mother as someone with "great integrity of style. . . . She always stood by what she wrote." She reminisced about a family friend, a nun, who had encouraged her to read, shared in the lively arguments at the family dinner table, and helped Dianne, after her mother's death, to use her journal to write out her grief and "put herself back together." And Dianne said, too, how our interviews had helped her become more aware of when she was suppressing her own feelings, especially anger, in her work. In our final conversation, she even seemed to be developing a salutary humor about self-censorship: "We—women—have always been the ones to make everything seem a little bit nicer than what it really is. The men get out there and say, 'We blew heads off, we did this, we did that!' And the women say, 'Well, it wasn't all *that* bad; we can still cook and clean.' " Despite the disappointing evidence of many of her late texts, I wanted to believe that comments like that pointed the way toward a new and unified feminist consciousness for Dianne.

Looking Backward

I originally read Dianne's case by confining my sense of context to the immediate one I could see—her conversations with me, her interactions with her teacher and classmates, her writing. I ended it aware that I needed a framework that would also account more broadly for how her struggles with language were also struggles to understand herself as a gendered subject. But I found myself exactly where Flynn places composition studies at that time—lacking any feminist theory of composing within the discipline itself. Why was this the case?

In raising that question again in a recent essay, Flynn notes that some of the field's "foremothers," particularly Janet Emig and Linda

Flower, adopted positions in the early 1980s that treated "the writer as an isolated individual divorced from social and political context" ("Composition Studies" 140). That seems an understatement: concerns for the relationship between cognition and composing processes shaped the work of many influential women in the profession (e.g., Nancy Sommers, Sondra Perl, Janice Hays, Mina Shaughnessy, Andrea Lunsford), while others were strongly influenced by the individualist expressivist theories popular at the time. Composition studies, in other words, was constituted as a discipline not just by an *absence* of social/contextual critique but by the strong *presence* of ways of reading that confined our attention to writers/readers and single texts and kept us from asking about contexts, at least those beyond the classroom.

My own work at that time was shaped by a set of assumptions and practices which Kenneth Dowst has called the "epistemic" approach, a way of reading writing as "the activity of making some sense out of an extremely complex set of *personal* perceptions and experiences of an infinitely complex world" (66; my emphasis). This pedagogy constructs the successful writer as someone who attempts to "push back" against the power of established languages to speak for the writer (to produce "themewriting," as William Coles calls it), while at the same time developing a resistance to closure that allows risk-taking and experimentation with language, learning (in Berthoff's famous formulation) "the uses of chaos." Writing cannot resolve conflict; but it offers a way, through the cultivation of a self-reflexive stance, of imposing, at least on paper, a kind of metadiscursive control over ambiguity and the threat of confusion. This pedagogy differed from others prevalent in the early 1980s, then, in that it addressed not the writer's "mind" or inner "self" but a discursively produced "textual self." The emphasis remained, however, on the individual writer struggling with language in the rhetorical context of the composition classroom.

These assumptions informed my original reading of Dianne's texts. Although I clearly saw her struggles as gendered, I also saw "gender" mainly in terms of a largely stereotyped, ready-made discourse for defining the self that a writer had to resist in order to "grow." I treated her as a relatively isolated individual whose work I read as a moral and epistemological struggle with and against language; I recognized her need to win approval by "making things nice" and her resistance to readings of the world that denied what she felt was true, and I defined her work, then, in terms of a conflict between self-censorship and self-assertion. I had a sense that Dianne had internalized contradictions that many other women also experience, myself among them, but she had no way either to read these contradictions more precisely or to account for the persistence of self-censorship in her work late in the term, even when she had herself become highly conscious of the issues and processes involved. Most crucially, I read evidence of reflexive language and metadiscursive irony in her writing as "growth" away from simplistic constructions of reality. I wanted Dianne's story to have a happy ending.

But even as I completed my analysis, composition studies was undergoing a re-vision, a shift in emphasis from, in Patricia Bizzell's terms, an "inner-directed approach" to an "outer-directed" one. By 1988, the publication date of "Composing as a Woman," new scholarship had *already* established in our vocabulary terms such as "social constructionist," "dialogical," "socio-epistemic," "contextualist," "interpretive communities," and "the ecology of writing." Although feminist scholarship in composition was still rare, the discipline was ready for the strong turn it has taken since in that direction. At the same time, however, this movement was far from monolithic. While many composition scholars confined these new ways of reading to work done by mainstream students in the academy, a dissenting strand of scholarship also developed in the discipline, often produced by scholars involved with nontraditional students—e.g., Marilyn Cooper, Shirley Brice Heath, Kyle Fiore and Nan Elsasser, Judith Goleman, Mike Rose. These voices have urged our attention to ways that all writers' "selves" are constituted not just by the discourses of the academy but by a whole range of different and even competing discourses in society—discourses of class, race and ethnicity, age, and religion, as well as local and regional "ways with words."

Failing to attend to this way of reading leads inevitably to idealization—and to illusions about ourselves and our powers. Richard Ohmann, of course, had argued this point in the 1970s in works such as *English in America*, but the expansion of the discipline around writer-centered pedagogies ensured his critique a limited effect. Bizzell offered a similar critique in 1982 (and helped to create a more receptive audience for it), observing that personal and institutional pressures for control and harmony make it easier for composition teachers to credit students' "innate" abilities (or lack of them) for success or failure in school than to ask if, in fact, performance has anything to do with whether or not we and our students share a common culture and history. In the English classroom, idealization hinges on how we judge acts of reading and writing: by reading "one community's discourse conventions [i.e., ours] as if they simply mirrored reality," she argued, we deflect attention away from the "political and ethical dimensions" of our own teaching (238). Seven years later, Linda Brodkey, writing "On the Subjects of Class and Gender in 'The Literacy Letters,'" suggested that this critique was still relevant. Her study documented the misreadings and miscommunications in letters exchanged by a set of middle-class teachers and working-class students, failures she attributed to the teachers' inability to read the students' letters in terms of cultural difference. This is evidence, Brodkey argued, that still, in "the dialect of educational discourse . . . a teacher's control over discursive practice is contingent on the ideology that classroom language transcends class, race, and gender" (139). Despite, in other words, our discipline's social-contextualist turn, it remains easier for many of us to read writing (ours and our students') in terms of what Dowst calls "personal perceptions and experiences of an infinitely complex world" than, as Cooper suggests, to know it as "one of the activities by which we locate ourselves in the enmeshed systems that make up the social world" ("Ecology" 13).

This critique of ways of reading, one developed within our discipline, provides a way to assess the "usefulness" of feminist developmental theory for composition studies—to make application of that theory the result of a genuine dialogue between disciplines. To what extent do these theories enable a fully contextualized analysis? In reading our work through the frames they offer, do we locate ourselves in that context as well? To show what I mean, let me turn back now briefly to my study of Dianne and reread it, first through the framing discourse of Gilligan's early work, *In a Different Voice,* and then through that of *Women's Ways of Knowing*—a work that I read as a critique as well as an extension of Gilligan's study.

Rereading "Dianne"

When I worked with Dianne's texts originally, I kept wondering: Why is she still unable to express publicly the anger and grief she shares with me and others privately? Gilligan also observed self-censorship among the women she studied, and offers a speculative conclusion that makes sense here as well. She suggests that when the discourse of the powerful either distorts or discredits what women perceive, they internalize this silencing, turning it on themselves; they "come to question whether what they have seen exists and whether what they know from their own experience is true. These questions are raised not as abstract philosophical speculations about the nature of reality and truth but as personal doubts that invade women's sense of themselves, compromising their ability to act on their own perceptions and thus their willingness to take responsibility for what they do" (49). This last problem is particularly evident in the way Dianne's revisions of paper 4 accomplish a manipulative but unacknowledged revenge: they reduce almost entirely the real power roles played by the female students, forensics teacher, and school principals, and give all the credit instead to the men. And in this construction, in which all males are oppressors and all females victims, it is sadly obvious in which role Dianne's writing continues to place her.

In emphasizing the need many women have to maintain a close "web" of relationships with others defined by an "ethic of care," Gilligan's work also enables me to imagine why Dianne found writing and talking about her experiences in high school ultimately frustrating rather than a way to lay the issues to rest: simply retelling a story that showed her acting according to a "morality of rights" would not resolve the depth of pain (and, quite possibly, guilt) she felt over the destruction of trust and support among the girls and women in her school. At the same time, I can read a positive connection between her sharing of this story with me and her various attempts to work out a more understanding relationship with her current female teacher and classmates, to shift her identification as a writer to her mother instead of her father, and to generalize her struggles with language as something "we women do." All can be understood as ways to compose a new community of supportive women as the context for her work.

Gilligan also argues that while the "morality of rights" orientation may be more associated with men and the "ethic of care" orientation with women, there is an "interplay of these voices within each sex" (2). She goes on to speculate that "development for both sexes would . . . seem to entail an integration of rights and responsibilities through the discovery of the complementarity of these disparate views" (100). Dianne, read this way, was struggling to reconcile her need for control and a sense of her rights as a person with her need for approval and relationships governed by an ethic of care. She wasn't there yet, but in what I saw as her increasing capacity for self-reflection and analysis (capped by the humor of our final interview), she seemed on the way to achieving what Gilligan calls "a new understanding of the interconnection between other and self" (74).

I also realize, however, even as I quote Gilligan's words, the seductive appeal her claim about development had and still has for me as a writer, the way it seems to offer, finally, a means to make sense of Dianne's case as a story about "progress." And I realize this because such treatment of development as natural and universal has been and is being questioned in my field by scholars such as Bizzell, Cooper, and Brodkey. Read in terms of their disciplinary critique, a crucial question is how a feminist theorist relates individual development and socioeconomic class. While Gilligan is not unaware of differences that might be attributed to social status, culture, and unequal distribution of power, she says in her introduction that she does not intend to make any generalizable claims about them (2). Her purpose, she insists, is mainly to demonstrate that there exists a mode of moral reasoning not accounted for by established developmental theory. Yet, having made that disclaimer, she writes often as if broad generalizations could be made about the moral development of "men and women," without reference to differences in class and culture. Her chapter on "Concepts of Self and Morality," for instance, draws on a study of women ages fifteen to thirty-three "diverse in ethnic background and social class" (71), yet ends with the statement I quoted above, that "development [singular] for both sexes . . . would seem to entail an integration of rights and responsibilities." Even if we keep in mind that Gilligan's work (like that of Belenky and her colleagues) constitutes an exploratory case study whose purpose is to *raise* theoretical issues, not a survey or experiment to test their generalizability, her lack of interest in any social determinant of identity other than gender is disturbing.[1]

While Belenky and her colleagues do not address Gilligan's methods explicitly, they distance themselves from developmental researchers like William Perry, arguing that his universalizing scheme of moral development was illusory because it was based only on the experiences of a "relatively homogeneous group of people" for whom the achievement of "maturity" means socialization into a common "system of values, standards, and objectives" (15). In contrast, the authors of *Women's Ways*, while looking in their data for any "common ground that women share, regardless of background," also say that "including women [in the study] from different ethnic backgrounds and a broad range of social classes enabled us to begin to examine and see beyond our own prejudices" (13–14).

Rereading Dianne's case now and trying to examine and see beyond my own prejudices in light of their work, I realize the extent to which many abilities and problems that I attributed to Dianne as an individual might be understood as the results of privilege and good fortune, albeit shaped, surely, by qualities of insight, good humor, and courage. In the technique- and audience-oriented writing abilities she brought to her college experience, she was like many of the women described by Belenky and her colleagues as "procedural" and "separate" knowers: learners who depend heavily on method, logic, objectivity, and external standards of judgment. Although the authors speculate that anyone might learn to think this way, in fact they nearly always found this epistemological stance among students who were (like Dianne) products of traditional, rigorous, liberal arts–centered, and elite schooling. Typical of such students, too, were the liabilities of her education that Dianne was beginning to realize, particularly the pressures she felt to "make things nice" (or as Belenky et al. put it, to be "a woman with a man's mind, but a woman nevertheless" [134]) and her contradictory desire "for a voice that is more integrated, individual, and original—a voice of [her] own" (124).

The efforts that Dianne made to move outside of the restrictions of her epistemological perspective—efforts to challenge the patriarchal discourses and structures of her high school, to state strong values in her work, to draw inspiration and support from caring intellectual women (while seeing her father as emotionally supportive of her efforts)—these, too, are most enabled by privilege. The final section of *Women's Ways*, "Development in Context," makes it clear how the lifestyles of middle-class families and the opportunities of advanced schooling are usually what provide the intellectual challenges, the occasions to read, write, and talk reflectively, and the sense of being taken seriously that encourage young women toward "connected" and "constructed" knowing. Conversely, the tentative moves Dianne made toward defining gender roles as negotiable, open to revision, can be recognized as "adaptive" strategies for the kind of success open to students so privileged. If, as Belenky and her colleagues note, "the perception of multiple perspectives on truth and values is almost unavoidable for advantaged children growing up today" (63), it is because "reliance on authority for a single view of the truth is clearly maladaptive for meeting the requirements of a complex, rapidly changing, pluralistic, egalitarian society" and, therefore, discouraged by those preparing such children for today's "educational institutions, which prepare students for such a world" (43).

Although occasionally, as Cooper notes, *Women's Ways* idealizes the achievement of multiple perspectives as more "mature" than other ways of knowing ("Women's Ways of Writing" 151), for the most part it resists the utopian tendency of Gilligan's work to suggest that such development leads to a resolution of conflicts via an "integration" of opposing ways of reasoning. Even the "constructivist" women, the ones most successful at such a resolution, see that "truth is a matter of the context in which it is embedded" (Belenky et al. 138), and, in our society, that means a context in which it remains difficult to integrate rather than "compartmentalize thought and feeling, home and work, self and other" (137). Such women "recognize the inevitability of conflict and stress and, although they may hope to achieve some respite, they also, as one woman explained, 'learn to live with conflict rather than talking or acting it away' " (137).[2]

Looking back now at my own attempts to make sense of Dianne's experiences, I see that much of my effort was, indeed, an attempt to "talk or act away" conflict rather than learning to live with it. The process was circular: by reading in Dianne's discourse the promise of "progress" and thus shaping her experience as unified and conclusive, I also brought my narrative to a unified and hopeful (if not quite utopian) closure; by creating the illusion, at least in writing, of a world of harmony and control, I could (more subtly) re-present the contradictions of my similar historical position as a highly educated woman in terms that transcended them. As Lester Faigley has argued in his essay "Judging Writing, Judging Selves" (1989), this unconscious projection onto student texts of middle-class fantasies about the unified, rational self may well be behavior I share with the majority of composition theorists whose work has shaped the field. Gilligan's work, I'm afraid, reinforces that idealization—and thus for me, its appeal.

Let me end this essay by suggesting why we might read my story, as my title promises, as a cautionary tale. We are seeing arguments now in composition studies that traditional academic discourse, especially as typically taught in beginning English, represents a "masculine" style or epistemology alienating to many women students— especially those in the positions of what Belenky and her colleagues would call "silenced" or "subjective" knowing. Drawing often on the work of Gilligan and (less often) of Belenky and her colleagues, proposals are being made (by, for example, Annas, Bleich, Peterson, and Hunter and his colleagues) that we teach an alternate style, one that would mix subjective and objective modes, public and private, exposition and narrative, "masculine" and "feminine" viewpoints. (In fact I've argued something like this myself.) It's not my purpose here to review these proposals in detail. I only want to suggest that if we proceed in that direction, we do so cautiously in light of our own problematic history of reading student work.

We might do well to ask ourselves questions such as these: In reading student texts as representative of moral or epistemological stances, do we base those readings on no more than brief samples of their work (the "snapshot" effect)? Or do our methods reveal the richness and conflicts in their lives? In advocating a revision of the "genders" of writing (or any other standard for written discourse), do we justify it as more "adaptive" to the demands of our institutions and/or empowering for our students, rather than idealize it as a more "mature" style? Do we recognize that what *we* define as adaptive or empowering may not be so regarded by students who do not share our histories, who may indeed want to resist the cultural identities we define for them? And how many of us read the work of those who might best address that question, the teachers of basic writing? Even if we do, do we still (as Faigley suggests) favor those student texts which achieve the closure of "rationality and unity by characterizing former selves as objects for analysis . . . rather than confronting the contradictions of present experience" (411)? In short, in reading the assumptions and experiences that inform our students' work, do we see ourselves as well?

Adrienne Rich argued nearly twenty years ago that the feminist project of discovering and re-vising our assumptions is "a difficult and dangerous walking on the ice, as we try to find language and images for a consciousness we are just coming into, and with little in the past to support us" (35). The challenge for composition studies today is to determine how much of what Rich said is still true for our discipline, while recognizing that we do indeed have a history that both supports and resists that effort.

Notes

1. Carol B. Stack, of the Institute of Policy Sciences and Public Affairs at Duke University, raises these issues concerning Gilligan's work in her essay, "The Culture of Gender: Women and Men of Color" (Kerber et al.). My point here, however, is that we do not have to go to scholarship outside of composition studies to make this critique.

2. Gilligan has come more recently to a similar position. Citing a number of follow-up studies to her work which have taken socioeconomic class into consideration, she has emphasized dissonance rather than harmony as the outcome of attempts to integrate different moral perspectives. While the more advantaged, better-educated women and men in these studies have generally *understood* and been able to use the logic of both the rights and care orientations, they will still *choose* one over the other as a way of behaving. Moreover, Gilligan adds, such critical awareness typically "brings women into conflict with current societal arrangements and often confronts them with painful and difficult choices" (Kerber et al., 328–30).

Works Cited

Annas, Pamela. "Style as Politics: A Feminist Approach to the Teaching of Writing." *College English* 47.4 (Apr. 1985): 360–71.

Belenky, Mary Field, Blythe McVicker Clinchy, Nancy Rule Goldberger, and Jill Mattuck Tarule. *Women's Ways of Knowing: The Development of Self, Voice, and Mind.* New York: Basic Books, 1986.

Bizzell, Patricia. "Cognition, Convention, and Certainty: What We Need to Know About Writing." *Pre/Text* 3 (1982): 213–43.

Bleich, David. "Genders of Writing." *Journal of Advanced Composition* 9 (1989): 10–25.

Brodkey, Linda. "On the Subjects of Class and Gender in 'The Literacy Letters.' " *College English* 51.2 (Feb. 1989): 125–41.

Cooper, Marilyn M. "The Ecology of Writing." In *Writing as Social Action.* Ed. Marilyn M. Cooper and Michael Holzman. Portsmouth, NH: Boynton/Cook, 1989. 1–13.

———. "Women's Ways of Writing." In *Writing as Social Action.* Ed. Marilyn M. Cooper and Michael Holzman. Portsmouth, NH: Boynton/Cook, 1989. 141–56.

Dowst, Kenneth. "The Epistemic Approach: Writing, Knowing, and Learning." In *Eight Approaches to Teaching Composition.* Ed. Timothy R. Donovan and Ben W. McClelland. Urbana, IL: NCTE, 1980. 65–85.

Faigley, Lester. "Judging Writing, Judging Selves." *College Composition and Communication* 40.4 (Dec. 1989): 395–412.

Flynn, Elizabeth. "Composing as a Woman." *College Composition and Communication* 39.4 (Dec. 1988): 423–35.

———. "Composition Studies from a Feminist Perspective." *The Politics of Writing Instruction: Postsecondary.* Ed. Richard Bullock and John Trimbur. Portsmouth, NH: Boynton/Cook, 1991. 137–54.

Gilligan, Carol. *In a Different Voice: Psychological Theory and Women's Development.* Cambridge: Harvard UP, 1982.

Hunter, Paul, Nadine Pearce, Sue Lee, Shirley Goldsmith, Patricia Feldman, and Holly Weaver. "Competing Epistemologies and Female Basic Writers." *Journal of Basic Writing* 7.1 (1988): 73–80.

Kerber, Linda K.; Catherine G. Greeno and Eleanor E. Maccoby; Zella Luria; Carol B. Stack; and Carol Gilligan. "On *In a Different Voice*: An Interdisciplinary Forum." *Signs* 11.2 (Winter 1986): 304–33.

Peterson, Linda H. "Gender and the Autobiographical Essay: Research Perspectives, Pedagogical Practices." *College Composition and Communication* 42.2 (May 1991): 170–83.

Phelps, Louise Wetherbee. *Composition as a Human Science: Contributions to the Self-Understanding of a Discipline.* New York: Oxford UP, 1988.

Rich, Adrienne. " 'When We Dead Awaken': Writing as Re-Vision." *On Lies, Secrets, and Silence: Selected Prose, 1966–1978.* New York: Norton, 1979. 33–49.

Wall, Susan V. "Revision in a Rhetorical Context: Case Studies of First-Year College Writers." Diss. U of Pittsburgh, 1982.

13 The Myth of Transcendence and the Problem of the "Ethics" Essay in College Writing Instruction

David A. Jolliffe
University of Illinois at Chicago

Many instructors portray college composition as a transcendent experience. These instructors rarely teach their students that a composition course is good for them in, of, and by itself. When students ask the inevitable "Why do I have to take this course?" these instructors respond that students must do well in composition for either or both of two reasons: (a) so that they may succeed in the reading and writing tasks in their other college courses, the "real" courses in their majors, minors, and distribution curricula; and (b) so that they may become "well-rounded," responsible, participating citizens. In other words, the value of composition as an enterprise transcends the actual composition classroom.

One could make a case that this notion of transcendence is both valid and useful. The first aforementioned reason represents the idea that underlies composition as a service course and that, ideally, makes the course relevant to the student's academic career; the second, again ideally, makes the course relevant to the student's life beyond the academy. My former colleague Thomas Masters has characterized transcendence as a central feature in the ideology that shaped writing instruction in American colleges in the decade following World War II. Indeed, the concept did gain currency then, as instructors attempted to justify instruction in *belles lettres* to the legions of new students who enlarged the postwar university populations.

But the notion of transcendence has roots that predate the 1940s, roots that allow it to persevere in contemporary composition classrooms. I try in this essay to explain these sources and to examine the concept critically, questioning whether composition instructors should continue to preach it. In particular, I critique one bit of pedagogy that grows

out of the notion of transcendence, namely the practice of asking
students to observe some feature of behavior or belief in their worlds
and draw an ethical lesson about it. I wonder whether the practice of
the "ethics" essay, like the notion of transcendence in general, has a
context that legitimately supports it in the contemporary college
composition class. I conclude by offering a perspective on college
composition instruction that allows instructors and students to understand both the benefits and the limits of believing in transcendence.

Can Students Really Believe in Transcendence?

Before examining its aforementioned ideological components individually, I want to pause and consider transcendence in general. Seen in
its best light, transcendence might motivate students taking composition
to do well: Here, after all, is a course that teaches them how to read
clearly and write correctly in all their college courses and prepares
them to deal with the world of the word outside college. Seen in a
worse light, however, transcendence denigrates composition instruction: Here is a class that is not really a class; it's more a lesson in
literacy calisthenics, an exercise in delayed gratification. But yet it *is* a
class: students must attend it regularly, read texts, participate in
discussions, write papers, and so on. They get a grade that figures in
their grade-point average, and the course counts toward graduation.

How do students today deal with this split personality of composition
instruction? When instructors justify the course by preaching the two-
plank, preparation-for-college/preparation-for-professional life platform, can students really believe them? My surmise is that there was
a time when they could, when transcendence made sense within the
curriculum and the students' perception of it. It might have made
sense when a university education was more of a unified whole, when
neither administrators nor students divided the curriculum into introductory "core" courses (the ones that bright, energetic students could
waive with precollegiate work so they could get on with "real" studies),
general-education distribution courses, major courses, minor courses,
and free electives. In such a unified curriculum, composition might
have existed on the same plane with, and even conceptually linked,
the student's study of history, philosophy, science, and letters. Transcendence might have made sense when the path from college to the
professions was more predictable, when a bachelor's degree would
certify a college graduate as one who had lived, for at least four years,
the life of the mind, and who could be expected to embody that life
with the power of the word.

Believing in the transcendence of composition is difficult, and it's a risk: It asks the student to withhold the troubling questions of immediate applicability and relevance—questions like the oft-posed "Why do we really have to write these kinds of essays?" It requires the student to see good writing as an abstraction, a skill which actually operates in other realms but which they must practice in composition courses. Students today are attending college in material, political, and social circumstances completely unlike those of earlier eras. I wonder whether today's student, who must pick up classes as they are available while working a part-time job, who knows that a bachelor's degree might lead to nothing more than a low-level service job, can really believe in the transcendence of composition.

A challenging answer to these questions comes from the historian Helen Lefkowitz Horowitz, whose 1987 study, *Campus Life*, examines how American college students have positioned themselves in relation to both formal coursework and informal education from the end of the eighteenth century to the present. Horowitz describes the development during this period of three types of student characters. Originally, these were "college men," for whom the extracurriculum was more important than the curriculum, who came to college not to study but to develop a social life and acquire connections for the future; "outsiders," who were "studious, polite, and respectful of authority," and who "focused on academic, not extracurricular, success" (14); and "rebels," who were "as excited by ideas as any outsider," but who "demanded the content, not the form" of academia and "identified keenly with artists and writers breaking conventions" (15–16). By the 1970s, Horowitz believes, "the culture of the outsiders triumphed" over the college men (and women) and the rebels. "But," she notes, for the new outsiders, "what had once been the province of aspiring youth, optimistic about their futures, became that of prosperous collegians fearful of downward mobility" (17). Today, she asserts, "few college students ask existential questions about the life of the mind" (3). Sounding a theme that Barbara Ehrenreich also develops in *Fear of Falling*, Horowitz explains further:

> The fear of economic and social erosion, of not being able to reproduce the comfortable world of one's parents, continues to dominate undergraduate consciousness. In this atmosphere, education is largely reduced to the quest for grades through the application of all the strategies of grinding that college men once imagined outsiders pursued. Despite their seriousness, today's New Outsiders do not connect to the life of the mind: ideas are far too risky in the game of grade-seeking they play. (20–21)

Such cautious "grinding" as the dominant mode of intellectual activity is, of course, frustrating to instructors in all fields who want students to take risks in order to grow as independent thinkers. It becomes frustrating to students and instructors alike, Horowitz points out, in writing classes, where instructors "judge the integrity of an argument—its logic, clarity, subtlety, and documentation" (270):

> Here is where the grinding fails. For here the students can no longer rely merely on memorized information or on the judgment of the professor, but must make imaginative connections on their own and create intellectual structures to support them. Although a few students accept and even welcome intellectual adventure, many become frightened by uncertainty and angry because they believe the professor is withholding knowledge. (270–71)

Whether economic, social, and political conditions, both within and beyond academia, will continue to nourish this New Outsider ideology is a larger question than this essay can answer. It seems clear to me, however, that faculty who teach and administer college composition must question whether students can really believe in transcendence in such an intellectual climate.

Does Composition Really Prepare Students for Other Classes?

Not only is transcendence in general a troubling concept, but these two tenets warrant much more careful scrutiny than they typically receive. The first tenet, that the value of composition instruction prepares students to read clearly and write well in their other courses, is regularly preached in general composition courses, but it has also been used to justify the long history of "linked" writing courses and the more recent writing-across-the-curriculum and writing-in-the-disciplines movements. Underlying this tenet is the idea that rhetoric, upon whose principles composition curricula are built, has no subject matter of its own, but is applicable to all subject domains.

The source of this attitude is Aristotelian, but nearly every major rhetorical theorist in antiquity—including Cicero and Quintilian, whose principles were more central than Aristotle's to the Western tradition of discourse education—says something to suggest that the art of rhetoric applies to no particular subject matter. Early in book 1 of the *Rhetoric*, Aristotle asserts that "rhetoric is not confined to any single and definite class of subjects; . . . the art has no special application to any class of subjects" (1355a). Cicero writes in *De Oratore* that "no man can be an orator possessed of very praiseworthy accomplishments unless he has attained a knowledge of everything important" (1:36), and Quintilian teaches in the *Institutio Oratoria* that the material of oratory is "everything that may come before an orator for discussion" (2:4).

Some contemporary observers also assert rhetoric's independence of subject matters and see in that independence a source of institutional strength for writing instruction. As Paul Kameen puts it, "It matters not, from an Aristotelian point of view, upon what turf/ground/territory rhetoric situates itself; it can pitch its tent, build its arena, inscribe its 'field' almost anywhere. It matters only that it finds a vantage point from which it can view the various 'games' that the rest of the arts and sciences play, the structure of which are its interest and its business to measure and appreciate" (218).

But rhetoric's apparent independence of subject matters is deceptive, and this notion of transcendence is troubling when instructors and students accept it in either of two simplistic forms. First, one could argue that a general art of rhetoric, based on classical theories, teaches students principles of invention, arrangement, and style that they can employ to write in all fields. But to use Aristotle, Cicero, and Quintilian too specifically as sources for such a general rhetoric would be naive. The rhetoricians of ancient Greece and Rome were concerned with preparing orators to speak to the legislative bodies, courts, and public ceremonial occasions of their times, and the features of their rhetorical theory are constrained by those contexts: the classical principles of invention, arrangement, style, memory, and delivery are principles for speaking and writing about Athenian and Roman politics and ethics. To adapt the ancients' teaching so that it applies to the arts and sciences of our own times is no mean task. What classical rhetoric taught about systems of invention, the structure of discourses, and figures and style cannot be applied, willy-nilly, to writing in twentieth-century academic contexts; after all, Aristotle, Cicero, and Quintilian were not teaching students to write in anthropology or business or home economics.

Second, one could argue that "good writing is good writing," no matter what the field, and that writing courses ought to teach students principles of good paragraph and sentence structure and rules of correct grammar and usage. Certainly, to write in all fields a student must know how to structure paragraphs and produce complete sentences without committing solecisms. But general composition instructors who preach the "good writing for all fields" tenet of transcendence have long been baffled by what to teach students about, say, the use of first-person pronouns, or the convention and functions of the passive voice, not to mention more subtle concepts such as stance, tone, and persona. The "rules" for all these concepts are not rules at all, but instead conventions of specific intellectual communities.

Thus, if instructors are concerned that what they teach students in general composition courses should be "transferred" to the writing they must do in other courses, they may find little "transferrable" material in either general rhetorical principles or in paragraph-, sentence-, or word-level skills. What *can* be transferred from general composition to other domains, I believe, is the idea that writing in all fields is shaped by an interactive relationship between the way an intellectual community constructs knowledge in writing and the genres it uses to configure that knowledge. In brief, here is how this dynamic works: Writers create texts to "do business" in certain communities of readers and writers. Within those communities, there are specific ideas, often tacit, about what constitutes acceptable subject matters to write about. About each of these acceptable subject matters, there are, within communities of readers and writers, certain *status quo* ideas, attitudes, and propositions, discursive entities that Chaim Perelman calls the "starting points of argumentation." Within these communities there are, in addition, specific kinds of rhetorical "moves" or "transactions" that a writer is expected to make in order to lead readers to perceive a central idea or adhere to a thesis. Aristotle, for example, in teaching the art of rhetoric for fourth-century Athenian orators, calls these "moves" *enthymemes*. Within these communities there are also definite ideas, again often tacit, about what functions written texts should serve—that is, the degree to which they should "shift the scene" from the written text at hand to some other arena of action.

All of these aspects of "knowledge work"—acceptable subjects, starting points, transactions, and functions of texts—are constrained by the kinds of genres within which the community has chosen to conduct its written business. Indeed, as I argue, the genres of different communities actually emerge from the knowledge-work its members must perform. In other words, whether a person writes about a specific subject matter, chooses to detail specifically what she believes her readers presently know and think about the subject, engages in certain kinds of rhetorical moves (for example, definition or comparison or causal reasoning), and urges some specific action depends on the genre she is expected to produce. The choice of genre also dictates, to a finer degree than other prescriptive rules, how the writer must construct paragraphs, sentences, and words.

This knowledge work–genre dynamic is what students can learn in general composition that can be transferred to the writing they must do in other courses. It is this dynamic that I believe ought to constitute the "content" of college writing instruction. But adopting this dynamic as the content of general composition courses means that they must have specific subject matters for students to read and write about. What should those subject matters be?

Should Students Write "Ethics" Essays?

Apparently, some instructors and composition scholars believe that an appropriate subject matter for college writing courses is the realm of contemporary moral and ethical issues. Requiring students to write about such issues manifests a belief in the second tenet of transcendence, the idea that composition ought to prepare students to be responsible, ethical citizens of the world.

Evidence from various sources shows how widespread the belief in this tenet is. In a chapter of her book entitled "Teaching Academic Writing as Moral and Civic Thinking," Sandra Stotsky takes it as axiomatic that "teaching . . . proceeds on the belief that individual development should have moral direction. Teachers are expected to develop—and evaluate—their students' moral thinking, not only for the students' sake, but also for the sake of their disciplines and the civic communities that support their work and their schools" (129). Recently, I asked writing program administrators at forty-five colleges and universities to share typical assignments that students in general composition courses at their institutions are given. My survey turned up these prompts: At a major public university in the Midwest, students wrote their final essays on the topic, "How do you account for love?" Students at an East Coast university were asked to answer the question, "What makes people happy in the 1980s?" At a major private university in the Rockies, students were given the topics, "Hypocrisy goeth before a fall" and "Relate a personal experience that taught you an important moral law." In a later study, I met twice a month with students from colleges and universities in the Chicago area who were expected to write about whatever they wished in their composition classes. For her final paper, a two-year-college student wrote on the evils of being lazy. At a comprehensive university in northern Illinois, students wrote argumentative papers on capital punishment and abortion; their instructor told them specifically not to acknowledge positions other than their thesis.

The assignment for the ethics essay generally asks students to consider some principle with ethical implications and to expatiate upon it. Usually students encounter the principle either as a kind of aphorism that they must explicate or as a single term for which they must provide an extended definition or illustration, terms such as "morality," "cheating," "patriotism," "leadership," "laziness," and so on. Such assignments suggest to me an invitation, if not a mandate, for students to observe the manners of their world and to turn from their observation to the task of shaping their fellow human beings' moral behavior.

The ethics essay as a pedagogical practice has roots in both major traditions that historically have shaped composition instruction, rhetoric and literary studies. As historians of education such as Henri Marrou and James Kinneavy point out, many of the principles of rhetorical education that influenced its development in Western Europe from antiquity through the nineteenth century—the principles set out by Cicero and synthesized by Quintilian—can be traced to the influence of the fourth-century Greek sophist, Isocrates. As Quintilian would establish in his definition of the orator as a "good man skilled at speaking" (*Institutio Oratoria* 12:1), Isocrates taught that the effective rhetor must treat morally edifying topics:

> . . . when anyone elects to speak or write discourses that are worthy of praise and honor, [the rhetor will support causes] which are great and honorable, devoted to the welfare of man and our common good . . . [H]e will select from the actions of men which bear upon his subject those examples which are the most illustrious and the most edifying . . . [T]he power to speak well and think right will reward the man who approaches the art of discourse with the love of wisdom and love of honour. (*Antidosis* 276–77)

Perhaps the most distinctive feature of the educational system that grew out of Isocrates' work was the pedagogical use of the *progymnasmata*, the preparatory exercises in composition that, as Edward P. J. Corbett notes, were common in schools throughout the Renaissance. The fourth of these exercises, the *chria*, specifically required students to expand upon a moral aphorism—for example, "Isocrates says that the roots of education are bitter but the flowers thereof are sweet"— in a series of eight prescribed steps.

A strong tradition in the teaching of literature, linked in varying degrees to composition instruction over the years, complements rhetoric as a source for the second tenet of transcendence and its application in the pedagogy of the ethics essay. This is the tradition that found its apostle in Matthew Arnold, who taught that the function of criticism was "to learn and propagate the best that is known and thought in the world" (595). Margaret Mathieson in *The Preachers of Culture* documents the development of this Arnoldian doctrine and its Leavisite extension in the first half of the twentieth century among English teachers who saw as their responsibility the task of refining their students' aesthetic and ethical views of the world by making them sensitive to literature. Janet Batsleer, Tony Davies, Rebecca O'Rourke, and Chris Weedon, in a challenging study of the "cultural politics of gender and class" in English teaching, note the British Schools Council's 1968 concern that most students showed a "regrettable indifference" to what the Council called "ethical values" in English studies (36).

So what's wrong with seeing moral development as part of English education, with asking students to read and write in order to refine their views of contemporary ethics? In essence, nothing; in practice, maybe lots. As Arthur Applebee has demonstrated, the collective wisdom of the progressive movements in English education in this century—progressivism itself in the 1920s, education for experience in the 1930s, education for life adjustment in the 1950s and 1960s, followed by values clarification in the 1960s and 1970s—has convinced most educators that young adults *can* profitably turn their attention, as they learn to read and write, to questions of what is ethically vital and important in their lives. Despite the increasing proportion of returning adults, most college composition students are still in their late teens, still working hard at developing their own positions on ethical issues vis-à-vis their parents' and families' ideas and attitudes. Writing essays about contemporary ethics could foster these students' emerging self-awareness.

The problem with asking students to moralize in college composition—the problem with the ethics essay as a genre—lies in the way most assignments that elicit the writing are construed. Striving to discourage hollow, formulaic, voiceless prose—an egregious *bête noire* in the literature of the writing-process movement—instructors present students with an ethical issue and ask, in so many words, "What does this mean to *you*? How do *your* ideas, attitudes, and experiences figure in your treatment of this issue? Don't worry about what other people think about the issue—we want *your* ideas, *your* sense, *your* personal voice."

This method of inviting the ethics essay is troubling because it is complicit with the very aspect of our culture that at least one contemporary philosopher and a major figure in modern rhetorical theory contend makes public discussion of ethical issues impossible. As Alasdair MacIntyre argues in *After Virtue: A Study in Moral Theory*, contemporary thinking about ethical issues is hopelessly clouded by what he calls *emotivism*, "the doctrine that all evaluative judgments are *nothing but* expressions of preference, expressions of attitude or

feeling, insofar as they are moral or evaluative in character" (11–12;
MacIntyre's emphasis). MacIntyre holds that embracing this doctrine
leads to a "gap between the *meaning* of moral expressions and the
ways in which they are put to *use*":

> Each of us is taught to see himself or herself as an autonomous
> moral agent; but each of us also becomes engaged by modes of
> practice . . . which involve us in manipulative relationships with
> others. Seeking to protect the autonomy that we have learned to
> prize, we aspire ourselves not to be manipulated by others; seeking
> to incarnate our own principles and stand-point in the world of
> practice, we find no way open to us to do so except by directing
> toward others those very manipulative modes of relationship
> which each of us aspires to resist in our own case. (68)

MacIntyre sees two paths for redeeming moral discussion in our culture.
First, participants in moral discussion must operate with a sense of
telos, a global sense of purpose for ethical behavior: "Unless there is
a *telos* which transcends the limited good of practices by constituting
the good of a whole human life, . . . it will be *both* the case that a
certain subversive arbitrariness will invade the moral life *and* that we
shall be unable to specify the content of certain virtues adequately"
(203). Second, participants in moral discussion must cast each human
life as part of a "narrative unity"; MacIntyre explains eloquently:

> I am never able to seek for the good or exercise the virtues only
> *qua* individual. . . . We all approach our own circumstances as
> bearers of a particular social identity. I am someone's son or
> daughter, someone else's uncle; I am a citizen of this or that city,
> a member of this or that guild or profession; I belong to this clan,
> that tribe, this nation. Hence what is good for me has to be good
> for one who inhabits these roles. As such, I inherit from the past
> of my family, my city, my tribe, my nation, a variety of debts,
> inheritances, rightful expectations, and obligations. They constitute
> the given of my life, my moral starting point. (220)

In a stroke of understatement, MacIntyre points out that "to think of
a human life as a narrative unity is to think in a way very alien to
the dominant individualist and bureaucratic modes of modern culture"
(227).

By linking the decline of effective moral discussion to powerful
individualist thinking, MacIntyre is echoing Wayne Booth, who holds
that one of the most damaging features of what he calls *modernism* is
the belief that "there are no good reasons for changing my mind,
especially in questions involving value judgments"; or, stated in more
"irrationalist" terms, "The heart has its reasons that reason ignores—
and therefore to hell with reason!" (23). Booth wryly casts himself in

this modernist stance and then prescribes what ought to happen to himself: "*My* preferences, *my* desires, *my* subjective states must again and again be modified and repudiated as I am dragged, kicking and screaming, out of infantile solipsism and into adult membership in an inquiring community" (13).

Toward a Pedagogy of Substance in College Composition

The problem of the ethics essay, I believe, is part and parcel of the most pressing problem facing college writing instruction: its lack of attention, in curriculum, pedagogy, and research, to *what* students are reading and writing *about* in composition courses. Students are asked to write essays about Subject X: happiness, love, capital punishment, abortion, you name it. But composition instruction too rarely offers students any kind of regimen, any planned method, for *learning* about these subject matters in the course of writing about them.

I think composition's unwillingness to consider issues of the content of student writing emerges from a belief in transcendence. If we are merely preparing students to write effectively in their other classes and in the world beyond the academy, composition instructors might ask, can we really *have* a content, a unified set of subject matters that students read and write about? To counter this question, I would offer another: Can composition instruction realistically operate *without* content, without specific subject matters for students to read and write about?

I propose that those of use who teach college composition see it in a highly untraditional way, not as a transcendent enterprise but as a class unto itself. Composition courses, I maintain, ought to require students to participate in an inquiring community, where they read, write, and learn about one subject matter (or perhaps a few related ones) for an entire term. As they learn about writing by investigating this subject matter—and the ethical issues inherent within it can certainly constitute part of the investigation—students can determine why it is important that they examine it; what are the *status quo* propositions that *other people* already know, think, believe, and feel about it; what kinds of generic, rhetorical transactions can effectively present key ideas and demonstrate theses about it; and what kinds of novel beliefs and new actions they can urge with regard to it. Adopting such a perspective toward composition will go a long way toward establishing it as a tenable course within college curricula, a course with bona fide content of its own, one that need not transcend its own legitimate, challenging boundaries.

Works Cited

Applebee, Arthur N. *Tradition and Reform in the Teaching of English: A History.* Urbana, IL: NCTE, 1974.

Aristotle. *The Rhetoric of Aristotle.* Trans. Lane Cooper. Englewood Cliffs, NJ: Prentice-Hall, 1932.

Arnold, Matthew. "The Function of Criticism at the Present Time." *Critical Theory since Plato.* Ed. Hazard Adams. New York: Harcourt Brace Jovanovich, 1971. 583–96.

Batsleer, Janet, Tony Davies, Rebecca O'Rourke, and Chris Weedon. *Rewriting English: The Politics of Gender and Class.* London: Methuen, 1985.

Booth, Wayne C. *Modern Dogma and the Rhetoric of Assent.* Chicago: U of Chicago P, 1974.

Cicero, Marcus Tullius. *De Oratore.* Trans. E. W. Sutton and H. Rackham. Cambridge, MA: Harvard UP, 1942.

Corbett, Edward P. J. *Classical Rhetoric for the Modern Student.* 2d ed. New York: Oxford UP, 1976.

Ehrenreich, Barbara. *Fear of Falling: The Inner Life of the Middle Class.* New York: Pantheon, 1989.

Horowitz, Helen Lefkowitz. *Campus Life: Undergraduate Culture from the End of the Eighteenth Century to the Present.* New York: Knopf, 1987.

Isocrates. *[Works of] Isocrates.* Trans. George Norlin. Cambridge: Harvard UP, 1928.

Kameen, Paul. "Composition: Inscribing the Field." *Boundary* 2.13 (1985): 213–31.

Kinneavy, James L. *A Theory of Discourse.* Englewood Cliffs, NJ: Prentice-Hall, 1971.

MacIntyre, Alasdair. *After Virtue: A Study in Moral Theory.* 2d ed. South Bend, IN: U of Notre Dame P, 1984.

Marrou, Henri Irenee. *A History of Education in Antiquity.* Trans. George Lamb. London: Sheed and Ward, 1956.

Masters, Thomas M. *Writing in the Margins: The Postwar Discourse of Freshman English.* Pittsburgh: U of Pittsburgh P, forthcoming.

Mathieson, Margaret. *The Preachers of Culture: A Study of English and Its Teachers.* London: Rowman and Littlefield, 1975.

Perelman, Chaim. "The New Rhetoric: A Theory in Practical Reasoning." *The Great Ideas Today, 1970.* Encyclopedia Brittanica. 1970 ed. 273–312.

Quintilian. *Institutio Oratoria.* Trans. H. E. Butler. Cambridge: Harvard UP, 1929.

Stotsky, Sandra. *Connecting Civic Education and Language Education: The Contemporary Challenge.* New York: Teachers College P, 1991.

14 The "Kinds of Language" Curriculum

David Bleich
University of Rochester

Lately, literary theory is enjoying unprecedented public attention. Most of this attention has come as a result of opposition to its raising of political questions. In part literary theory's political orientation derives from several views of language, such as those of Husserl, Wittgenstein, and Derrida, which stress its subjectivity, its flexibility, its ludic potential, the transience of its uses and meanings, and, often, its ability to betray us. In America, some well-known critics have extended these views of language to literature and have made an industry of formulating self-questioning meanings for works previously understood in stable ways. When this style of interpretation became associated with political advocacy, the style and the advocacy threatened traditional ways of doing business in the academy and in popular politics. The term "politically correct" originated as a note of self-interrogation among politically awakened academics. But now it is a taunt used by threatened traditionalists in and out of the academy. This appropriation of the "other's language" by the opposition is one sign that something new is happening in the relationship between the academy and politics as usual.

Their own progressiveness notwithstanding, advocates of "theory," "cultural studies," and "postmodernism" are justifiably viewed by teachers of writing as themselves seekers of power: the actual social relation of writing teachers to "literary theory" people has not changed very much, as Susan Miller discusses in her 1991 treatise, *Textual Carnivals*. There are still the "sad women in the basement" (a group associated by gender with the mostly female teachers of primary and secondary school) who do most of the teaching of writing. Similarly, in a recent doctoral dissertation at the University of Maryland, Mary Alice Delia describes a distinct and traditional class structure in the population of those participating in a recent summer meeting of Dartmouth's School of Criticism and Theory. While the interests of literary theorists have helped to make reading lists more culturally comprehensive, these interests have not changed the class structure within the academy. Many compositionists acknowledge a more pertinent set of theorists—such as James Berlin, Susan Miller, Stephen North, and Louise Phelps—but those who do most of the actual teaching are still in a (lower) class by themselves. The presumably progressive idea of "writing across the curriculum" still refers to the expansion of a service performed by the lower academic class for those who finally don't consider teaching and curriculum to be authoritative categories. Meanwhile, literary theorists, who have spent many pages explicating the poststructuralist sense of writing as referring to any semiotic activity (such as speaking), separate their theory from their teaching, and separate both their theory and their teaching from the total enterprise of teaching writing. No matter how much opposition these theorists may have claimed against the class structure in Western corporate-governed society, the same theorists maintain a similar class structure in the academy.

Consider the term "curriculum," which identifies this "class" situation further. In the academy, it is a term most often used to describe departments of teacher education in schools of education: Curriculum and Instruction departments. In primary and secondary schools people often refer to the curriculum, as if there is a fixed set of subjects that counts as a universal, fundamental preparation for something else— work, or "life," or college, for example. In the university we instead speak of "core courses," "distribution requirements," and "majors." "Curriculum," if used to describe what is taught in the university, would be considered to have devalued the status, the freedom, the depth, and the subtlety of the study that takes place there. The university is the site of research, reflection, speculation, and perhaps training. So one use of this term "curriculum" depends on a contrast between the alleged fixed status of pre-university learning and the constantly researched status of college subject matters.

At the same time, because "curriculum" remains a Latin word, it indirectly aligns itself with the language of medical and legal "experts," and can sometimes seem to elevate the work of teacher educators (education teachers?) toward the higher status of other faculties in universities. You don't say, "I teach teachers"; you say, "I teach curriculum and instruction." So another use of this term is to conceal the hierarchical relation of teaching to the other main activity of academics—research.

Many colleges and universities have accepted the need for the category of "writing across the curriculum." But because of the class status of writing and the conventional uses of the term "curriculum," it tends to be treated mostly as a response to the demands of people in non-English disciplines (and many in literature and literary theory as well) that university students in all subjects need intensive training in something like "learning how to write a clear and coherent sentence or paragraph." Faculty in many disciplines reluctantly attend workshops and seminars, often taught by professional outside consultants expert in the teaching of writing, which these faculty members then "apply" to their own subject matters as best they can. Writing across the curriculum, like writing and like curriculum, remains a service to the university yet not a part of it.

For a number of years now, Louise Phelps has argued strenuously that we should think of composition as a "human science." She cites a wide range of established sources, such as Aristotle and Paul Ricoeur, to provide a credible scholarly basis for us to rethink composition as a subject matter. Her own erudition is an instance of how a writing teacher can be as authoritative a scholar as anyone else in the academy. In the December 1991 issue of *College English*, she offers an elaborate, detailed (and literal) chart of how to organize theoretical and practical knowledge in the field of composition, striking an optimistic note to counter Stephen North's doubts about the subject as presented in his 1987 *The Making of Knowledge in Composition*.

While Phelps's work is energetic, committed, and documented, she aims to legitimate, so to speak, a part of the academy—composition teaching—whose identity requires, as Susan Miller argues, an illegitimate status. Disenfranchised groups have always known that their own enfranchisement will entail a fundamental transformation of society as a whole. Such groups only initially wish for legitimacy: by now most African Americans, nonheterosexuals, and women, as well as other, smaller groups, understand that fair and full citizenship for them entails a major transformation of the entire society. "Writing across the curriculum," following my analogy, is more or less like wishing for legitimacy: a sensible wish given the circumstances, but still not decisive enough an answer to the current, unbalanced conditions of academic life. Terms like "good writing," "composition," and "curriculum" are attached to the academic ideology that requires their reduced status. Within this ideology, science and technology form a priestly class, predominantly masculine in population; other subjects, even humanistic ones, aim to emulate science, while society's ruling class of military and corporate men preside over—and fund, partly through their roles on boards of trustees—the traditional academic pyramid of status and authority. Miller's view of the profession recognizes this arrangement and actively works to deauthorize it; Phelps's view of the profession tacitly respects its terms. In contrast to Phelps's sense of the benign relation of the academy to society, Susan Miller's sense of the discipline as geared toward transforming ideological expectations of political hegemony suggests a more promising heartbeat for our profession than the reconciliation of "theory and practice" that characterizes Phelps's work. Nonetheless, both efforts are welcome.

Under the influence of literary theory, the fashionable term for writing and language lately is "discourse." It is a useful term, especially to us academics. It is a term now used the way "text" is used: as a universal. Everything is discourse, everything can be textualized; and, not coincidentally, everything can—and ought to be—"theorized." This faddist style is itself a derivative of scientific ideology, since science is where the search for universals acquires its immunity to political and social criticism, a problem treated at length in the work of Sandra Harding, Evelyn Keller, and several other feminist epistemologists. When we who honor "textuality" and "discourse" as terminological advances also seek to confer legitimacy mainly by "theorizing" a subject, we unwittingly affiliate ourselves with the existing hierarchy of academic life. We adopt the ideology of science by accepting a separation of knowledge from individual lived experience and collective social relations. A "universal," after all, is not just a name of something but an accepted category which predicts and explains as well as describes. When "text," "discourse," and "theory" become jargonized, it is a sign we have lost touch with "books," "talk," and "thought." The task of teaching writing across the curriculum teaches us that we are not simply wringing our hands over terms: it teaches us that the language we use marks our interpersonal and societal interests and relations. So I want, even if temporarily, to think about kinds of language as an enlargement of writing across the curriculum. My comments are addressed to offering a writing subject matter whose classes and categories are rooted in questions of society and knowledge, to changing the social relations of the classroom, and, I hope, to integrating the memberships of the different academic interests and classrooms more fully. To begin these tasks, let me describe a recent classroom experience I had.

I was a guest teacher for about six months in a ninth-grade classroom in an urban high school in Rochester, New York. One of our early subjects was the difference between proper and improper English. We had class discussions and essays on this topic. There was an essay assignment which asked students to *discuss* what they considered the difference between proper and improper English. Here is Ms. K's contribution:

> I miraculously bit into one of my sister's rock-hard meatballs and crunched noisily. I'd seen my brother try to feed a meatball to the dog who had turned up his nose and started eating the cat's food.
>
> "Tommy pass me the sauce please," my sister asked kicking the meatball that my brother left on the floor. When my mom and dad left the dinner table, my brother rudely said, "I ain't passing you nothing." I passed her the sauce and said, "Ain't ain't a word."
>
> "Yes it is," my sister piped up, "I saw it in the dictionary."
>
> "So?" my brother snapped.
>
> "Hey," my mom said peeking her head into the kitchen, "who's saying 'ain't' "?
>
> "Mom is ain't a word?"
>
> "Well it all depends on what you think proper English is."
>
> "Proper English is not talking slang," my sister said clearing the table and rolling her eyes.
>
> "Yo girly stop sweating my talk," my brother said grabbing his glass.
>
> "See mommy that's improper English," my sister said babyishly.
>
> My father pushed past my mother and said, "There is no proper or improper English, as long as you talk so that someone can understand you." Everyone glared at my brother.
>
> "Yo," he said loudly, "ain't no proper or improper English."
>
> My sister stuck her tongue out at my brother before saying, "Yo, young blood how's about if you let me whip the sneakers off you in a game of king's checkers."
>
> Everyone laughed.

There are two sets of issues presented by this essay: those connected with proper and improper English in the situation presented by Ms. K, and those presented by the fact that this was Ms. K's response to the essay assignment. The scene at the dinner table has five people, the two parents and the three siblings. The use of "ain't" here is connected with the difference between black English and standard white English. Both are spoken in this family. Ms. K characterizes the sister's complaint as "babyish." She herself in the scene, as in the dialogue, takes both sides of the argument: "Ain't ain't a word," she said. But she portrays the sister and the mother as holding an opinion different from the brother and the father. The female family members are concerned with propriety; the males with spontaneity. At the end, the sister understands both sides and reconciles with the brother. On top of the issues of sibling rivalry and adolescent and adult relationships, this family is dealing with black and white, male and female, rich and poor. At some level, the author of this vignette is acutely aware of all of these issues and represents each in a different kind of language.

Ms. K, a precocious and gifted student of fourteen, obviously speaks and writes perfect "white" English: "I miraculously bit into one of my sister's rock-hard meatballs and crunched noisily." This keynote of her "essay" is given to the two white teachers of her class. She has authorized herself immediately. She is also an imaginative writer, however, and one who has been reading a great deal, so she includes the secondary comedy about the dog and the meatball on the floor. In making these moves, and in presenting a story with a dramatic dialogue embedded in it, she bypasses the discursive essay assignment that most other students wrote. While respectful of school, teachers, and white standard English, Ms. K actually made one kind of language (the reflective commentary) into another: a, shall we say, fictionalized narrative dialogue that addresses the assignment metaphorically.

Classmates of Ms. K had other observations about proper and improper English. Two male students said outright that proper English is what the rich speak, or what those who went to college speak. Another female student wrote, "When the women used to wear those big dresses they talk very proper they say things like 1. yes Madam, 2. yes Sir, 3. no Madam, 4. no Sir." For the two boys, the class identification *precedes* the identification of the language: the economic and social classes *determine* the propriety of the language. The girls, while indirectly identifying the determining class—the women in "big dresses"—further identify *obedient* language as being the sign of propriety.

Such samples suggest that these students have a good basis for learning to distinguish different kinds of language and what each kind means. Both accomplished students and less-accomplished ones are acutely aware of not only who speaks what language, but of the qualities and characters of those different kinds. Like all students, these lack only the experience and discipline to think through their knowledge at some length. The curriculum, however, does not ask them to do this thinking. It asks them simply to master white standard English, a necessary task, most teachers, white and black, agree, but not a task which responds to the strongest forces that motivate these students. In most classes, "Yo girly stop sweating my talk" is confined to the marginal conversations of students. In many classes, particularly crowded ones, there is no space to stop and think about the fact that Ms. K, like most other African American students, habitually shifts between (at least) two dialects, each marked by race and class and often by gender. There is no time to recognize, in fact, that *all* students speak different kinds of language as they move among different classes and communities. In the university, there is no time to think that even the most homogeneous group of students enters college with a comparable array of language kinds, each living in its own context, each governed by social and political conventions that are taken for granted and not considered parts of the language curriculum.

The many subject matters and social zones and groups in university communities create an excellent atmosphere for study of the many kinds of language in society as a whole. Most students can describe and document the phenomenology of how to function in college. Their knowledge, however, does not correspond well to the local and technical kinds of writing demanded by their different subject matters. Rather, the social psychology of students' intellectual life has to do with the getting of grades and their pursuit of whatever ability is necessary to enhance their successful certification. Toward this goal, their attention is less on the kinds of writing needed relative to the subject matter than on the kinds of writing needed to ingratiate themselves with the teacher. As a result, writing becomes identified as a form of compliance rather than as a form of exchange, communication, expression, or initiative. Let me discuss the work of two female students who are trying to present this situation to me (in my first-year writing course) in as respectful a way as possible. The first student is somewhat more at ease with the situation than the second. Here are some of Ms. S's comments. She is a cognitive science major and an accomplished, conscientious student.

> It seems that all people who are involved in academics in some form have a "split personality." . . . I am as guilty of having two personas as everyone else. There is definitely a difference between the writing I do for classes and the writing I do for pleasure. Generally, my writing for classes is "proper." By this, I mean that my grammar is excellent (I think), my vocabulary is relatively sophisticated, and my work has a specific structure—there is an opening, a body, and a conclusion. Also, my work has to be thought out prior to actually starting the writing; everything must follow a logical order. On the other hand I would say that my letter writing is very informal when compared to my school work. I'm generally not concerned with the correctness of my grammar, even though it tends to be fairly good, the level of vocabulary that I use, which is usually simpler than the vocabulary that I use for school, and the structure of my letters—I tend to write them spontaneously.

Ms. S engages the issue of academic writing by viewing it to be all in the same genre, and by comparing this genre with another—letter writing. Toward the end of her eight-page essay on this topic, Ms. S observes, "I don't think that my writing style changes much when writing for the sciences, humanities, or the social sciences."

> I think I consider academic writing to be good because it seems to fit all occasions in which I need to use it. Also academic language utilizes correct grammar and impressive vocabulary, so it is easy to call this writing "good." It is hard to find anything wrong with it except that it can be boring. I would much rather read a letter from my mother than a textbook. But that is simply my opinion.

It looks as if Ms. S has a benign and straightforward sense of just what academic writing is, particularly with regard to the old standards of propriety: grammar, vocabulary, and logical development of ideas. This view accords with the views of many academics who do not teach writing, but who demand it in the written work in their courses. The jarring note in Ms. S's presentation is her remark that academic writing can be boring, and that the counterpoint to it is in letter writing, which is personal and spontaneous. Shortly, I will elaborate on her preference for reading her mother's letters over reading a textbook.

But let me look more closely at what Ms. S is reporting about academic writing. The "meat" of her essay describes the utterly strict compliance of students with what teachers want. "Students assume that they are expected to write a formal essay unless otherwise specified." In turn, this formal essay is defined, *for each course*, by each teacher: "Teachers . . . expect their type of academic writing." After noting that in this class (the one in which the essay was written) people are encouraged to "take liberties," she nevertheless observes that my handouts are "written in an academic style, and they imply that we should also write in an academic style. Teachers are always giving examples of what they consider to be good writing in their handouts." While this conclusion is a speculative inference, and not necessarily true, it is certainly a rule-of-thumb for students: what kind of writing is "good writing"? Why, the kind of writing done by the teacher, of course. Ms. S, a successful student, is indirectly announcing her own secret of success—the pursuit of which seems to be a decisive preoccupation for most students, and perhaps especially the successful ones.

Ms. S perceives a kind of uniformity in academic coursework based on the "common" standard of propriety plus whatever a particular teacher requires: "Even though students follow teachers, each teacher has a different style . . . students have to adjust their style so they can get better grades." In addition, "certain teachers will downgrade students for expressing a different opinion from that of the teacher." Thus, mostly in style, but also in opinions, Ms. S describes a writing situation in which compliance, enforced by the grading system, is the mark of the writing process. But Ms. S does not believe that things are very different in this class, either: "Even in this class, in which the students do not receive direct feedback on each paper, I think that all of us still try to conform to what is 'expected' of us. . . . I know from my own personal experience that I am trying to conform to Bleich's suggestions for me by asking questions in my essays. I am even explicitly stating them so that Bleich sees that I am trying." Moreover, aware that this class permits the "taking of liberties" such as inventing new vocabulary and criticizing events in other courses, Ms. S nevertheless wonders: "Although the students are taking liberties, they are endorsed by the teacher, so are they really liberties?"

It is true that I urged Ms. S to depart from her usual declarative essay style and indulge what I thought was her own ability and tendency to ask or raise questions. But then she uses this opportunity to present, in interrogative form this time, her suspicion regarding what constitutes a liberty in the classroom. From her viewpoint, there is no way out: if there are no explicit instructions on how to write, students will infer what the teacher wants indirectly. If "liberties" are given, then they may not really be liberties because they are authorized by the teacher. She considers: "Maybe some higher authority has decided what is acceptable and what isn't. I don't know." In any case, Ms. S cannot be wrong in any choice, so long as she is able to guess what kind of language in her essays will result in the best possible grade. Before further discussion of Ms. S's work, let me consider a stronger set of statements by another female student who I also consider did excellent work.

Ms. R distinguished between her academic writing and her own "true voice," a distinction somewhat more emphatic than between academic and letter writing—two written genres as opposed to a written genre and a "voice." Ms. R says, "I think I sound least like myself when I am answering the essay questions on my philosophy tests." While she distinguishes between the style of English and religion classes as opposed to those in philosophy and statistics, she nevertheless observes that "the style that I use [in each of my courses] is a reflection of the type of language that is in my texts and that the professor uses in lectures." That Ms. R's perspective has somewhat more of an edge than Ms. S's comes across in her characterization of academic writing as "impersonal and (for lack of any other words) 'snooty.'" In her examinations, she says, "I try to sound like the wise philosophers that I am reading, and in turn I try [to] use the same type of formal language that they use."

Although Ms. R, like Ms. S, seems to have a general policy of trying to adopt the discourse that each teacher speaks and teaches, unlike Ms. S she seems tacitly to oppose this situation. She is more critical of the texts themselves, even though she feels she must emulate their language use in addition to the faculty members'. In the statistics text, for example,

> the structure of the text lets the student do last-minute memorization with all of the summaries and italicized words. The student never really "learns" because the book promotes short-term learning rather than long-term. Granted, I am supposed to keep studying and using the terms, but a year from now I will be lucky if I can recall half of what I learned. I find that I learn more when I have to figure out what the text is trying to tell me, but this text just gives facts, formulas, and procedures that I don't question. . . . the nature of the material does not let the language lose that sense of formality. . . . even though the teacher tries to explain things in a less formal manner, it still seems as if he is reading from the text. . . . the language used gave the feeling that it was telling "the absolute truth" and there was no questioning it.

Although I am not sure that Ms. R would question the statistics textbook if given the chance, there is a kind of resigned frustration expressed here, where teacher, subject, text, and lecture represent a ball of material that Ms. R feels she must swallow. Even if she hated statistics as an isolated subject, her presentation and its sarcastic use of a term like "the absolute truth" suggest a deeper discomfort with the academic scene and the kind of response it is demanding from her. She may not be quite old enough to actually challenge a course's requiring "short-term" learning over long-term, but she obviously considers it a serious flaw in the course. While Ms. R and Ms. S have similar perceptions of academic writing and what it takes to succeed in it, it is worth inquiring further into why Ms. R seems angrier and much less patient with the situation, and I would suggest that the "kind of language" perceived in academic writing by each student is occasioned, at least in part, by the kind of language they reported having been used in their homes.

My perception is based in part on essays class members wrote on "language use in the home." It was noteworthy that almost every student reported fights, disputes, and arguments. Some tried to characterize the language-use style in general. In the process of their reports, the family structures of authority emerged, and almost always with some reference to the circumstances of gender and culture. I will cite a few excerpts from Ms. S's and Ms. R's essays that suggest what I consider salient features of their reportage, particularly features which help explain how each student perceived academic writing and her relation to it. Here is part of what Ms. S reported:

> Our conversation usually commences during this [dinner] preparation period. My mother and I talk about whatever comes to mind. My father is in the kitchen, watching the news on TV (the TV usually remains on during dinner). My mom and I ask Dad to set the table, but he usually doesn't hear us ask. So Mom has to raise her voice in order to get through to Dad (she will have to raise her voice quite a few times over the next hour or so). We've discovered that when the TV is on, there is only one way to get Dad to hear us and that is to yell at him. In fact, most of the fights in my house are due to the fact that Dad never hears what is going on. Our dinner fights are very reminiscent of the typical fights in the house. . . .
>
> From our dinner conversations, it is easy to see that my mom is the boss of the family. She is the one who yells at both Dad and [the dog]. She cooks dinner and supervises the cleanup. My dad just does what Mom tells him to do, but usually not until Mom yells at him. This is what happens all the time, even when we're not eating dinner. . . .
>
> My family does not generally talk about their emotions. However, I notice that I do talk to my mother quite a lot about how I'm feeling, especially when I'm depressed or sad and she tells me what she is feeling. I don't think that I could talk to any other member of my family like I talk to my mother. . . I don't feel I have that relationship [of friends] with any other member of my family and I don't think that any other family members have this relationship either.

In view of this account, Ms. S's casual opinion that she would rather read letters from her mother than academic prose takes on more consequence. Her mother is the "boss" of the family. She reported that her father is a civil service worker whose job is the same every day. From her standpoint, not only is her mother the "boss," but she is perhaps more interesting and varied as well as generally more involved in her daughter's life than the father is. Although feelings are not discussed in Ms. S's family, they are discussed in conversation with her mother. Her father's relatively passive removal from the scene "is what happens all the time," even when the family is not eating dinner.

Perhaps Ms. S's good relation to the authority figure in her home accounts for her relative equanimity in discovering the principle of grade-motivated compliance in school: authorized ways of doing things are negotiable. Furthermore, because it is she and not her brother who went on to college, education and advanced training are not associated with privileged masculine choices. Ms. S claims no strong gender consciousness in her household, no taboos about how women can or cannot relate to men. She even reports that she learned not to be provoked by her brother's opinions by deciding that he was entitled to them. We also should probably not overlook the fact that if in this family the female members are more authoritative and educationally advanced, it still leads Ms. S to the view that hers is a "normal" family.

The situation is much different for Ms. R. Here is her description of the analogous situation in her home:

> Whether it is on an important topic or on who will win a football game, my family almost always manages to turn the discussion into a disagreement. One particular argument . . . took place right before I left for college.
>
> . . . This time [Mom] asks me, "What are you going to study in college?" Not that this is an unusual question, it is just that she had asked me about fifty times before and it was beginning to get irritating. . . . so I said to her, "Mom, leave me alone."
>
> After my comment, Mom started in on how I should be an economics major like my brother had been. . . . I hate it when she starts to think I should follow in my brother's footsteps. . . . Dad was telling Mom to leave me alone . . . This just upset Mom even more and she started yelling at my Dad to talk to me and tell me what I should do with my life. . . .
>
> I started yelling at my Mom, telling her that I will decide what I want to do in my own time and that if she left me alone I wouldn't feel as pressured. Then I told my brother that he should mind his own business and that it was between Mom and me . . . I started yelling that she is always on my case and that she is always trying to tell me what to do with my life. Then I said that she is always trying to turn me into a replica of my brothers, especially Ron because he is her perfect son. This was said purposely because he was involved in the argument, but I also said this because I come from a male-dominated family and I always feel I have to rebel against them. My Mom comes from a very traditional background, and she shows this whenever she talks to my father or brothers. She rarely defends herself against them, and treats what they say and do as some sort of law. . . . My Dad telling me that I shouldn't yell at my Mom comes from his very traditional background where the child never went against the parent. . . .
>
> Being the only girl in my family, my arguments almost always end up criticizing my parents for favoring my brothers because of their gender.

Ms. R reports self-consciously how her family is caught in the wider social process of the changing of roles. She is on this occasion more urgently affected by these changes than is Ms. S, and she is more ready than Ms. S to render her own judgments about the resulting adversity in her life. When Ms. R's family "yells," it emerges from anger and impatience at specific acts of others. When Ms. S's family "yells" it is to get through to the father, who is relatively withdrawn. Even though both students report "yelling" by the female members of the family, there is a different style of yelling in each case, and in turn, the different styles are related to the different distributions of authority in the family. In Ms. R's family, the men also take the option of yelling.

The salient situation for Ms. R is male domination and her mother's participation in it. On the one hand there is opposition between parents and children, but she being the only female child is in a doubly reduced status, a situation which results in her much-more-suspicious attitude toward several forms of authority. From what Ms. R reports, her intellectual life in college is connected with—or purposely separated from—the authority and gender configurations at home. In view of the home situation, as well as her independent personal style, Ms. R reacts sarcastically to the implicit demands of textbooks: she is individually sensitive to implications that she may not be independently able to cull from a textbook a thoughtful and critical knowledge of the subject. She perceives the textbook and instructor as more in league with one another whereas Ms. S generalizes perhaps more generously across academic life: academic writing "seems to fit all occasions." While both students are duly aware of the need for compliance on a relatively major scale, Ms. R responds more to the individual styles of the various subjects and tends not to separate out the individual teachers as the main point of orientation for whatever level of compliance might be indicated.

One sees, furthermore, why Ms. R might express her perspective as a function of "voice." The oral scene at home is the site of conflict where her actual voice is endangered. For Ms. S, both voice and letter writing are subsumed into a personal venue in which she and her mother participate productively. But for Ms. R, a very reluctant speaker in class, her "true voice" is the last refuge of individual independence and therefore cannot be risked in a public situation. The distinction between these two students' orientations toward writing is more than a matter of style. I want to suggest further that their current vocational orientations—Ms. S toward cognitive science and Ms. R toward religion and the humanities also helps to associate them, respectively, with the kinds of writing often considered characteristic in science and the humanities—a distinction that Ms. S did not include in her valid existing category of "academic writing." I will try to describe several features of each student's "kind of language" that represent the beginnings of the kind of language conventionally associated with science and with the humanities.

On page 201 above, Ms. S reported her view that people in the university have a "split personality" with regard to writing and that she is as "guilty" as anyone else of this trait. Her division of personality corresponded to the conventional division of public and private. At the end of the semester her course evaluation essay included the following observation about herself:

> . . . writing is not my favorite activity, and the amount of writing that I have had to do for this course has been a great weight for me to bear. I would much rather write a computer program than write an English paper.

Throughout the semester, in discussions of vocation both in class and in my office, Ms. S was steadfast in her intention to become a cognitive scientist. While she is able to write well and copiously, the use of language as an easy and pleasurable activity is for her somewhat cordoned off in an interpersonal context of family and friends. Writing a computer program is in a special class for her, at least at this point in her life. This suggests how her intellectual energy is configured: into two major but largely separate areas, one vocationally privileged and more intense and urgent than the other. She perceives, however, that "all people involved in academics" participate in this division of personality marked by two kinds of language.

Ms. S's division of language into these two kinds resembles Chomsky's division of language into competence and performance, where the former follows rules and can be studied scientifically and the latter follows choices and cannot be studied scientifically. In a recent interview, Chomsky offered the following descriptions of himself and his work:

> I have two full-time professional careers, each of them quite demanding, plus lots of other things [such as correspondence]. . . . I discovered over the years that probably my only talent is this odd talent that I seem to have that other colleagues don't, and that is that I've got sort of buffers in the brain that allow me to shift back and forth from one project to the other and store one. (Olson and Faigley 64)
> . . . but let me tell you what my own choices and priorities are. Like any human being, I'm interested in a lot of things. There are

things I find intellectually interesting and there are other things I find humanly significant, and those two sets have very little overlap. Maybe the world could be different, but the fact is that that's the way the world actually is. The intellectually interesting, challenging, and exciting topics, in general, are close to disjoint from the humanly significant topics. . . . The use of language to impose authority . . . [as a topic] has no intellectual depth to it at all, like most things in the social sciences. Also, it's of marginal human significance as compared with other problems. (87–88)

His description of his "talent" refers to imaginary "buffers" in his brain which separate his political from his linguistic interests. His more personological style in the second paragraph divides the "intellectually interesting" from the "humanly significant." These two divisions correspond to one another, as they are both describable as being, approximately, in scientific and humanistic categories. Chomsky claims that the intellectually interesting topics, such as the linguistics which he practices, are "close to disjoint" from the humanly significant topics, which he also studies. Doesn't this correspond pretty well with Ms. S's division of academic language from other, informal, language, such as that in the letters from her mother that she prefers reading to the language of textbooks?

As part of her work in the course, Ms. S compared the language of her multidimensional calculus textbook with the language of the teacher in whose course the textbook was used. She cites an explanation from the text, which she describes as "extremely formal and rigid." She then offers the following observation:

I think that part of the informality of the class is due to the actual interaction between students and teacher. . . . The lack of communication between the authors and students and the ability to communicate with the teacher is a major reason why the textbook is more formal than lectures. (3)

In view of other statements and observations given by Ms. S, this seemingly superficial one takes on considerable weight: within the "purely" mathematical context, Ms. S separates the human situation of interpersonal interaction between students and teacher from the textbook situation of no communication, which necessitates the "extremely formal and rigid" language in the text. From Ms. S's work, we have "derived" a very clear sense of different kinds of language governed by two different social configurations: a living or interactive relationship such as between mother and daughter, teacher and student, and a scientific, presentational situation in which an author (does not) communicate(s) with an impersonal audience.

Ms. R had not made a vocational choice. She was taking three humanities courses and a statistics course. She was taking religion because "I am hoping to learn more about the religion I was brought up in." She was taking philosophy because "it deals with questions that I have been asking myself for a long time. The question of God's existence has always plagued me. . . . I am hoping I will be able to think more logically about the questions I have." The foregoing citations come from Ms. R's second essay in this class. Although the statements seem ordinary, they accurately describe the truly interrogative state of mind in which Ms. R came to college. There is religious concern in her own family, and its treatment at home created doubts about her parochial precollege education. While she was as alert as Ms. S was to the constraints on writing given by the instructors of her various courses, her way of identifying the constraints was to gauge their distance from her "true" voice or "true" style, an interior standard of authentic feeling and tone. Here is how Ms. R discriminates:

> I think I sound the least like myself when I am answering the essay questions on my philosophy tests. The language that is used in the class is all very logical. . . . The kind of language that I use in my papers in English . . . is more casual; there is more feeling behind the words, and it is a reflection of how I speak (not for friends, but in classes and a less social setting). In my papers I like to make a lot of generalizations, and I like to comment on what I am saying within the paper itself. I also like to make it seem that I am speaking to the reader by using the second person. . . . In this course I get to escape from the "academic" language that I described before. I don't feel I am writing in a certain style to prove I know the topic, and I feel that I am writing without any of the constraints I feel in my other courses.
>
> The topics that I write about in English do lack a certain creativity. I think this lack does put somewhat of a constraint on what I write. I think if the topics were more personal, and if I didn't have to try and explain the language use, my style would be even more different.
>
> In some respect, I am very responsive to the demands of academic writing. I adopt the style that is expected in the class, and even when I am given some freedom to write what I want, I still try to make it sound like "academic prose."

Ms. R has a good ability to make fine distinctions among different language-use situations in college. In her own writing she is better able to use subjunctive moods than most other students in this class. Unlike Ms. S, she needed only a minor prompt (a public instruction, as opposed to private urging for Ms. S) to use a discourse of feeling, doubt, hope, and uncertainty. More easily than most others she was willing and able to make *tentative* generalizations about language and experience and to present them for discussion. Her ability to make subtle but substantive discriminations was, perhaps, unique in this group of students. These fluencies in rendering judgments may be in part related to her need in her own family to decide on the differences among the competing values among parents and siblings, in order that she might better preserve her autonomy and independence: "Mom, leave me alone." Unlike in Ms. S's family, difference is more exposed in Ms. R's and occasions more open dispute. The tendency to arguing existed in her family, in part, because the two parents were from different national and cultural backgrounds, whereas Ms. S's parents were from the same background. In addition Ms. R's parents' background clashed more directly with the growing emancipation of women; in Ms. S's home the emancipation seemed to cause no problem.

Whereas vocation and science were established areas of major interest for Ms. S, the inner voice was a locus of greater certainty as a kind of language for Ms. R. Though she is as alert as Ms. S to the need to adapt to the "going" language style in courses, Ms. R also *judges* that she is "very responsive" to the demands of academic writing. I get the impression she feels that she has more of a choice in what kind of language to emulate than Ms. S feels she does, since Ms. S makes fewer distinctions among the language-use styles in different subjects. While both Ms. S and Ms. R perceive that even in this English course, which has removed certain constraints, the teacher still exercises considerable influence, Ms. R makes an intermediate distinction: English writing is closer to her voice than other writing, but still not permitting her "true style." While Ms. S relaxes her academic style somewhat, it continues in its mode of presenting declarative information in excess of the suggested length, but remaining relatively modest in its willingness to draw conclusions and make judgments. Ms. S did continue, and knew she continued, to use academic writing in this course, the liberties allowed perhaps not being taken too seriously.

Both students have something true to say and to enact about academic writing: Ms. S stresses its scientific function, its aim to present information as carefully and accurately as possible—this is what she tries to do in her writing. Ms. R stresses its more humanistic side—the presentation of provisional judgments for discussion. While neither student advocated any one way of writing or kind of language, their work was inflected by individual personalities already immersed in changing cultural backgrounds and processes of vocational orientation. In spite of these complex foundations for the kinds of language they used, we should, like Ms. R, pursue provisional conceptualizations of these kinds. They continue to exist and function as identifiable kinds of language because of the conventions of social life in which they exist and change. If we place the question of kinds of language in the classroom context, *these kinds are always identifiable yet also always in a process of change.* While Ms. S makes Chomsky-like distinctions and establishes relatively strong boundaries between two kinds of language she usually uses, the classroom can become an active forum for the interrogation of these kinds, for the collective critique of their use and their history. Ms. R's kind of language, which seems more of the "humanly significant" style, is also available for critique and reeval- uation, particularly as part of the individual process of seeking a vocation during the college years. Ms. R's own style actually does question the division of kinds that Ms. S's style takes for granted.

A "kind of language" is the language-use style associated with any group of people, from a pair like a mother and a daughter, to a special group, like male athletes or urban African Americans, to a larger institution, like the academy or a whole nation. Always, students in a class are members of several groups, all of which have, to one degree or another, their own kinds of language. The "curriculum" in a district, a school, a university, a department, or a classroom can always be built on the various kinds of language in use by, and of possible value and consequence to, its constituents. But in any case it is a curriculum grounded in the social relations of its constituents, and not on the moral abstractions of a "liberal education" or a "well-rounded person."

The kinds-of-language curriculum both accepts the widest variety of existing "kinds," such as proper and improper, culturally masculine or feminine, private and public, scientific and humanistic, and the principle that these kinds are continuously changing and often com- bining. Moreover, I wish the word "curriculum" could refer to the responsibility of classrooms to review these kinds on each occasion: the kinds-of-language classroom both discovers the kinds that people are using, and evaluates, criticizes, and judges those kinds in the cause of promoting active individual and collective authority over language use and the social relations in which they are found.

Finally, then, a "kinds-of-language" curriculum is one that can be drawn from the kinds of language that students bring to class. Everyone will know what writing and language use is and that it pays to practice both, cultivate them, and let them grow as other organic things grow— in a friendly ecology. But members of a class will not know what kinds of language other members bring unless the "curriculum" stipulates that this discovery is part of the project of the school or course. By thinking of this investigation as part of the curriculum, I mean to specify it as a principle of schooling: ask, discover, disclose, and study what members of a class bring into the class, and let this existing knowledge become part of the subject matter. If this is a curricular principle, it follows that what the teacher brings to class is specific, to one degree or another, to that teacher, so that curriculum, which may be treated in a general way, must always come down to its specific form in any class or school. Although, perhaps more than any other subject, literacy studies is susceptible to this particularization, in fact students bring knowledge of many subjects to many classes, and the idea of curriculum should begin to refer in a principled and disciplined way to the use of students' and teachers' existing knowledge in the seeking for new knowledge.

Works Cited

Miller, Susan. *Textual Carnivals: The Politics of Composition*. Carbondale: Southern Illinois UP, 1991.

North, Stephen. *The Making of Knowledge in Composition*. Portsmouth, NH: Boynton/Cook, 1987.

Olson, Gary A., and Lester Faigley. "Language, Politics, and Composition: A Conversation with Noam Chomsky." In *(Inter)views: Cross-Disciplinary Perspectives on Rhetoric and Literacy*. Ed. Gary A. Olson and Irene Gale. Carbondale: Southern Illinois UP, 1991. 61–95.

Phelps, Louise Wetherbee. "Practical Wisdom and the Geography of Knowledge in Composition." *College English* 53.8 (1991): 863–85.

15 Writing Academic Autobiographies: Finding a Common Language across the Curriculum

Rhonda C. Grego
University of South Carolina

Intellectual order is not simply an instrument of domination; it involves just as much a capacity for reliving our thoughts. It is perhaps more like housecleaning, a rearrangement which in welcoming others leaves more room for ourselves. . . . The integrity of our beginnings is the source of our welcome. It also strengthens our speech and the commitment of our interests and thereby reminds us of our freedom. For in thinking and speaking we choose paths much as in life we choose careers and marriages, that is, as ways of resolving the history and geography of our lives.

—John O'Neill, "Mind and Institution"

The Integrity of Our Beginnings

Over the last ten years we have all read of and been witness to writing-across-the-curriculum programs designed to help faculty institute more writing in their courses. The challenging task faced by compositionists has been to develop vocabularies that help us and our colleagues across the curriculum identify and discuss the salient features of written communication in many different disciplines. To do so we initially turned to the latest composition theory: we relied on the research and theory of the "James triumvirate"—Moffett, Britton, and Kinneavy. We used their categorization of writing purposes, aims, and types as we ventured into the unfamiliar territory of writing-across-the-disciplines to help us (and our colleagues) identify and develop common names for the kinds of discourse we found therein.

An even more challenging task has been to develop vocabularies that help both us and our colleagues understand the part played by writing and discourse in the learning processes of our students. Developing such vocabularies has required a considerable leap: moving from the perspective of a full-fledged member of a discipline to that of an entering novitiate (or even that of someone who is *not* seeking to enter that field per se, as most undergraduates do not go on to graduate study). The shift in composition studies from "composing product" to "composing process" promised to help with this task. The process approach seemed to give us a more "interdisciplinary" content *and* pedagogy because of its focus on the similar processes involved when people (in this case, students and their professors) write, rather than on the differing products. Thus, as the work at Michigan Technological University reported in *Writing across the Disciplines* (Young and Fulwiler) shows, compositionists could use both an academically researched content to teach colleagues about writing (from cognitive research on problem-solving behaviors and the composing process), *and* experiential learning techniques to bring academically submerged knowledge about the "composing process" to the surface for workshop participants. As workshops led participants through an assignment and discussions of how they got from "point A to point B," workshop leaders could lead participants to experience for themselves the cognitive "stages" and difficulties entailed in accomplishing writing assignments.

What, we might ask, has the most recent trend in composition theory and research added to the evolution of writing-across-the-curriculum programs? At least one social constructionist has been working on the history of such programs; he stresses the importance of bridging the gaps among disciplines, although he also makes clear the difficulty—perhaps even the impossibility—of doing so. In "Writing across the Curriculum in Historical Perspective: Toward a Social Interpretation," David Russell argues that there are no longer any linguistic forms shared by the various disciplines and that the lack of shared linguistic forms, languages, and values is a substantial roadblock to the progress, implementation, and staying power of writing-across-the-curriculum programs:

> The academic disciplines are in one sense united through their common missions—teaching, the advancement of knowledge, and social service. But disciplines have been so diverse, so independent, and so bound up with professional communities outside academia that they require no common language or even shared values and methods within the university in order to pursue those missions.

The various disciplines have grown to constitute the modern university through accretion, as Gerald Graff has forcefully argued, and by their relevance to concerns in the wider society, not through their logical relation to each other—so much so that interdisciplinary study is always a notable (and often suspect) exception. Indeed an academic is likely to have more linguistic common ground with a fellow professional in the corporate sector than with another academic in an unrelated field, except in regard to purely institutional matters (governance, academic freedom, teaching loads, etc.). (54)

Russell admits that there are recent hopeful moves and possibilities for development of shared languages: grant agency funding of inter-disciplinary and teaching topics, faculty development programs, and increasing recognition of the importance of reaching across interdis-ciplinary boundaries. The purpose of these hopeful moves and pro-grams, given his view of the problem, would be to straighten out the relationships among disciplines, to realign those relations along more "logical" lines, perhaps enabling us to find the "shared linguistic forms" that presumably might exist once we attend less to the "concerns of the wider society" and more to our common existence within the university. According to Russell, the divisions among disciplines, which create the problems of communication faced by writing-across-the-curriculum programs, originated in the wider society, while efforts to reunite the disciplines must originate from within the university.

Unlike Russell, I don't believe the disciplines within the modern university have grown apart *solely* because of their different responses and responsiveness to "concerns in the wider society." Given the character of graduate student education and faculty development— both of which focus on research prowess—it seems likely that the research mission of the university has actually fostered the gaps among disciplines by promoting a high degree of individual research special-ization within disciplines. If writing-across-the-curriculum programs can be saved only by reestablishing the "logical relations" among disciplines, then we must also realize that the modern research uni-versity exerts substantial pressure at the level of individual career development *against* such a realignment. Publication of a coherent, specialized body of research is a much more significant requirement for tenure and promotion within most modern research universities than is teaching or service within one's own department, much less to the "wider society." And although the requirements for tenure and promotion may be oriented more toward teaching and service at smaller institutions, the faculty at those colleges and schools are more often than not *trained*—and their attitudes shaped—at larger research-oriented institutions like the one at which I teach.

There is, I believe, another possible avenue for realizing what John O'Neill calls the "integrity of our beginnings." We all know that there are other walls to be breached in our search for shared languages and values, walls more within the immediate power of the individual to tear down or at least to question. What walls am I referring to? At an NCTE Convention workshop, I asked a group of participants to freewrite for fifteen minutes about a recent writing experience, then to go through and circle those words they used that were a part of the cognitive or rhetorical lexicon used to describe composing processes. They found few such words in their freewritings, though most participants were familiar with those bodies of research. What they did find were many words that described emotions associated with the writing experience, emotions that tied other people (past teachers and fellow students, colleagues, families, friends), places (both academic and nonacademic), and interpersonal relationships to the remembered writing experience. In such accounts, I have learned, lies a significant body of shared language and shared experience, social and interpersonal, which composition studies and the university itself have trained many of us to ignore, or at least not to value in "intellectual" ways.

When we help our colleagues reexperience (relive) their writing processes, when they recall intuitions and common writing experiences from their pasts, we begin to tear down walls between what is counted as valuable, "intellectual," and influential experience (or "knowledge") in the academy and what is not. Here I will argue that having colleagues recall their particular writing/learning experiences (their frustrations and successes) as students, undergraduate and graduate, perhaps also as young professors, might enable us to better see that the issues Russell relegates to the *purely parenthetical*—institutional matters of governance, academic freedom, promotion criteria, etc.—are themselves the residue of submerged personal/interpersonal relationships, feelings, and values that provide the powerful (though largely unrecognized and undiscussed) common ground of our lives as academics. Unearthing and collaboratively reconstructing these underlying relationships might lead us to "ways of resolving the history and geography of our lives" that have been ignored by the standard histories of our specialized disciplines. Institutional matters such as these, after all, give us important guidelines for how we treat one another (governance), what we are allowed to say when opinion and knowledge blur in the classroom and in our writings (academic freedom), and how we value each other (tenure and promotion).

As our understanding of the social, political, and psychological dimensions of written communication increases, it becomes clear that the pursuit by writing-across-the-curriculum programs of ideas about "writing to learn" means asking ourselves and our colleagues to bring to the surface those discounted, submerged, "unacademic" parts of our lives as academics—to recognize their influence on the knowledge that universities produce and teach to their students. The difference between the abstracted content knowledge that we point to when we begin with "I *know* x" and the peopled and placed knowledge which we acknowledge when we say "I *remember* x" defines the difference between what academic institutions value and define as the "professional" or "objective" and that which they reject as the "personal" or "subjective." It is not the "logical relations" among disciplines that need to be rediscovered or redrawn. Rather it is the relations among the individual, the personal, the professional, the institutional—among *these* roles, these boundaries—that need to be explored and better understood if writing-across-the-curriculum programs are to survive and prosper.

Writing-across-the-curriculum programs can focus not only on developing *student* skills but on helping *faculty* develop their awareness of the very human "beginnings" they share with their students and with their colleagues in the academic setting. Writing experiences both past and present offer us important learning opportunities—opportunities ending in success or frustration, shame or pride. These are the experiences (and the emotions) that emerge as significant events in the "history and geography of our lives" in academia.

Exploring the History and Geography of Our Lives

As "model-givers," we lend our colleagues assignment formats to try out, but we give them very little in the way of a philosophical framework for discussing or exploring the failures or successes involved in the use of these models: we assume shared values and languages about what writing is, what writers do, and who writers are—values and languages which actually need further work and care. As interdisciplinary "experts" on the cognitive processes of writing, we've adopted an approach which carries with it all the problems associated with cognitive psychology's general failure to adequately account for the influence of social factors (past and present), resulting in our case in a failure to account for the influence of such factors on writing processes and decisions and on the use of writing-to-learn techniques.

As "experts" on the workings and uses of expressive languages, we have worked in writing-across-the-curriculum forums to introduce our colleagues to the potential value of expressive, subjective uses of language, such as journal writing, poetry, and narrative. But our colleagues tend to see these as literary forms of writing—as "literature"—no matter how much we stress the thinking and learning aspects of such writing. When we use terms from Britton, Moffett, and Kinneavy, we set ourselves up as the "experts" once more, a stance, unwitting though it may be, that can leave our colleagues feeling dependent upon a discipline with which they feel unfamiliar and uncomfortable (English). As long as we keep the philosophies from which these vocabularies arise to ourselves, our colleagues can and do fall back vociferously on what they generally feel most confident about: their knowledge of the mechanics and forms of "good writing," which they got from their own teachers in the past. In other words, as long as we keep our programs and our conversations about writing across the disciplines working on the level of our own self-possessed research vocabularies and theories, we retain for ourselves a position of power at the expense of those colleagues who enter our writing-across-the-curriculum programs.

We might define a change by looking more at the "microsociology" of writing and writing-to-learn experiences across the curriculum. "Microsociology" is a term used by Thomas Scheff, a sociologist who argues that traditional sociology looks too broadly outward and traditional psychology too narrowly inward to understand the relationship between an individual's actions and perceptions and larger group/societal/institutional pressures on and perceptions of that individual. Scheff is interested in the ways in which groups within society use the emotion of shame (and its opposite, pride) to control the individual and in ways in which individuals might be empowered to act and speak on their own behalf. Empowerment, according to Scheff, is gained when any individual uses discourse tactics to force into the open "underlying [power] relationships," relationships which the content level of a discussion tends to mask or ignore.

In *Microsociology: Discourse, Emotion, and Social Structure*, Scheff gives the example of an encounter between a patient and her therapist. The patient is frustrated by the therapist's lack of response to the despair she has felt and voiced during the session. The therapist keeps throwing the patient's questions back to her, keeping her in the dark as to the attitude of the therapist while he receives information from the patient and speaks according to the dictates of a theory to which only he has access. Scheff discusses how the patient can empower herself by breaking this cycle: she can ask the therapist why he is responding in such a way to a fellow adult and can ask him to reveal the bases of his responses. Once the therapist does so, then those bases are potentially opened up for discussion and perhaps renegotiation between therapist and patient. Scheff urges people to force recognition of and clarification of "underlying relationships" in speaking with professionals, whether therapists or teachers, whose job is to help them achieve some goal (186-89).

We might see the writing-across-the-curriculum forum as a human development service for faculty where the underlying, unacknowledged, and undiscussed relationships between the individual faculty members and the university-as-institution can be made available for discussion (and perhaps renegotiation). Such discussion and renegotiation might begin through collaborative explorations of the participants' own learning and writing experiences, experiences which could then be brought into the discussion to clarify and construct ideas about the relationships between the academic contents and the academic discourses of the various disciplines.

The "underlying relationships" among institutionalized academic disciplines (which on the level of content or subject matter seem no longer to possess "shared linguistic forms") is constituted by our individual, "forgotten" pasts: by our forgotten or unvalued struggles to gain membership into "Club Academe," by our struggles to talk the talk and walk the walk, by our forgotten friends who didn't make it or who didn't value the higher levels of graduate study we entered on the way to our professorships. In the social and interpersonal relationships that contextualize our academic learning/writing experiences lie the institutionally forgotten ties and responsibilities of academic professionals to the work which will be done by the individuals whom we educate at the undergraduate level (and *not* beyond). The difference between "I know" and "I remember" often marks the part played by the *personal* (the subjective, the past, the extraneous, untethered understanding of the social and interpersonal contexts of our academic knowledge) in the *professional*. Seen in this light, the question of vocabularies and of shared linguistic forms with which I began this discussion of writing-across-the-curriculum programs might be rephrased this way: How are we to begin resolving the history ("I remember") and the geography ("I know") of our lives as academics? Or, when will academics intellectually and professionally acknowledge the role played by the underlying *human* relationships of academia as a *social* context for the development of their *content* knowledge?

Writing Autobiographies

Feminist sociologist Dorothy Smith argues that there is no sociology from the standpoint of women, no sociology which takes the everyday world of women's work and women's lives seriously, as "problematic." I would argue that we lack much the same kind of sociology from the standpoint of student learners in the modern university. I have often wondered, "What difference would a sociology of academic knowledge developed from the standpoint of student learners (past and present) make to writing-across-the-curriculum programs?"

One difference is that we would better understand student perceptions about writing and writers and the ways in which those perceptions contribute to the success or failure of writing-to-learn assignments in the various disciplines. Over the last two years I have been using what I call a "writing history" assignment to collect stories from my students—autobiographies of their reading and writing experiences (both academic and nonacademic). I see this work as building toward a sociology of writing from the standpoint of students, but for now I use their stories simply to understand why it is that so many students do not like writing, or feel that they are inordinately bad at it, particularly junior and senior computer science and statistics majors in my technical writing courses.

What has stood out most is that the majority of these students see a dichotomy in their experiences as readers and as writers. Many have found reading outlets (Stephen King, science fiction, comics, and so on) that allow them a feeling of participation in a creative work, a feeling of joint creativity that they often contrast with their experiences as writers in school or on the job. Although a few note that they do creative writing (outside of academic writing) for the feeling of control and freedom it allows them, most see a big division between creative writing/reading and the writing that they have done in school or that they imagine doing in their disciplines or professions. What has struck me the most about their testimonials is that they have very literary and canonically old-fashioned ways of defining who writers are (published fiction writers and poets) and what writers do. One student, for example, began his writing autobiography with a "critical analysis of fictional writing," arguing that "in this form of writing, reality is the point of view of the writer. Writers create their own agenda and branch out in whatever way they desire." He then contrasted fictional writing with what he termed a "realist" position, where "events and situations must be justified," and noted that "fictional writing almost always fails to provide tangible or perceptible effects." Notably, the student never labeled someone taking the "realist position" a "writer" or what he or she did as "writing." Another student's writing autobiography equated being good at English with being good at grammar. He described a painful car trip during which his father tried to "teach" him grammar, leaving both of them unhappy and frustrated. Only with "the addition of a few years, a few more hormones in my system, and a few good teachers" was the student "finally able to understand grammar."

There is a sharp division in these students' minds between "Writers" and the writers they are by virtue of the writing they do in school or on the job. They see academic or professional writing as important, yes, but as mundane and formal nonetheless. They do not see the writing done by the "writers" that their professors are as "creative." Likewise, those tasks we might see as writing to learn, as fostering the student writer's creative construction of knowledge about or within a discipline, students see as merely following a form or discovering the form desired by the teacher. They do not equate the construction of knowledge through discourse with the exercise of creativity; nor would they be likely to see academic writing as the social construction of knowledge, because they are not part of the "society" of professionals in the discipline who are actively involved in this construction. Do their professors ever learn anything from their writing? Probably not, most students would say.

I realize that what I have begun working on is a sociology of student writers/learners of the *present*—something which might be very different from a sociology of academic knowledge from the standpoint of our colleagues across the curriculum (the student writers/learners of the *past*). But I would venture that a number of those colleagues would relate stories somewhat like those offered by my students, at least in relation to the mechanical nature of writing and the creative freedom of reading. From conversations with colleagues in other disciplines I know that assumptions about who writers are and what writers do are largely shaped by the values assumed to be held by English department faculty, faculty whose own views of authorship and good writing are still largely influenced by conceptions of the literary canon.

Though for many of us the canon debate is old hat, I want to redefine that debate within the terms of a sociology constructed from the standpoint of these student learners/writers past and present (the unempowered within the academy). The canon represents another way of keeping the conversation about writing away from underlying relationships, another way of masking or ignoring personal histories and values. These underlying relationships and the sources of our "professional" values have been called into question by the canon debate for most of us in the field of English. But these questions simply haven't been raised for many of those outside English departments, whether students or professors. Rather than trying to persuade students that the professional world expects them to be "good writers" in a literary sense, the opening chapters of technical and business writing texts should concentrate on defining "writers" and "writing" rhetorically, in noncanonical terms, so that our students (and our colleagues) across the disciplines can identify themselves as writers and their work as writing.

We should keep in mind that students' reluctance to see themselves as writers is shared by many faculty participants in our writing-across-the-curriculum programs, who see compositionists as English department members with canonical criteria for "good writing." Many of our colleagues will confide that as students they chose a nonwriting (or nonhumanities) major because they "weren't as good at it," or were made to feel that way. Others got caught up in the intellectual discourse communities of their disciplines, which, as Russell points out, act on a day-to-day basis as if their languages, their discursive constructions of knowledge, are invisible. We need to be careful that whatever stance we take in writing-across-the-curriculum forums, we work against stereotypes—stereotypes that entail attitudes about writers and writing as well as attitudes about who we as compositionists are and our colleagues are not.

Indeed, we compositionists have barely skimmed the surface of our *own* past experiences; we have only begun to ask questions about the influences of other life roles on the learning we do in our research and teaching. Insofar as we consider composition an academic discipline, we, like our colleagues across the curriculum, little recognize the influence of our many other life roles—past and present—on our own writing practices and on our research and theorizing about composing. When we do, the experience is often powerful. Nancy Sommers's "Between the Drafts" has as its point and theme that the academic life *in*cludes, but academic discourse seems to *ex*clude, the personal experiences of the researcher. She notes that personal histories, issues, and experiences are an inextricable part of anyone's research, including her own extensive work on revision—yet it has taken her years to recognize, let alone give voice to, these influences.

Discourse Tactics for Empowerment

What tactics might we use in writing-across-the-curriculum programs to counter stereotypes about writers and writing? Scheff's tactic of bringing out underlying relationships for clarification or renegotiation of the content level of discussion seems important in such a situation. In the case of writing-across-the-curriculum programs and changing attitudes about writers and writing, the underlying relationships to be brought out for discussion have rhetorical rather than canonical bases: the social contexts in which and for which writing is done and knowledge discursively constructed. So why not just teach current rhetorical theory and vocabularies for analyzing writing? Simply put, teaching rhetorical theory and its vocabularies places compositionists in a position of power rather than a situation of empowering others; we retain the position equivalent to that of Scheff's therapist in the example I cited earlier. In addition, rhetorical theories themselves have a disciplinary content and unity which can, in the name of community or group or institution, draw attention away from the fact that each individual is multifaceted, participating not only in many discourse communities—as Patricia Bizzell tells us—but in experiences which he or she identifies *not* through the recognized and valued discourse of a coherent community, but by that which remains unvalued and "silenced," as feminist critiques of that which has been "left out" of so many disciplines make so clear. In other words, a priori theory and vocabularies themselves will not necessarily tap into the underlying relationships that academic mnemonics train us to forget, to be silent about: the interpersonal, peopled contexts of our individual academic experiences. Yet these relationships must be brought out and discussed before the renegotiation of our definitions and valuations of writers, writing, and writing to learn can begin—for reasons I hope I have made clear. We all need to seek better understanding of the discursive construction of knowledge from the standpoint of the individual who can be and often is aware of the underlying, unvoiced, perhaps "silenced" relationships between himself or herself and the other members of a discourse community.

In discussing their survey of how writing-across-the-curriculum workshops changed faculty attitudes toward writing, Toby Fulwiler, Michael Gorman, and Margaret Gorman have said,

> Subjectively, we feel that the writing-as-learning concept created the most frequent "Ah ha!" experiences of the workshop. A colleague in philosophy wrote that the most important thing the workshop taught was that "writing is an integral part of cognitive

growth. I grasped that intuitively years ago—I used to see essay tests as a learning experience—but I really did not put the concept to work very much." An historian wrote the following about the workshop itself: "I am most pleased to see perceptual wheels turning, and I sincerely hope we are truly listening to one another as well as discovering, or rediscovering, the basic common sense behind the personal, active experience of learning and helping others to learn." (57)

Although recalling such intuitions and rediscovering some basic common sense are wonderful outcomes, what our workshops need to do is to help our colleagues and ourselves bring those intuitions and "basic common sense behind the personal, active experience of learning" into *public and professional* being for discussion. If we do not recognize (by examining and reliving and collaboratively discussing) those intuitions and common sense, then we will ensure that the real, human experiences (histories) which support those submerged intuitions and common sense will continue to be discounted as "knowledge" within the academy.

By way of applying Scheff's basic discourse tactic for empowerment to the writing-across-the-curriculum forum, I will briefly mention the work of Peter Reason and John Rowan as a further resource in developing these alternative approaches. Their book, *Human Inquiry: A Sourcebook of New Paradigm Research*, and Reason's *Human Inquiry in Action* outline an approach that they call "co-operative experiential inquiry," a style of inquiry growing out of action research in modern sociology and American phenomenological methods of experiential learning adapted to group research situations. Reason and Peter Hawkins's work on storytelling as a collaborative, action-research methodology would be particularly useful for writing-across-the-curriculum programs. Insisting on experiential processes of research and the application of that research, their central concern, as Reason points out, is not furthering theories, but *action*:

> ... knowledge is formed in and for action rather than in and for reflection. This idea has been around for a good time. . . . From a feminist perspective it is argued that an over-reliance on analytical, theoretical knowledge contributes to an oppressive patriarchy, and is part of the alienation of Western Man; what is needed is a recovery of the muted feminine which is both more intuitive and more grounded and practical.
>
> Co-operative inquiry seeks knowledge in action and for action. Co-operative researchers may write books and articles, but often the knowledge that is really important for them is the practical knowledge of new skills and abilities: a more holistic practice in the surgery, or more efficient and safer stoves for cooking. And

> thus in co-operative inquiry, education and social action may
> become fully integrated with the research process. (*Human Inquiry
> in Action* 12–13)

It is this "integration of education, social action, *and the research
process*" that leads us back to the social constructionist interpretation
of the history and future work of writing-across-the-curriculum programs with which I began this essay. The parallels between the tenets
of human inquiry and what I have earlier outlined as the needs and
deeper significances of the writing-across-the-curriculum movement
should be clear. As workshop facilitators, not "experts" on all writing
and writing processes, we need to claim and empower our colleagues
as co-researchers. Because of the high degree of specialization in
academic disciplines today, it is likely that the only shared languages
available to us are the languages of primary subjective experience we
have as writers and learners. As we collaboratively examine those
experiences, we construct knowledge legitimated by our critical subjectivity, by the conscious application of the comparisons and ques-
tionings allowed by intersubjectivity itself.

Teacher-Researchers across the Curriculum

A glance at the bibliography at the end of Reason's *Human Inquiry in
Action* shows how much this radical sociology and method has developed out of modern American phenomenology. It is no small
coincidence that champions of the teacher-researcher movement have
also pointed to or relied on phenomenological approaches as holding
promise, as a way of privileging the knowledge which comes from
individual experience, and as a means of bridging the academic gaps
between research and teaching and between thought (research) and
action. In "Knowing Our Knowledge: A Phenomenological Basis for
Teacher Research," C. H. Knoblauch and Lil Brannon have suggested
that phenomenological research methods present teacher-researchers
with a field that values languages and stories excluded from other
kinds of academic discourse. Janet Emig also turns to phenomenological
approaches, largely through references to Michael Polanyi's work on
personal knowledge, in developing her discussions of the tacit tradition,
inquiry paradigms, and reflective inquiry in *The Web of Meaning*.

These approaches also tap into a growing body of feminist theory
and methodology that has the potential to revolutionize academic
research and teaching and to bridge the gap between the two. The
"writing histories" approach which I have presented here—having

faculty write about and share and collaboratively analyze the significance of their own writing experiences as students and the interpersonal and social contexts which those memories call up—is very much like a feminist research method called "memory-work." "Memory-work" is discussed and used by a group of women—June Crawford, Susan Kippax, Jenny Onyx, Una Gault, and Pam Benton—in their recent book *Emotion and Gender: Constructing Meaning from Memory* (1992). Here is how they describe the three phases of memory-work within small groups:

> Memory-work involves at least three phases: First, the collection of written memories according to certain rules. Second, the collective analysis of those written memories. There is also a third phase in which there is further reappraisal; a reappraisal of the memories and their analysis in the context of a range of theories from academic disciplines. We are still involved in that third phase; in writing this book we have reappraised much of our work in the light of theories of emotion as well as the memories and memory-work of other groups. *In the process we have also reappraised the theories.* (43; emphasis added)

I find it fascinating that their "memory-work"—the very unacademic business of remembering and sharing their "unintellectual" perceptions about "everyday" experiences from the past—led these women to actually reconsider the academic theories and ideas and assumptions about emotion and gender (from many different disciplines) valued by their different fields of study. I would hope that such work could also lead us and our colleagues across the disciplines to reconsider and enrich theories about writing and writing to learn as well. If we could do this jointly with our colleagues, we might begin to bridge some of the gaps among disciplines.

But I'd like to push this point a bit further and end this essay with a kind of visionary wish for bridging the gap between "teacher" and "researcher" which also exists across the curriculum in our modern university. What if college undergraduate education began to reconstitute itself as cooperative research undertaken between students and professors, as memory-work in the undergraduate classroom? If feminist perspectives have begun to introduce different silenced or unvalued interpretations of phenomena in various disciplines, might not student perspectives likewise enrich our thinking/rethinking of our research vocabularies and theories as well? Might not cooperative research or memory-work in the undergraduate/graduate classroom define *another* source for the social construction/creation of knowledge within a discipline? Perhaps we can enrich our "I know" thinking with questions raised by collaboratively undertaken "I remember" ruminations.

In other words, perhaps the teacher-researcher stance is not limited to the discipline of composition. This grassroots movement began by seeking to empower the pre–higher education teacher who conducts research in the classroom through a system of notes, observations, teaching and learning logs, etc., thereby contributing to and shaping developing theory and practice in the field of composition. But at a deeper level the teacher-researcher movement seeks to recover the excluded stories of *all* the citizens of academe and to exhibit the value of this remembered, recollected knowledge.

The teacher-researcher movement thus offers evidence of the beginning of what will likely be a long struggle to redefine what it means to be an academician, an intellectual, an educator. In fact, I believe that collaborative construction of faculty writing histories, coupled with comparison to student writing histories—and the encouragement we would thus offer our colleagues across the curriculum to take on the teacher-researcher stance toward writing across the disciplines— might itself be the first step toward the adoption of teacher-researcher stances toward the "contents," the "subjects," and the "vocabularies" of other disciplines. It is in the spirit of this hope that I urge us all to revise our academic autobiographies.

Works Cited

Bizzell, Patricia. "Cognition, Convention, and Certainty: What We Need to Know about Writing." *Pre/Text* 3 (1982): 213–43.

Crawford, June, Susan Kippax, Jenny Onyx, Una Gault, and Pam Benton. *Emotion and Gender: Constructing Meaning from Memory.* Newbury Park, CA: Sage, 1992.

Emig, Janet. *The Web of Meaning: Essays on Writing, Teaching, Learning, and Thinking.* Ed. Dixie Goswami and Maureen Butler. Montclair, NJ: Boynton/ Cook, 1983.

Fulwiler, Toby, Michael E. Gorman, and Margaret E. Gorman. "Changing Faculty Attitudes Toward Writing." Young and Fulwiler. 53–67.

Fulwiler, Toby, and Art Young, eds. *Language Connections: Writing and Reading across the Curriculum.* Urbana, IL: NCTE, 1982.

Knoblauch, C. H., and Lil Brannon. "Knowing Our Knowledge: A Phenomenological Basis for Teacher Research." *Audits of Meaning: A Festschrift in Honor of Ann E. Berthoff.* Ed. Louise Z. Smith. Portsmouth, NH: Boynton/ Cook, 1988. 17–28.

O'Neill, John. "Mind and Institution." *Interdisciplinary Phenomenology.* Ed. Don Ihde and Richard M. Zaner. The Hague: M. Nijhoff, 1977. 99–108.

Reason, Peter, ed. *Human Inquiry in Action: Developments in New Paradigm Research.* London: Sage, 1988.

Reason, Peter, and Peter Hawkins. "Storytelling as Inquiry." Reason 79–101.

Reason, Peter, and John Rowan, eds. *Human Inquiry: A Sourcebook of New Paradigm Research.* New York: Wiley, 1981.

Russell, David R. "Writing across the Curriculum in Historical Perspective: Toward a Social Interpretation." *College English* 52.1 (Jan. 1990): 52–73.

Scheff, Thomas. *Microsociology: Discourse, Emotion, and Social Structure.* Chicago: U of Chicago P, 1990.

Smith, Dorothy. *The Everyday World as Problematic: A Feminist Sociology.* Boston: Northeastern UP, 1987.

———. *The Conceptual Practices of Power: A Feminist Sociology of Knowledge.* Boston: Northeastern UP, 1990.

Sommers, Nancy. "Between the Drafts." *College Composition and Communication* 43.1 (Feb. 1992): 23–31.

Young, Art, and Toby Fulwiler, eds. *Writing across the Disciplines: Research into Practice.* Montclair, NJ: Boynton/Cook, 1986.

16 "So Happy a Skill"

Robert Scholes
Brown University

My title is a borrowed expression, a quotation. And that is appropriate, since I mean to take up the topic of how texts are made out of other texts. Part of my aim in this discussion will be to argue that this whole matter of intertextuality should be central in any attempt to do what is usually called "teaching writing." For reasons that I shall try to make apparent, I do not believe that we can actually "teach writing," though I do indeed believe that we can help people to improve as writers if they desire such improvement. Though I think this holds true for all writing, I am only claiming here that any course designed to help students negotiate the challenges of academic writing should give a central place to the theory and practice of intertextuality. I am also very much aware that, as I write this, I am also producing a piece of academic writing myself, one that will be read aloud on at least one occasion and then appear in print later on. In this discussion, though I hope to avoid becoming paralyzed with self-consciousness, I intend to connect my problems in producing an academic paper such as this one to the problems faced by every student who writes an academic paper.

Like any student's paper, this one was produced in response to an assignment and for a deadline or series of deadlines. After agreeing, in a general way, to speak at the University of New Hampshire's conference on composition, which is very like enrolling in a particular course, I received a letter from Pat Sullivan, giving me a more specific assignment: a paper that could be delivered in thirty minutes and that would draw upon my "interest in issues of text and context and in processes of reading and writing." I was also given a deadline for submission of a title and an admonition not to "report on work that has been promised for publication elsewhere." Borrowing some terminology from Michael Baxandall's book on the interpretation of artworks, *Patterns of Intention*, I was given not just a *charge*—"Write a paper, deliver a talk"—but a *brief* that put the charge in terms of what Baxandall calls "local conditions in the specific case" (30).

230

At the risk of disrupting both your and my continuity of thought here, I must stop and ask, "Why Baxandall?" What has an art historian's discussion of the building of a bridge over the Firth of Forth in Scotland got to do with the problems of writing? That is—why did I, as a writer working on an assignment, feel a need to call upon Baxandall's aid? Well, "Had to fill up those thirty minutes," to be sure, just as our students feel they must fill up whatever quota of words or pages they are asked to produce. But there is more to it than that. I want to suggest that much of what students have to learn about academic writing comes down to the process that brings something like my citation of Baxandall into this text. As I was trying to find the words to explain the intertextual situation of every writer, Baxandall's explanation of the compositional process simply drifted into my mind, as a simple, clear, and powerful way of describing how texts actually get produced. What I liked about his book when I first read it was that it took a problem in civil engineering as a model for discussing the production of paintings, moving from the building of the Forth bridge to paintings by Picasso, Chardin, and Piero della Francesca.

Part of what interested me in Baxandall's book was the fact that he used the model of a utilitarian work with some aesthetic dimension— a bridge—as a way of getting a clearer look at the production of more fully aesthetic visual texts. It was this way of connecting the practical and the aesthetic, I now understand, that made Baxandall's book memorable for me, because it was connected by analogy to problems of reading and writing that I regularly face as a writer and a teacher. For my citation of Baxandall to be justified in the present circumstance, however, I shall have to work with it, do something with it, to make it productive in terms of my particular brief on this occasion. I will go further and say that if I couldn't find anything to do with it other than to cite or mention it, it would be an error to bring it into my text. We academic writers must learn both that we have no choice but to be intertextual and also that we are obliged to add our own labor to these intertexts in order to make them do productive work in helping us with our own textual problems. We need them. We cannot do without them. But we must use them, work them, in order to get beyond mere quotation. In the case of my use of some words of Baxandall's, my effort takes the form of adapting his terminology to my rather different context. Often, in academic writing, borrowings from a field just beyond our own are most productive, precisely because they must be adapted and cannot simply be taken over unchanged.

In this case, I want to say that the distinction between "charge" and "brief" is crucial in the compositional process. What I mean by this is that we teachers who assign writing projects to our students have a responsibility to assist the student of writing in moving from the vague charge to write a paper on this or that occasion to something that is more intelligible because it involves an appreciation of the "local conditions in the specific case." Put simply, teachers should assign not charges to write but briefs for writing—or, they should make the development of a brief a part of the assignment for which they will serve as consultants. The operative principle here—and it applies to all the arts and sciences—is that constraints are the necessary stimuli to creative work. But this is only one dimension of the compositional problem, and the simplest at that. Now we must turn to a matter of greater complexity.

In Baxandall's discussion of composition, the charge, reduced to a brief, makes just one angle of a triangle or vector of forces in which the final angle or point is the work itself. The second point, which together with the brief forms the base upon which the maker or builder constructs the text or object, is what he calls "culture," by which he means "the general range of *resources* offered to the agent," including "resources of medium, of models (both positive and negative), and of 'aesthetic' " (35). He makes no large claims for this triangular structure—either for its originality or for its general applicability—but with some modification to suit our specific situation, we should find it useful. Let us start with a question. When we give students a charge and a brief, what cultural resources must we assume they can use? The first of these resources, obviously, must be the medium itself, the written language. The teacher of writing must have a fairly good idea of the student's level of ease and fluency in this medium, so that assignments can be calibrated for the specific purpose of developing this fluency. That is, assignments must not be grossly beyond the capacities of those asked to perform them, and yet they should extend and develop those capacities. A major purpose of writing courses is precisely to expand these elements of "culture" for students taking such courses. This is a mere platitude, however, unless we can be more specific about how to undertake such expansion. Once again, Baxandall can help us.

His notion of "culture" specifically includes "models (positive and negative)." You don't build a bridge without knowing something about how bridges have been built, including those that have fallen into the rivers they were supposed to span. An important negative model for the Forth bridge was a bridge built not long before across the Firth of Tay, which "blew over in an easterly gale, taking a passenger train with it" in 1879 (17). This negative example proved to be extremely helpful in planning a bridge designed for similar conditions, but one that would not fall down. The successful designer of the Forth bridge also, of course, knew of many good examples of bridge building, although none of them exactly matched his brief. Translated to our own situation, the proper use of models means that students of writing should see and discuss some examples of good and bad writing of the sort required by their own assignments. We are, of course, very familiar with the use of good examples. In our literature courses we habitually teach only good examples, since our notion of literature does not allow us to modify that noun with the adjective "bad." There is no bad literature. The result of this is that English teachers are accustomed to finding only good things in the works they assign and lots of bad things in the assignments students compose for them. What do you do with a student's assignment? You "correct" it, do you not? But how often do you "correct" a poem, a play, a story, or even an essay that is part of your syllabus? Not very often, I should think.

This is a real problem. Verbal texts seldom fall into the Tay, carrying a train of readers with them. We are more familiar with essays resembling trains that huff and puff a lot but never seem to get out of the station. (At this moment, for instance, I am worrying about whether my own engine has enough power to make it up the gentle slope we are presently climbing.) If we accept Baxandall's view that bad examples are important, how can we ensure that our students encounter some of these and understand the causes of their badness? To begin with, I want to reject as counterproductive the two most obvious ways of finding bad examples to use in a writing course. I do not think we can do a good job of finding published essays that are bad in useful ways. Even Brooks and Warren had a terrible time finding bad poems to discuss in *Understanding Poetry* and they fell all over themselves trying to show why such poems were indeed bad. If we select material that we simply don't like, we run the risk of selecting what other people, including our students, may like very well—which can lead to mere debating of prejudices rather than useful criticism. On the other hand, if we select writing by students to serve as our bad examples, we may simply reinforce the frustration and hostility of those students. Such writing may also fail to be bad in instructive, which is to say creative, ways.

No—to find really helpful sorts of badness, we shall have to produce bad texts ourselves. First of all, however, we must face the fact that badness is never absolute. It is always a matter of context, purpose, function. If one wished to design a bridge so as to create a disaster, the Tay bridge would have been an excellent solution. Similarly the most feeble and ungrammatical sentence might, in the proper context, be a perfect example of a feeble and ungrammatical sentence. (Let me point out, parenthetically, here, that once I have introduced the good and bad bridges into my text I can keep drawing upon them for illustrations that lend specificity and point to my discourse. The bridge and the train have been working for me in more ways than one: as analogies, metaphors, and concrete illustrations of the points I am trying to make—including this one. I did not know, when I brought the train into my text, how it would be used, but once it was in my text I could use it to get from there to here. Such use is what I mean by making borrowed textual matter earn its keep to justify the borrowing.)

Returning from my metadiscourse, I want to argue that teachers and students of composition need examples of specific kinds of badness relative to specific verbal tasks. The best way to come by such examples is to make them, and the easiest way to make them is to make them out of already existing good examples. If teachers are going to give students briefs to write on a particular topic, they should prepare the students by examining with them some good examples of solutions to similar briefs. To offer bad examples, however, may be a more productive place to begin. That is, we, as teachers, should also take at least one clearly well-formed example of a solution and deform it creatively before presenting it to our students. In doing this we may lop crucial paragraphs, introduce feeble sentences, weaken connections, alter evidence—do whatever we wish that will enable us to analyze the resulting text with critical authority—because it is our own. I would recommend performing such an analysis, then taking questions about it, and finally producing the original as a good solution to the problems noted in the analysis. Having made the errors ourselves, we are in a position to resist claims that they are really improvements, since we know the ways in which they have weakened the original text we have warped to our purposes.

As I have suggested, preparing our malformed text requires some creative ability. Do all teachers of writing have this ability? My answer to this crucial question is that they must—they simply must. If we cannot make bad texts out of good ones, how can we hope to aid our students in improving their own written work? In actuality, I think many teachers have creative talent that may presently be unused and frustrated when they teach what we have called composition, or may even be misused simply because it cannot be repressed. In the example before us, in which a weakened piece of writing is discussed before the original is presented, a creative teacher may then be tempted to go further and subject the original itself to a devastating critique. I would resist this temptation for one simple reason. We do not want to set perfection before our students as their goal. We should not want to do this because we cannot teach perfection. Our range, our capabilities, go no further than craft. Even in "creative" writing courses, craft is all that can be taught. Any snatching of graces beyond the reach of art—as a crafty poet once put it—our students must do on their own. Our aim should be to help students learn how to produce a good, workmanlike job with a written essay whenever they need to. And this means what it means in any trade or craft. It means knowing what to avoid. It means using rules of thumb and tricks of the trade to accomplish basic tasks without having to think them out from scratch every time. It means mastering a medium through the study of models. In this particular case, it also means that we should select a good essay to deform rather than one we consider faulty.

The use of negative models can actually be taken one step further. After one such model has been discussed, it may be extremely helpful to ask students themselves to produce a deformed version of one of the positive models under discussion. This means involving students in a creative process of the negative sort, which can be as much fun as knocking down a tower of blocks or a house of cards—and requires a higher degree of skill. To learn not by doing—but by undoing—is the idea here. Specifically, in this kind of assignment, we should give students a brief that requires them to take a text that performs its function well and sabotage it creatively so that it fails in ways that can be discussed as plausible examples of how writing can go astray. This can be done with whole texts or parts; it can be limited to certain features, such as diction or transitions. Many variations can be played on this basic theme. The point is to learn how a certain kind of text works by deliberately sabotaging that kind of text—not just writing another text about the first one, which we usually call textual analysis, but by actually intervening in the first text to produce another that exhibits certain carefully defined problems or weaknesses. This is analysis with a vengeance—a more effective form of analysis because more creative.

Up to now, we have been considering one dimension of what Baxandall calls "culture": the medium itself, as it may be studied through the use of positive and negative models. We must now consider at least one other major aspect of culture, in order to complete even a rough sketch of the model of instruction on which we are working. Culture, as we are using the word here, means knowledge about the topic to which the brief is addressed, including, in particular, previous treatments of it. It is to avoid the problems of culture that writing instructors so often resort to assignments in which students are asked to write about themselves and their personal experiences, or "what they know." There are two problems with this kind of assignment, although it has a place in the teaching of writing, of course. The first problem is that, though one may possibly know something about oneself, it is a far from routine accomplishment. Still, even assuming that one did, would it be right to assume that this knowledge necessarily entailed the ability to write about it? We are not born knowing even how to think about ourselves—which turns out to be one of the hardest projects of our entire lives, so hard that most of us give it up early, if indeed we ever try it in the first place. Furthermore, writing about the self, which is implicated reciprocally in thinking about the self, is not something that takes place in a cultural vacuum. What we know about ourselves is largely what our culture has enabled us to know—just as those selves are mainly the selves that our culture has enabled us to have. What is "real"—what is permanent—about ourselves may be only our resistance, our negation, our fear, our depression, our boredom. Finding a way to textualize these resistances is never easy. It requires effort, and a knowledge about the culture in which we have come to selfhood. That is one reason we go to school: to come into possession of our selves by learning about our culture.

The second problem is that the writer's self is simply not what most academic writing is about. Most academic writing specifically extends beyond the writer's self because it directly involves the extension of knowledge. Writing in the academy is a major way of extending knowledge by subjecting mere information to the disciplines of a particular discourse, with its attendant grammar and rhetoric. This means that most of the time when we write, in the academic lives of both students and faculty, this writing is not directly about ourselves, nor even about something that we already know entirely, but is directed toward the boundaries of our knowledge, where discoveries may be made. The more we know about a field of study, of course, the more our discoveries are likely to be of interest to others, but the process of discovery can be exciting in itself. It has a formal quality that can give even a beginner's discoveries a structure that is engaging for the reader. Every writer, then, and especially a beginner, must start with some sense of how a given discourse is conducted and what its major presuppositions are supposed to be. How to tackle a relatively new field of study is one of the things we have to teach. This is why intertextuality must be at the center of our teaching.

Texts are made mainly out of other texts. This does not mean that there is never anything new under the sun but that even something very new indeed must be presented in a textual form that is largely borrowed from other texts. In the academy the introduction to intertextuality received by most students takes the form of a stern warning against plagiarism. In a culture organized around property, patents, and copyrights, plagiarism has become a sin, occasionally a crime. In other cultures, or in certain contexts within our own, this sin does not exist. Certainly Chaucer and Shakespeare never worried about it. Alphonse Legros, who directed the Slade School of Art in London at the turn of the last century, used to advise his students, "Si vous volez, il faut voler aux riches, et pas aux pauvres" ("If you steal, you must steal from the rich and not from the poor"). That is, he advised them to steal from the old masters of visual art and not from inferior artists. And T. S. Eliot is famous for having observed that "immature poets imitate; mature poets steal." If even painters and poets must operate intertextually, how much more so must this be the case with writers engaged on more academic topics.

At this point I want to reproduce some remarks on our topic by a writer who had a great success almost a century ago, writing on an astonishing range of subjects, although he is not much remembered now. He was a schoolmaster under trying circumstances; he earned a degree in medicine, but did not practice for long; he suffered the ignominy of having a book successfully prosecuted for obscenity by the British government. He wrote on literature and on scientific subjects. He wrote essays and poems. He even wrote on writing, and it is from an essay of his called "The Art of Writing" that I have taken the title for this piece. Let me quote the relevant passage from this essay. In this passage the author has been considering the notion that great writers seldom quote others. He acknowledges that this may often be the case but then goes on to make a rather different point.

> The significant fact to note, however, is not that the great writer rarely quotes, but that he knows how to quote. Schopenhauer was here a master. He possessed a marvellous flair for fine sayings in remote books, and these he would now and again let fall like jewels on his page, with so happy a skill that they seem to be created for the spot on which they fell. It is the little writer rather than the great writer who seems never to quote, and the reason is that he is really never doing anything else. (Ellis 145)

The happy skill invoked here is that of a specific case of intertextuality, the actual quotation of one author by another, done in such a way as to make the old gems appear to have been designed for their new setting. We must assume something like this notion to be operating in Eliot's admonition to steal rather than imitate, which is really advice to make the old textual material thoroughly a part of the new one. But we, as writers and teachers of writing, do not have to do with greatness, since we can neither aim at it ourselves nor claim to lead our students to it. We have everything to do with littleness, which is why the last part of the quoted passage may be more important for us than the happy phrase I have borrowed for my title. The little writer, we are told, seems never to quote because "he is really never doing anything else."

The author I have been quoting here considered himself an original genius, I am sure, and with some justice, even though he is now scarcely more than a footnote in those disciplines to which he contributed. Still, we can learn something from his admonitions—if we are willing to face up to the littleness of our task. We academics are mainly little writers ourselves, who are attempting to guide our students into the ways of successful littleness as well. Fluency within discursive bounds is the goal of academic writing, and staying within discursive bounds involves a lot of semiconscious quotation. We have as our goal—and the goal of each student—the achievement of littleness. Our students must learn to write as the Others write, in order to survive in academic life. That is one side of our dilemma. The other side is that without some feeling of moving beyond the already written it is scarcely possible for a writer to write. This problem is particularly acute for students, who are often poignantly aware of the limits of their own knowledge and are confronted by academic discourses that seem to be boundless. The dilemma, then, takes the form of the inevitability of littleness versus the need of every writer—even a fledgling writer—to feel that littleness is not inevitable.

This is a dilemma that immersion in a discipline over a long period of time is designed to solve. By long study we academics hope to reach the margins of our disciplines where our methods and our learning come face to face with the raw chaos the discipline is designed to master. Many of us never quite reach this boundary, although we sometimes convince ourselves that we have done so. Some of us come to believe that, like the beast in the jungle, raw chaos does not lie in wait at the end of our journey but paces beside us every step of the way. And others come to think that there has never been any raw chaos, except what we have invented as the untamed Other of our disciplined thinking. But whether the beast is real or invented, beside us or distant, the trick is obviously to find it and capture it in our textual nets, alive, if possible.

(I have been driven to metaphor, here, as a way of inducing a discursive beast into my textual net, but that action itself—the making of a metaphor aided by a dim recollection of Henry James—is, even as I write this passage, leading me to reformulate the textual and pedagogical problem itself, rejecting the sharp distinction between great and little, between quotation and originality.) The "happy skill" needed by every writer struggling in the net of textuality is not so much the art of quotation as the ability to push language toward its metaphorical limits. Perhaps there is no way to get beyond quotation, to stretch the bonds of littleness, that is not metaphorical. What is outside textuality may not be there waiting for us to throw our perfected net of language over it, but may be brought into being only by the charm of the net itself, appearing only where we have playfully weakened or stretched the fabric, shaping the material of the net itself into the beast we need to find. (If I may draw back parenthetically from my own writing, once again, I find that the textual play of the words I have brought into my discourse is leading me toward an unforseen conclusion. I got to this point in my text driven by a brief and drawing upon a culture or discursive field that includes my experience as a teacher and writer, but in attempting to solve the problem set by my brief, I was led through a process of revision and rethinking in which I learned to loosen up a bit and play with my metaphors until their object came more clearly into view. This part of my text has been the most revised and has become for me the most interesting. Even here, however, I would not claim to have escaped littleness and quotation, but I have rearranged my textual furniture a bit.)

In the course of writing these words I, like any student, have kept one eye upon my brief, including the length of time allotted me. Thirty minutes translates into fifteen pages, which translates into 27,000 characters, helpfully counted for me by my Macintosh. At the moment we stand at 29,330. I shall conclude, then, with just two bits of advice. We must find topics for our writing courses that enable students to focus on their culture at the points where it most clearly impinges upon them, where they already have tacit knowledge that only needs to be cultivated to become more explicit. And in our teaching we should focus on the way that the topic of any course exists as the object of a discourse, a body of texts connected by a certain way of naming its objects that is ultimately metaphorical. The academic writer must learn to understand, use, and ultimately play with those metaphors. The skill of a writer is a happy one because it is based upon play.

Works Cited

Baxandall, Michael. *Patterns of Intention: On the Historical Explanation of Pictures.* New Haven: Yale UP, 1985.

Brooks, Cleanth, and Robert Penn Warren. *Understanding Poetry.* 4th ed. New York: Harcourt Brace Jovanovich, 1976.

Ellis, Havelock. *The Dance of Life.* Boston: Houghton Mifflin, 1929.

Index

Editors

Patricia A. Sullivan is associate professor of English and director of composition at the University of New Hampshire, where she teaches graduate and undergraduate courses in composition studies, critical theory, and American literature. She is co-editor of *Methods and Methodology in Composition Research* and the 1991 recipient of the James L. Kinneavy Award, and her work has appeared in journals and essay collections that explore both ideological and practical issues in the study and teaching of writing.

Donna J. Qualley is assistant professor of English at Western Washington University. Her interests include composition theory, feminist studies, and reading and writing as reflexive methods of inquiry. She co-authored an article on collaborative writing for *Journal of Advanced Composition*, and her chapter "Using Reading in the Writing Classroom" appears in *Nuts and Bolts: A Practical Guide to Teaching Composition*.

Contributors

David Bleich teaches in the Department of English and the College of Arts and Sciences of the University of Rochester. He supervises the preparation of second-year graduate students in English for the teaching of first-year undergraduate writing courses. He also teaches in Women's Studies and in Jewish Studies. His publications include *Readings and Feelings* (NCTE, 1975); *Subjective Criticism; Utopia: The Psychology of a Cultural Fantasy;* and *The Double Perspective: Language, Literacy, and Social Relations* (paper, NCTE, 1993). Forthcoming in 1994 are *Writing With: New Directions in Collaborative Teaching, Learning, and Research,* edited with Sally Reagan and Tom Fox, and a guest-edited issue of the *Journal of Advanced Composition,* "Collaboration and Change in the Academy."

Elizabeth Chiseri-Strater is assistant professor of English at the University of North Carolina at Greensboro, where she teaches in the doctoral program in composition and rhetoric and is involved with English education. She has taught in and directed the New Hampshire Writing Program for Classroom Teachers. Her book *Academic Literacies* is an ethnography of writing across the curriculum at the University of New Hampshire, and she has written articles and book chapters on portfolio assessment and the evaluation of writing, non-mainstream literacy practices, and collaborative writing. She is currrently planning a book on field writing strategies and research practices for first-year English courses.

Karen Fitts is assistant professor in the Writing and Media Department of Loyola College in Maryland, where she teaches writing and rhetoric. With Alan W. France, she is co-editor of a forthcoming anthology entitled *Writing Dialectics: Cultural Studies, Rhetoric, and Composition Theory.*

Alan W. France is assistant professor of English and director of composition at West Chester University. His latest essay, "Assigning Places: The Function of Introductory Composition as a Cultural Discourse," appeared in *College English.*

Cinthia Gannett is associate professor of English and Women's Studies and coordinator of the writing program at the University of New Hampshire at Manchester. She is the author of *Gender and the Journal: Diaries and Academic Discourse* and various articles, including "The Stories of Our Lives Become Our Lives: Diaries, Journals, and Academic Discourse," to appear in *Feminine Principles and Women's Experience in American Composition and Rhetoric,* edited by Emig and Phelps (forthcoming 1994). She is currently on sabbatical researching unpublished women's diaries in New Hampshire for a project called "Unlocking the Diary."

Maxine Greene is professor of philosophy and education and William F. Russell Professor in the Foundations of Education, emerita, but still teaching at Teachers College, Columbia University, where she has taught since 1966. She is the author of about one hundred articles and chapters in various anthologies in the fields of aesthetics and education, social theory, literature, ethics, curriculum, and educational philosophy. Her books include *Landscapes of Learning* and *The Dialectic of Freedom*. She is a past editor of the *Teachers College Record* and past president of the Philosophy of Education Society, the American Educational Studies Association, and the American Educational Research Association.

Rhonda C. Grego is assistant professor of English in composition and rhetoric at the University of South Carolina, where she spends much of a day's time teaching, writing, and talking about teaching/writing with friends, students, colleagues, her statistics professor husband John and his colleagues, and her four-year-old daughter Caroline. Along with collaborator Nancy Thompson, she co-directs the Writing Studio, a small-group writing workshop program designed to build productively upon the "writing histories" of basic and other student writers by collaboratively examining their ways of talking about, understanding, and approaching the tasks of academic writing. Her research focuses on memory, emotions, and writing: recent scholarship includes a book manuscript—*Recollection and Its Return*—that explores how ideas about memory influenced classical rhetoric (thereby influencing modern composition) and the implications of feminist rhetorics of "rememory" or "re-membering" for contemporary revisions of composition pedagogy and research.

David A. Jolliffe is associate professor of English and director of English composition at the University of Illinois at Chicago. He holds the Ph.D. in English, with a specialization in the teaching of writing, from the University of Texas at Austin, and has taught English at Texas, West Virginia University, Bethany College, Wheeling (West Virginia) Park High School, and Jilin University of Technology in the People's Republic of China. He is co-author of *Scenarios for Teaching Writing: Contexts for Discussion and Reflective Practice* (NCTE/Alliance for Undergraduate Education, 1993), co-author of *Assessing Writers' Knowledge and Processes of Composing*, and contributing editor of *Advances in Writing Research, Volume 2: Writing in Academic Disciplines*. He is also the author of *The Content of Composition: Subjects and Genres in College Writing Instruction*, forthcoming, and *Writing, Teaching, and Learning: Incorporating Writing throughout the Curriculum*.

Michael J. Kiskis is associate professor of American literature at Elmira College. Prior to his move to Elmira, he served as assistant dean at SUNY Empire State College, where he worked with adult/returning students. In addition to articles on program administration and planning he has published on issues related to adult students and autobiography. He is editor of *Mark Twain's Own Autobiography: The Chapters from the North American Review*, has published on Mark Twain, and has been a program participant at AAHE, CCCC, MLA, NCTE, and NEMLA conferences.

Elizabeth Klem is currently finishing her doctoral work at the University of Massachusetts at Amherst. She has taught most recently in the Writing Program's computer-equipped facility. She has collaborated with Charles Moran on a number of projects, including an ethnographic study of a networked writing classroom which appeared in *Computers and Composition*.

Linda M. LaDuc is director of business writing programs in the School of Management at the University of Massachusetts at Amherst. Previously she has taught language arts in public schools, trained teachers, and worked in business as a manager and consultant. A recent article published in the *Journal of Technical Writing and Communication* was nominated by NCTE for an award for excellence in technical communication philosophy and theory. At present she is collaborating with Amanda Goldrick-Jones on a special issue of *Technical Communication Quarterly*, while also completing her dissertation study of women entrepreneurs' leadership discourse. Because her research is cross-disciplinary, she makes presentations regularly at rhetoric, composition, communication, and management conferences.

Sharyn Lowenstein has taught writing at the University of Massachusetts College of Public and Community Service, the University of New Hampshire at Manchester, and Lesley College. She is currently director of the Lesley Learning Center. Her published work on the journal includes "Journal Writing," in *Writer's Choice*, Teacher's Edition, and "A Brief History of Journal Keeping," in *The Journal Book*, edited by Toby Fulwiler. She has also presented papers on the journal at regional and national conferences

Charles Moran is professor of English at the University of Massachusetts at Amherst. He is co-director of the Western Massachusetts Writing Project and author of articles in *Computers and Composition, College Composition and Communication,* and *College English*. With Elizabeth Penfield he edited *Conversations: Contemporary Critical Theory and the Teaching of Literature* (NCTE, 1990), and, with Anne Herrington, *Writing, Teaching, and Learning in the Disciplines*. In 1993 he received the Ellen Nold Award from *Computers and Composition* for the best article in the field of computers and writing.

Peter Mortensen is assistant professor of English at the University of Kentucky. His research investigates representations of illiteracy in popular and literary discourse at the turn of the century. With Janet Carey Eldred, he also publishes on issues of women's rhetorical and literacy education in the early Republic. Mortensen teaches rhetoric and composition courses for graduate students in English and for undergraduate English Education majors. He sits on the advisory board of the Bluegrass Writing Project, the National Writing Project affiliate in central Kentucky.

Daniel Reagan is associate professor of English and coordinator of first-year English and writing across the curriculum at Saint Anselm College in Manchester, New Hampshire. He has written articles on various aspects of nineteenth-century American literature and African American literature. His current project is on Melville and nineteenth-century theories of reading.

Mariolina Salvatori is associate professor of English at the University of Pittsburgh, where she teaches undergraduate and graduate courses in the composition program and the literature program. She holds a degree in the languages, literatures, and institutions of Western Europe (English, German, and Spanish) from the Orientale University in Naples, Italy and a Ph.D. in nineteenth- and twentieth-century English literature from the University of Pittsburgh. She has written on twentieth-century Italian literature, literary perceptions of aging, and the immigrants' experience. Her most recent work concentrates on the interconnections of reading and writing, theory and practice, literature and composition. Her essay in this volume is part of a larger project, *Pedagogy, 1820s–1920s: Disturbing History,* currently under editorial consideration.

Jean Donovan Sanborn is associate professor of English at Colby College in Maine, where she also directs the Writers' Center and co-coordinates the writing across the curriculum program. Her research interests are the essay, as both literary and academic genre, and feminist issues in writing. She has presented papers and workshops at CCCC, the Wyoming Conference, the UNH Conferences, the Miami University Conferences, the National Conferences on Peer Tutoring in Writing, and various regional meetings. Among her publications is an essay related to her chapter in this volume: "The Academic Essay: A Feminist View in Student Voices," which appears in *Gender Issues in the Teaching of English,* edited by Nancy Mellin McCracken and Bruce C. Appleby.

Robert Scholes is Andrew W. Mellon Professor of Humanities at Brown University and director of the Forbes Center for Modern Culture and Media. He is the author of many books on modern literature and literary theory, as well as textbooks for courses in writing and literature. His book *Textual Power* received awards from NCTE and the MLA. He is also chair of the Pacesetter English Task Force, sponsored by NCTE, the College Board, and the Educational Testing Service, a group which is working on a new plan for twelfth-grade English.

Susan V. Wall is associate professor of English at Northeastern University and a specialist in composition studies. One of her abiding interests has been pedagogy for urban schools and colleges: she has (with Nicholas Coles) contributed a chapter on basic writing to *The Politics of Writing Instruction: Postsecondary,* and is currently a fellow at Northeastern's Center for Innovation in Urban Education. Her other interest is teacher education: she has established a National Writing Project site and is currently associate director of the Institute on Writing and Teaching at Martha's Vineyard. She directs the M.A. degree program in writing offered through the institute, and her most recent research includes a book on teacher-researchers as writers.